A

SHORT ROAD

BACKWARDS

G. A. J. Coleman

ISBN: 1484088158
ISBN-13: 9781484088159
Library of Congress Control Number: 2013907325
CreateSpace Independent Publishing Platform
North Charleston, South Carolina

CONTENTS

INTRODUCTION

This is a story about the rise and destruction of Southern Rhodesia, a small, land-locked country in Central Africa, now known as Zimbabwe. In many respects it reflects a period of major shift in world politics and philosophy, going from the independent, hardworking, God-fearing culture of the Victorian era to the secular, liberal, entitled culture of today. My grandfather arrived in Southern Rhodesia in 1896, only six years after the original 196 members of British Pioneer Column staked out their first settlement as Fort Salisbury. He had no health insurance, no pension plan, no unemployment insurance, no welfare to fall back on and very little money. He was tough, adventurous and willing to take risk. He did not expect help from anyone. The story lays out my life in the context of growing up in a prosperous and successful country, only to see it destroyed by the United

Nations and the government of our own mother country Britain, to whom we had shown great loyalty and allegiance through two world wars. Five of my uncles fought for Britain in the Second World War, one of whom never returned. Ironically the fight to preserve responsible government in Rhodesia was not against the indigenous population, who in fact would be the biggest losers. It was against the politicians of civilized nations who, having never lived in Africa, arrogantly believed that they knew better than those who did. This is the first time in history that a mother country has deliberately and voluntarily sacrificed its own people and loyal allies in favor of a vicious dictatorship whose allegiance is for sale to the highest bidder.

In order to put the period in perspective it is helpful to give a brief history of the region. I have also given my philosophy as I saw it. Many will disagree with this philosophy and for them I take the strategy of Ronald Reagan running for president in 1980 against Jimmy Carter, "Are you better off now than you were four years ago?" Is Africa better off now than it was under colonial rule? It is a fact that those countries in which the English colonizers retained control, the USA, Canada, Australia, and New Zealand, great progress has been made and the future is bright. Those countries which were colonized by the British and returned to indigenous control have deteriorated to various degrees and the future is very uncertain.

Although it is instructive to refer to certain political events during the time period there is no intent to present these as precise history. Regarding my own experiences, I have related things as I remember them and others may have different memories. The people mentioned are real but I have generally used only first names or nicknames. They will know who they are and I trust that I have kept everything positive and without offense. I regard "political correctness" as a failure to accept reality and therefore have made no effort to abide by this illusory fad.

PROLOGUE

In 1874, at the request of Portugal, Count Otto von Bismarck of Prussia convened a conference in Berlin of virtually all the nations of Europe to discuss their aspirations on the African continent. It was clear that there was going to be competition for control of this vast area and the objective was to apportion it in a rational manner. Aside from the Boer occupation of the Orange Free State and the Transvaal, the interior was largely untouched and sparsely populated by many different African tribes living in the iron age. Britain was a major player in this initiative and lost no time in staking its claims. It already had control of large parts of coastal northern and southern Africa and aspired to connect the two regions to give an unbroken line of control from Cape to Cairo.

At about this same time Matabele chief Lobengula was wreaking havoc amongst the tribes north of the Limpopo

River. His father, Zulu induna Mzilikazi, had broken away from the main Zulu tribe in the early 1800's and with his powerful impi had ranged north. The Boers' entry into the territory north of the Vaal river drove him over the Limpopo river and in about 1840 he established his kraal near a range of hills called Matopos. It became known as Buluwayo, "place of slaughter" for very valid reasons. In punishment for a plot to replace him with his eldest son, Mzilikatze had his two sons from the senior wife and all suspected collaborators thrown to their deaths off a cliff known as The Hill of Chiefs. Lobengula was a son from a lesser wife but became king shortly after Mzilikatze's death in 1868. Lobengula continued the Zulu custom of total annihilation of other tribes. The Zulus were physically impressive and totally ruthless. From their homeland in the coastal hills of south eastern Africa they had ranged into the interior and virtually wiped out all human inhabitants in the *mfecane*. With their short stabbing spears and long cowhide shields they surrounded their opponents in the classical crescent formation and then moved in for the kill. They spared only the young marriageable girls and young boys who could be trained to fight. Older women were used to transport captured goods and then clubbed to death. All the captured livestock were driven off and added to the Zulu herds. This offshoot of the Zulu tribe called themselves Matabele.

It was inevitable that Africa would be colonized. Europe was hungry for new territory and supplies of raw materials and the interior of Africa was the last untouched part of the world. Whereas some European colonizers were harsh on the local tribes, Britain was sympathetic to their situation and sought both to protect them and educate them. For this reason certain areas were designated Protectorates and Britain played the role of mentor and protector until such time as the indigenous tribes could fend for themselves in a dangerous world. In other areas it was understood that permanent British presence would endure. Southern Rhodesia and South Africa were designated as colonies and the Europeans who settled there expected a permanent presence. They invested and built accordingly.

Cecil John Rhodes was the son of an English vicar who had come to South Africa for health reasons and to join his brother farming in Natal. He was a very shrewd businessman and made a fortune in consolidating much of the diamond mining in Kimberly, where, with financing from the Rothschild family and partner Alfred Beit, he formed the de Beers Consolidated Mines Company. He became Prime Minister of the Cape Colony in 1890. His dream was to extend the British Empire through the whole African continent and using his wealth and influence he set his sights on the lands north of the Limpopo River. He formed the British South Africa Company for this purpose. After arranging the signing of several mineral concession treaties with Matabele chief Lobengula, he felt that the time was ripe for occupation. With the support of the British government, in 1890 he made plans to take control of the Shona lands north of Bulawayo, by-passing Lobengula's kraal. Lobengula was in failing health by this time, obese and plagued by gout.

In keeping with this strategy, on June 7th, 1890, a twenty three year old Englishman named Frank Johnson crossed the Limpopo River at Camp Cecil on a quest to take possession of the territory of Mashonaland. Under contract to Rhodes, he had assembled a Pioneer Corps of 196 hand-picked men with enough porters, drivers, 117 wagons and supplies for one year. They were accompanied by a contingent of 400 mounted British South Africa Police who were to occupy and defend the forts that were built along the way. Johnson's main weapon was a 10,000 candle-power searchlight powered by a steam-driven dynamo. He also had two war-rocket tubes, a Gatling gun and Nordenfelt gun. On July 1st the column reached the Tuli River which constituted the border with Matabeleland. While building a fort there they received a messenger from Matabele chief Lobengula enquiring why an armed force was about to enter his territory. Johnson replied that he had permission from a more powerful chief, Queen Victoria, and to make the matter clear, he gave an impressive demonstration, firing rockets and powering up his searchlight at night. The Matabele were very superstitious and reported to Lobengula that this force had supernatural powers and should not be attacked.

After establishing two more forts along the way, Victoria and Charter, Johnson arrived at a small hill high up on the watershed divide between the Zambezi and Limpopo rivers which he considered the best site on which to establish a settlement. On September 12th, 1890, this site was proclaimed Fort Salisbury after the Prime

Minister of England. The Pioneer column had trekked 360 miles from Fort Tuli through virgin bushveld, cutting its own roads and fording the rivers. The entire expedition had cost Rhodes ninety thousand pounds. Fort Salisbury was the nucleus of the country that was to become Southern Rhodesia, named after Cecil Rhodes. The pioneers and those that came after them were tough men looking for adventure and opportunity. They were willing to take risk and endure hardship, disease and attacks from the natives. They built a great country for all its inhabitants and at no time did they commit any atrocities as other European colonizers had done. They did not take the risks and suffer the hardships so that Robert Mugabe and his ministers could live in opulent luxury. After 90 years of progress, in 1980 this country became the independent nation of Zimbabwe and started moving backwards.

Chapter 1:
COLONIZATION

For those unfamiliar with Rhodesia's history, it should be mentioned that when the first pioneers set up camp in what became the capital of Salisbury in 1890, the area was effectively ruled by the Matabele chief Lobengula. You could say the Matabele were colonizers, but not benevolent ones. By all accounts the Matabele rule was ruthless. Life of any kind had no value whatsoever and Matabele impis raided the local tribes at will, killing everything except young marriageable maidens, young boys who could be trained to fight, and livestock. They appeared to do this without any compassion and apparently had absolutely no comprehension of suffering unless it was inflicted on themselves. The reality is that the now predominant Shona tribe were virtual slaves to the Matabele and would have remained so had not the colonists taken control. The early hunters who traversed the area in the mid 1800's reported very little sign of habitation in Mashonaland, most of the Shona villages had been pillaged by the Matabele or abandoned, with terrified survivors living in hiding.

As more and more settlers moved into the area north of Bulawayo, Lobengula realized he was at risk of being constrained to ever-decreasing hunting grounds. To reinforce his claims he increased his raids upon the Shona and in 1893 one of his his impis attacked a Shona settlement near Fort Victoria. Some of the Shona tribesmen sought refuge with the small detachment of whites at Fort Victoria. The whites drove off the Matabele impi, killing their leading Induna. This incensed Lobengula, who then embarked on a rampage against all the whites in the country. The whites assembled a larger force to punish Lobengula and advanced on Bulawayo, which they burned to the ground. Although the odds were overwhelming, by this time the white forces had acquired five Maxim guns which mowed down the closely packed Matabele warriors with devastating effect. Although the Matabele were well equipped with Martini Henry rifles supplied by Rhodes as part of the mineral rights negotiations, they were not good marksmen and no match for the Maxims. Lobengula and his army fled north and Lobengula died of natural causes during the retreat. Jameson had offered Lobengula peace terms but his reply was evasive and it was believed he was just playing for time. It is also claimed that Lobengula sent two tribesmen loaded with gold to buy peace but they inadvertently delivered it to junior troopers who stole it. After the massacre of Major

Alan Wilson and his 33 troopers Captain Forbes persuaded the Matabele army to surrender.

Without their chief, the Matabele were in disarray. Feeling secure, in late December 1895 Jameson decided to take most of his forces on a raid into the Transvaal Republic to incite insurrection amongst the many foreigners and stake British claims to the newly discovered gold fields. Perceiving weak opposition, the Matabele staged one more rampage and slaughtered many whites on isolated farms. The fighting men returned from Jameson's ineffective raid and subdued the tribesmen. Rhodes subsequently met unarmed with the Matabele indunas near Bulawayo and negotiated a lasting truce. The British South Africa Company was now effectively in control of the lands between the Limpopo and Zambezi rivers.

By today's standards, the concept of a commercial enterprise conquering and administering a country sounds quite bizarre, but of course this had been a fairly common practice by many nations, including the original settlement of the Cape by the Dutch East India Company a couple of centuries before. It worked pretty well, as the rulers had to be fiscally responsible, unlike most governments.

Chapter 2:
FAMILY HISTORY

When my grandfather arrived in Southern Rhodesia in 1896 he found an unspoiled land, sparsely populated but torn by regular conflict between the Matabele and Shona tribes. There was no infrastructure at all. At the time of my birth, this land had been transformed into a paradise by hard-working and highly principled Englishmen and Afrikaners. They had put a stop to the Matabele aggression, built railways, roads, cities mines and farms. The government was democratic with a qualified franchise. English law prevailed. Everyone benefited.

We never got to know our paternal Granddad very well as he passed away while we were very young. He was born in 1873 in Somerset, England, in the good old days of Queen Victoria's reign, when England ruled most of the world. Granddad felt he should do his part in helping to rule the world, so in 1894 at the young age of 21 he bought a passage to Cape Town, South Africa, and entered into the postal service there as a telegraphist. After two years he learned of exciting opportunities being offered by the British South Africa Company in the newly occupied territory of Southern Rhodesia.

Right after the 1896 Matabele uprising, Granddad caught the train to Mafeking, which was as far as it went, and then continued his trip by mule cart to Bulawayo to work as a telegraphist in the fledgling postal system. He and some friends set up house in the tiny settlement and started work establishing the postal service in the new territory. His housemates were two brothers from a family he had known in England and after a short time they sent for their sisters to join them to keep house. Thrilled at the prospect of adventure and patriotism, Grandma and her sister accepted the challenge and took the long and dangerous trip to England's newest conquest. The twin sisters were imaginatively named Ada Lizzie and Lizzie Ada. Grandad must have been impressed with Ada's cooking, for after an appropriate period of courtship, Granddad and Ada were married in Bulawayo in 1900.

Dad was born in 1912, in Hatfield, an area just outside the new capital, Salisbury. He was the fifth of seven children, but the first, a daughter, had died of dysentery at the age of two. Shortly after his birth, the family moved to Gatooma, a tiny farming community 70 miles south of Salisbury, where Granddad was given the responsibility of Postmaster. Dad and his siblings had a fine time growing up in Gatooma. The surrounding country was virgin bushveld, and the youngsters spent their free

16

time roaming the bush behind their house, collecting butterflies and birds' eggs, hunting and fishing. Gatooma consisted of a cluster of quite nice brick houses with the traditional corrugated iron roofs. The bricks were made locally, but all the steel and any manufactured items had to be brought from South Africa. Southern Rhodesia now had rail service to Salisbury from the south and to Umtali from the Mozambique port of Beira in the east and a network of dirt roads. The new colony had attracted adventurers from all walks of life and many different nations and soon a thriving mining and farming economy developed. Life was tough in many respects, but the English tradition at the time demanded high standards and a responsible government was put in place. Dad attended a proper school with well qualified teachers from England, following a strict English curriculum. As money and luxuries were in short supply and the climate was temperate, shoes were not required but pupils wore practical garb of khaki cotton. At that time there were about 3,000 whites and 500,000 blacks.

The white settlers had put a stop to most of the intertribal warfare and for the first time in their histories the black population could go about their business without constant fear of attack. The black civilizations had been based on livestock with limited crop production and were nomadic to some extent, as grazing became scarce and land became barren. The wheel was unknown, and heavy items were moved by cattle pulling crude sleds made of wood. Shelter was normally in the form of circular huts made from tree limbs with mud caulking and thatched roofs. Aside from the dubious ministrations from the witchdoctor there were no medical facilities and infant mortality was high.

Traditionally the blacks had lived in groups, each headed by a chief. The chief was not elected democratically, he simply acquired the position by force or descent. Aspirants were not above murdering their fathers, brothers or sons to get there. Once in place, the chief ruled autocratically and did as he saw fit. His main objective was to increase his own power and possessions. His subjects accepted this and understood that their lives lay in his hands. In many respects he was regarded as their father and indeed they used the name baba (father) with respect when addressing him. It was a paternalistic system which they were accustomed to. The whites did not interfere with this system and dealt respectfully with the chiefs when negotiating common interests.

The blacks were astonished as the whites set up their towns, mines and farms because they had not been exposed to any of the facets of European life, and understandably they were in awe. Dad remembers the average tribesman in Gatooma dressed in nothing but a loincloth and carrying an assegai (crude spear). Probably because of this, apart from a small number of minor attacks in the first few years, the blacks did not continue to resist occupation. Early Rhodesia was a very safe place, with the main threat coming from animals and disease, not humans. Malaria, dysentery and typhoid were common and Dad got malaria almost every wet season. Dad remembers no old whites, all the pioneers were young, vigorous people who had adventurous spirits and let nothing daunt them.

When Dad was nine years old, the family moved to a small town called Umtali, nestled between the mountains on the eastern border with Portugal's colony of Mozambique. Granddad became postmaster here too, and the children attended Umtali Junior and High Schools. Sports were very important in the lives of the new Rhodesians, and rugby and cricket were mandatory for all male pupils. On weekends the schools from different towns played against one another and the weekend sport formed a major part of the social life. Upon finishing high school at the age of 17, Dad was offered a job in the civil service. As times were hard because of the Depression and there was no money for college, he took it and moved to Salisbury. Over the next few years the rest of the family moved there too except for Dad's elder brother Rufus. Dad lived in various men's messes enjoying the sporting and social amenities until he married Mum in 1940.

In October 1923 Southern Rhodesia became a self-governing colony of Britain, with a 30-member Legislative Assembly. Legislators were elected by qualified voters. Any inhabitant who met the requirements of property ownership, income or education could vote, regardless of race. Britain retained control over foreign policy and had veto power over any legislation involving the indigenous peoples. In 1930 parliament passed the Land Apportionment Act which reserved 51% of the land for white purchase, 30% as tribal land with option to purchase by blacks only and the remainder held by the state.

Mum's family had a quite different story. Her maternal ancestors came to South Africa from Scotland shortly after the 1820 Settlers from England, arriving in Algoa Bay which is now the city of Port Elizabeth. They spread out over the country from there and became prominent in various walks of life. Her father was born in South Africa, the grandson of an Irish immigrant, from Cork. Old Jack, as we affectionately called him, was a great character and worked as a magistrate in many towns throughout South Africa. He fought on the British side in the Boer War. Mum was born in 1906 in the small Eastern Cape town of Keiskammahoek, but in her teens moved to Cape Town where she attended Rustenberg school and the South African College of Music. After graduating, she moved to London to continue her studies at the Royal College of Music. She was a talented pianist, and spent some time touring in other European capitals. While in Germany she ordered a brand new Bluthner piano which she had shipped to South Africa. After teaching music there for a time, a friend persuaded her to move north to Rhodesia. As many of her relatives had already moved there, she decided to give it a try. South Africa was still suffering from the aftermath of the Boer war and she felt Rhodesia would offer more of the English lifestyle she was accustomed to. She taught music at schools in Bulawayo and Umtali before moving to Salisbury, where she met Dad through his sister Madge, also a pianist. They were married at the Anglican Cathedral on Second Street in 1940.

I should draw attention to the wonderful union Mum and Dad developed. From my earliest memories until

Mum's death in 1973 I can honestly say I never detected anything but a fantastic love between them. They were both naturally kind and considerate to everyone and their marriage worked perfectly. Mum had a very happy and sunny disposition which her twinkling brown eyes revealed clearly. She was seldom sick but did suffer from bad migraine headaches, during which time she would quietly rest until they passed. I never saw her in a bad mood and she never nagged Dad. She tended to us kids with great love and kindness and there was nothing we could not tell her. She had a busy social life, mainly with family and her many music friends and our house was always open to visitors. She also took it upon herself to take care of old people who were alone and she brought them home for tea frequently. Some of our friends had children in boarding school and on weekends when the parents could not visit, Mum would invite these kids to spend the time with us. Mum left most of the worrying to Dad, which he was very good at.

Dad was the solid rock in all our lives. He worried a great deal himself, which probably gave him the duodenal ulcer which plagued him for most of his life. He was the disciplinarian, financial manager, planner, handyman and gardener. He consulted Mum gently on all major decisions and between them they agreed upon the best course of action. We loved Dad but were very aware that he was the boss. He was a wonderful father who regarded his family as his greatest treasure and did his utmost to give us everything we needed, both material and psychological. We knew exactly where we stood with him. Although he never earned a lot of money, he was an excellent money-manager and with careful planning he was able to give us very good lives with few luxuries but every necessity. He instilled in us the basics of honesty, integrity, hard work and fiscal responsibility. I do not have any statistics but from our perspective most of our friends were brought up like us. We knew very few divorced people, for us divorce was a rarity.

The majority of whites in Rhodesia were middle class with modest incomes sufficient to support themselves in reasonable comfort. The more wealthy had the good manners not to flaunt their riches and the poorer were treated with kindness and respect. All the schoolchildren wore inexpensive and practical uniforms so that no child would feel disadvantaged. The junior schools in poorer areas offered one healthy meal per day available free to all. Schools were segregated because of the vast cultural differences and also because of proximity to the pupils' homes. The government instituted a program to both build schools and train teachers to educate the black children and these schools set the same academic standards as the white schools. The missions also offered schooling to blacks. Robert Mugabe attended a mission school.

Chapter 3:
THE HILLSIDE HOUSE

I was born at the Lady Chancellor nursing-home in Salisbury in May of 1945. This was a pretty good time to be born, because the war had ended and everyone was in a celebratory mood. Dad had been at sea returning from a trip to England when war was declared in 1939, and by the time he arrived home in Salisbury, all his contemporaries had already enlisted and gotten their assignments. He signed up for the Royal Air Force, but because the main contingent from Rhodesia had already shipped out for training, he was held back until the next intake. Well, that never happened, and Dad was eternally bitter because in his words, he spent the war serving tea to the officers in the air-force mess-hall. His air-force aspirations were probably thwarted by his very serious stammer, although he never led us to believe this. Dad's life was divided into two periods; before and after the war.

He correctly believed that the war changed the balance of power in the world and led to the dismantling of the empires of Britain, France, Belgium, Holland and Portugal.

We lived in a rambling house on a fourteen acre lot in the Hillside suburb of Salisbury, with our southern boundary on the Macabusi river. The house was solid brick with the ubiquitous corrugated-iron roof. At the rear of the house were two huge jacaranda trees, which provided good shade and were perfect for us youngsters to climb. We had a detached garage for Dad's 39 Chevrolet and another detached complex for servants' housing and Dad's workshop. Further away were the chicken and duck pens and a large barn for the cows. Mum maintained a huge vegetable garden and we had various fruit trees and a multitude of mulberry trees, so we had a very healthy diet.

The kitchen was very large with an electric stove and a long counter with sink. As we had no refrigerator, the kitchen had no glazed windows, but large openings along two sides covered with mosquito mesh. This allowed the cool breezes to pass through and avoided cooking odors from permeating the rest of the house. We had a separate pantry to keep food. Meat, butter and milk were stored in a mesh covered "safe" which had its legs immersed in cans of water. This kept the contents reasonably cool and the cans of water discouraged ants from raiding the perishables.

Because of the lack of refrigeration, milk, meat and bread were delivered each weekday by delivery men riding bicycles with large baskets in the front. The butcher, baker and dairy each had their crew of delivery men who fanned out over the town each morning delivering fresh supplies. These delivery men not only had to be strong and fit, but also needed to be adept at fending off dogs with a skillful swift kick. For unknown reasons, most dogs detested these men and waited with great eagerness each morning in the hope of getting at least one quick bite in. We generally confined the dogs during the delivery period, but occasionally one would escape for some sport. It was uncanny how the dogs knew the delivery man was approaching long before we could either see or hear anything.

We had one bathtub inside the house, and hot water was supplied by a forty-four gallon petrol drum on its side which was built into a crude brick furnace outside. A wood fire was kept burning here stoked periodically by the garden boy. The water itself came from a deep well, and once a day one of the servants would man the hand-pump and pump water from the well into a five-hundred gallon tank raised high on a metal platform. The toilet was another matter. At that time Salisbury suburbs had no central sewer system, so the city fathers set up a very effective routine of bucket collection. The outhouse was a brick structure located a hundred yards downwind from the house. It consisted of a very spacious bench seat with a suitable hole and a large bucket positioned strategically beneath the hole. At about eight pm every night, a stinking truck would pull up in the driveway and a strong young fellow would leap off it carrying a clean bucket and pick up the full one. We called these crews the Zambezi

Boys, I guess to avoid calling them a name more closely associated with their vocation. These buckets had no lids, and one never wanted to imagine what happened each time the truck lurched or braked hard. The Zambezi Boys were aware of the hazards of their chosen profession, and dressed appropriately in mealie sacks which could be discarded at the end of each night's work. The buckets were all hauled to the municipal sewage farm which produced a wonderful array of tasty vegetables which were sold in the city market.

The plot itself was rectangular and rather flat, as is most of the Salisbury area. It actually had two houses on it, the one we lived in and the other rented to another family. The two houses were about 300 yards apart and because of the large syringa and mulberry trees, one was not visible from the other. We had a very large front lawn and a homemade tennis court had been built to the left of the house. The rear was simply a packed earth clear area with the two large jacaranda trees. We walked down a long dirt path to the chicken-run and barn and beyond lay Dad's fields, going all the way down to the river.

At that time Salisbury was a thriving town of about 75,000 whites. It had been carefully and tastefully laid out with avenues named after various heroes running east-west and numbered streets running north-south. The city center was First Street between Jameson and Manica Avenues. At the time of my first memories, all the roads were tarred, the Jacaranda trees along the avenues were quite large and the Salisbury Park and botanical gardens were well developed. Mum used to take me to the park in the mornings to play with the other kids and enjoy a fine selection of swings, roundabouts and bucking horses. My favorite area of the park was a scaled replica of the Victoria Falls, complete with arched bridge and railway line. The park had a nice tea-house and on Sunday afternoons the military band would play rousing music from the bandstand.

Salisbury is situated high on the watershed of the country at an altitude of about 4,800 feet above sea level. It has a very temperate climate, never very hot or cold. The summer rains normally start in October, with big cumulus clouds building up before midday and a short, heavy downpour in the afternoon. After this, the sky would clear and everything would smell fresh and clean. As the summer progressed, periods of rain became longer and gentler, ending in April or early May. The afternoon storms at the beginning of the rainy season could be quite violent. The heat and static would build up in the morning and after lunch the skies would become black and lightning and thunder would flash and rumble. The heavens would open and deliver about an hour of heavy rain. The fork lightning was impressive and one afternoon our houseboy was ironing clothes in the kitchen when the house was hit, sending him flying across the room with blue sparks coming from the iron. He picked himself up and broke into a huge smile, the African philosophy celebrating his near brush with death.

My early memories start at our house in Hillside, although my parents moved there after I was born. My sister Jennifer was two and a half years older than me.

Next door, Dad owned the second house which he rented to friends who had a son my age. JD, as we called him, was my constant companion and we played together all day. Apart from the farm animals we had dogs and cats and from time to time rabbits, guinea-pigs, white-mice and nagapies. I shared a room with my sister in the big old house. We had solid iron bedsteads and mattresses filled with coia, a fiber derived from the cactus plant. The floors were solid concrete, topped with a dark red cement and polished to a shine. As was popular in colonial houses, a wide verandah ran around two sides.

The daily routine at this time was breakfast at about seven am, consisting of either brown or white corn or oatmeal porridge with milk and sugar. On Sundays we had eggs, kippers, kidneys on toast or haddock. After breakfast Dad would leave for work by bicycle and Mum would get ready for the day's music lessons. I would be entrusted to the nanny and taken outside to play in the dirt yard at the back of the house. Dad would come home for lunch at one o'clock and we would all sit at the table for the main meal of the day. We had a very good black cook named Herbert who prepared a great variety of meals under Mum's direction. Lunch was quite formal, with Dad sitting at the head of the table and carving the meat. As I grew older, he also took the precaution of placing a short reed stick next to his side-plate. Dad correctly believed that teaching his children good table manners and general polite behavior was important. Any slight or blatant deviation from his proscribed ideas on these subjects was immediately corrected by a swift application of the reed to the closest part of my anatomy. Dad was not reticent in assisting other parents in fulfillment of their duties, so any of my friends who happened to be dining with us were held to the same standards. Interestingly, this never caused any resentment and Dad was well liked and respected by all our friends.

Mum spent a lot of the day giving piano lessons, so our house was generally filled with various levels of music according to the skill of the pupil. Although Mum was an exceptionally good pianist, I never appreciated piano music while living at home, I think because my ear had suffered so much from very imperfect playing and the endless repetitions of scales and other exercises of her pupils. The standard of music was high in Salisbury and periodically Mum and her fellow musicians would put on a fine concert in one of the halls in town. Many talented musicians and singers from Eastern Europe and Russia had immigrated to Rhodesia before and during the war and they loved nothing better than playing together. Rhodesia had also become a favorite stop for renowned touring musicians, and Mum accompanied some world-famous singers.

One of Mum's favorite music friends was a Jewish violinist named Leo from Lithuania. His family had suffered terribly during the Russian and Nazi occupations and he was happy to be safe in Rhodesia. Two other lady friends played both piano and stringed instruments, both Russian Jews who had fled during the revolution. Mum was also a competent violinist and these four frequently got together to play quartets at one or the other's houses and this music was wonderful at close quarters. Leo was the finest violinist Mum had ever heard and her dream was for him to teach me to attain the same standard. Alas, despite Leo's best efforts for several years, it was clear to us both that my efforts were an affront to the instrument and all within earshot.

Salisbury maintained a high standard in all the arts and drama and music played a large part in our lives. When Mum had a concert to prepare for she put her music students on hold and practiced the piano for up to eight hours per day. We kids have various concertos indelibly imprinted in our minds after listening to the same pieces day after day for several weeks. Mum played long solos in the concert halls and I once asked her how was it that with two lines of music to read and ten fingers and two feet to send independent instructions to at high speed, she never hit a wrong note? She looked at me incredulously and proclaimed that this was the point of all the practice and it would be unthinkable to have errors. Her main concentration was not the notes, but getting exactly the right expression into the music so it could be enjoyed to its fullest extent. I still believe that good piano players must be some of the smartest people in the world.

Dad would arrive home about four thirty each weekday and I looked forward to this hour eagerly. When I was very small I would assist him with changing from a collar and tie to his preferred khaki shorts and shirt. Dad hated ties with a passion and couldn't wait to tear his off each evening. Once freed of his encumbrances he would be off outside to attack the project of the day. Dad was a good farmer and good with machinery, so most afternoons were spent ploughing, planting, cultivating or maintaining his various machines. I didn't care much for the farming part as I could do little to participate, but the maintenance jobs I loved. Dad was very patient (which was very difficult for him) and explained each step of the process as he dismantled or assembled the machines. He gave me small tasks which made me feel very useful. I think at this early age I developed my respect for logic, reason and engineering.

Dad had two farm machines. His favorite was a vicious mechanical tiller which bucked and reared as it dug into the sun-baked soil. It had to be started with a pull-cord without any rewind mechanism, so each pull was a laborious affair. Dad was not a cussing man, but sometimes repetitive pulls drove him very close. Once the engine had started, Dad would seize the two long handles with all his strength and engage the wicked dog clutch. The tiller would take off with a wild jerk and Dad had to lean far backwards to get the tines to bite. Once they reached the desired depth he would walk forward down the field, hoping that the tines would not strike any roots or large rocks. If they did, the torque would try to drive the handles into the ground, and Dad had to be quick on the clutch or be dragged down too. I always thought the machine was dragging Dad along against his will.

The second machine was a crude harvester with lethal reciprocating blades on a long boom in the front. It was also a walk-behind machine but not nearly as unmanageable as the tiller. I got the impression that Dad didn't enjoy this harvester quite as much as the tiller as he found it boring. As both machines were procured third or fourth hand, they required a great deal of tender loving care. Dad had a nice workshop out back and was skilled at improvising solutions to most problems. I liked this workshop very much and was very happy when the machines broke down.

Just before sunset each evening we would all go for a walk. Both Mum and Dad enjoyed nature and the exercise they got during these walks. Having been raised in the bush, Dad would not venture very far from the house without his stick. He took great care in selecting his supply of sticks. They had to be the right wood, dead straight and preferably slightly tapered. He would remove the bark and let them dry for a period of time, after which they would be smoothed with a pen-knife and lightly sanded. He swung them in his right hand, not using them for support. The main purpose of the stick was protection against snakes. Most snakes flee long before one sees them, but a couple of varieties are lazy. The puffadder is one of these. It is a short, fat snake which hisses quite loudly when threatened. If one does not hear the hiss, it is easy to step on one. The puffadder was very common at that time, and it is a very poisonous snake. Dad had eagle eyes in the bush and if he saw any snake he would first try to go around it or scare it out of the way using the stick. Occasionally he would judge it too late for avoidance, and the stick would crash down on the unfortunate reptile's back.

During these walks Dad would point out many things along the way. Having been raised in the bushveld himself, he had keen knowledge of African fauna and flora. The sandveld paths we walked along were narrow and smooth, as the blacks who had created them always walked in single file. There were always interesting things to see, depending on the time of year. In the wet season the grass would be lush and green and the streams would flow strongly. Occasionally we would see a small duiker antelope but more often we encountered guinea-fowl, partridge, mongoose, field-mice and a variety of birds.

Once back from the walk, Mum and Dad would occasionally enjoy a drink before dinner. Mum's tolerance level was very low, and one glass of sherry was all she would ever touch. Dad would have a beer at room temperature (he had little choice without a frig). We would have dinner about seven, served by the cook. The family would always dine together in the main dining table and everything was done correctly according to English etiquette. The cutlery was silver and crockery of good English china. Dinner was usually three courses; soup, main course and desert. After dinner we kids would take our baths in the big metal bathtub and Dad would tune in to the BBC for the English six o'clock news, which was eight o'clock our time.

Dad aspired to farming, but lacking the resources to buy a farm, the fourteen acres was the best he could do at the time. Fourteen acres might sound like a rather large urban property, but at that time Salisbury was sparsely populated and only the city center was divided into smaller lots, even those usually being at least half an acre. The farming was a hobby, as Dad still had his civil-service job from eight in the morning until four in the afternoon, with an hour for lunch. Apart from raising maize, he had four head of cattle and a multitude of chickens and ducks. The oldest cow was called Black because she was completely black. Her daughter was appropriately called Blackie for the same reason. The other two cows were Daisy and Dainty, both good-natured Jerseys. The black cows were a bit cantankerous and we approached them with some trepidation. The Jerseys were very sociable and would allow us kids to pet them and milk them with no objection. We were more or less self-sufficient on the plot except when we wanted non-poultry meat, which was supplied from the butcher shop nearby. The farm "boys" milked the cows each day and we had plenty of fresh milk. Mum always boiled it before we were allowed to drink it, and after the boiling we were able to skim a rich layer of cream off the top which was kept in a separate jar for use on scones and deserts. Mum was a first-class scone cook and there was nothing we enjoyed better than fresh scones with cream and jam.

We collected a good supply of eggs from the chicken run each morning, some of which we ate fresh and the rest of which Mum immersed in animal fat to preserve them for a later date. Every Sunday that we had lunch at our house, Dad would catch a nice plump chicken or duck and it would be roasted for the meal.

One day we noticed that our chicken count was diminishing at a faster rate than our own consumption. At first we suspected human thieves, but on closer investigation, Dad spied jackal tracks in the vicinity. He went down to the farm-supply store and bought a wicked jaw-trap which he tethered near the chicken-run and baited with some leftover raw meat from the kitchen. Sure enough, the next morning we all went down to the trap and discovered a very unhappy jackal with its front paw caught firmly in the jaws. We felt rather sorry for the unfortunate beast, but Dad was not encumbered by any sympathetic feelings at all. He sent me to fetch his two-two, a 0.22" caliber rifle, and put the jackal out of its misery.

As young children we were allowed to roam more or less freely. Our fourteen acre property had many attractions for us and we thoroughly enjoyed them all. At the bottom of the property the Makabuzi river divided our lot from the neighbor's. One of the first admonitions by our parents was never to have contact with the water in the Makabuzi. Most African rivers are infected with the water-borne parasite bilharzia. This is an ugly little worm that is carried by certain snails and can enter the body through any wound or damaged skin. Once in the body, it makes its way to the kidneys and starts devouring them. If detected early it can be eradicated with heavy doses of penicillin, but if left untreated for a long period it can cause irreversible kidney damage and death. It is the curse of Africa because it renders most of the rivers and lakes off limits to swimming and other water sports. The only exceptions are fast-moving, deep or cold water where the snail cannot survive. Regrettably we did not follow orders too well and inevitably waded or swum in the Makabuzi.

Whereas most of my friends got bilharzias, some several times, for whatever reason I never did.

The Makabusi was by normal standards not a river but a rather miserable stream. Most of the year it was very low, but during the rainy season after a big storm it could suddenly transform itself into a raging torrent. There were small bream and barble in the river which we liked to catch. Getting the bait was a dirty business however. We used the larvae of the large horseflies, which were readily available in the fresh dung of our cows. We had to hand-pick through this dung to get them, and maybe the residue was as unattractive to the bilharzia parasite as it was to us. The bream were generally too small to eat and we threw them back. We did catch some reasonable-sized barble, but they tasted like the mud they lived in, so we generally gave them to the servants who had developed a taste for the fish. The African barble is a very hardy fish. Adapted to the wild swings in rainfall and water-level, it can survive for months buried the moist mud of the riverbed. Once the rains arrive and the river flows again, it wakes up, wiggles free and starts swimming normally. It can survive out of the water for several hours. A few times we caught a barble and left it on the riverbank, where it became hard and dry. Some hours later we threw it back in the water, where after a few minutes it loosened up and swam away happily.

One of the family's favorite evening walks was along the banks of the Macabuzi. Here we could check on the status of the neighbor's immense black and white pig, which we held in great awe. He was a splendid specimen, bad-tempered and filthy and he hated nothing more than small boys. We formed small catapults with rubber bands looped across our thumbs and index fingers and fired small pieces of orange-peel at his impressive testicles. He did not like this at all and rushed the fence of his sty in fury, but fortunately it always held strong.

Along the small path there were many thorn trees. These had sharp thorns up to three inches long. The butcher birds would catch field-mice and skewer them on these thorns to kill them. They would return later to eat the sun-dried mice. We felt very sorry for these mice but nature is cruel in many ways and we had to accept this.

Rhodesia was home to a vast variety of poisonous snakes, and from birth we were taught to kill all snakes anywhere near our house. This was rather unfair to the harmless varieties, but was considered prudent for those not educated in all the species. For the time honored reason, Dad chose to situate his woodpile close to the outdoor latrine. The logic was that each trip to the latrine could also serve as a wood hauling trip. We kids didn't like this arrangement at all, not only because we didn't like hauling wood, but because the woodpile was a favorite shelter for snakes. The most common variety in our area was the cobra, a large and very poisonous snake. Like most wild things, the cobra does not go out looking for trouble, and if possible, will flee if it feels in imminent danger. After a few nasty experiences seeing the large snakes slither between the toilet and the woodpile as we made our trips to the latrine, we never could have a relaxing experience whilst doing our legitimate business.

Generally the servants would kill snakes close to the house. Once a dead snake became available, we placed it nicely coiled in the corner of the latrine. The latrine was unlighted, so normally the snake would not be noticed until the occupant's eyes had adjusted to the darkness. To make sure we got a rewarding performance, once we perceived that the occupant had sat down, we jerked on a piece of string tied to the snake's head and dragged it across the floor. The occupant definitely felt disadvantaged in the compromising position, so the first reaction was to flee from the latrine with the minimum of decorum and seek assistance. By the time this came, we and the dead snake were long gone, returning to sympathize with the victim only after our laughter had subsided .

We had another equally gratifying routine for this latrine. When an adult visitor had purposely or inadvertently insulted or scolded one of us, we would wait until he or she made the inevitable trip. Rhodesia had some very nice natural grasses which grew thick and tall. One of the varieties had a nice bushy head of seeds at the top. We would equip ourselves with a couple of these stalks and quietly open the bucket trap-door at the back of the latrine. This gave an unobstructed view of the posterior of the candidate. Depending on gender, we would gently apply the bushy end of the grass stalk to the appropriate area of the victim's anatomy. This was a risky business, but generally delivered spectacular results. We had to be sure to have impeccable alibis for the time involved, but I believe nobody was fooled.

There were all kinds of interesting things to do at home and our parents and the servants took pleasure in showing these to us. When I was very small, Dad showed me how to catch ant-lions. Ant-lions trap ants by digging a conical hole in loose sand and waiting at the bottom. The ant would stumble into the hole and find itself unable to climb out because of the steep, loose sides. The more it struggled, the deeper it fell until it hit bottom, where the patient ant-lion would move in for its meal. Dad showed me how to take a short piece of jacaranda twig and make circular movements with it in the ant-lion hole. Sure enough, the rotary motion would drive the poor insect to the center and up, where it could be grabbed with the fingers. We generally replaced them in their desecrated holes afterwards and they would repair them in a short time.

The other very plentiful species in our area was the chongalolo. These were millipedes ranging from one to 8 inches long. They were dark brown with lighter brown rings and had thousands of little legs all nicely synchronized. We would collect these to see who could find the biggest, and occasionally race them. They came out en mass after the rain, and were one of my favorites.

Chameleons were plentiful and when we came upon one we brought it home. The blacks did not like them at all because of an ancient legend in which the chameleon was chosen to represent them at an important race. Notwithstanding the fact that this was undeniably a poor choice, the blacks blame the chameleon for moving too hesitantly and losing the race, which left them disadvantaged. The blacks will not go near the chameleon, so there was a certain amount of conflict when we caught them and brought them into the house. Chameleons feed by quietly approaching insects and then rolling out their incredibly long, sticky tongues and catching the insect. Their skin color adapts to most natural surroundings, and this camouflage, coupled with the very slow and hesitant motion, allows them to sneak up very close. Our kitchen had screens instead of windows to allow the air to circulate and keep flies out. However, some flies and mosquitoes inevitably got in. We would place the chameleons on the screens, where their sharp claws could support them very well, and they would be very happy there for weeks devouring the supply of captive insects. These chameleons are normally very passive fellows and will allow themselves to be caught easily, mainly because they are incapable of fleeing. They walk happily over one's body and don't seem to mind being handled. Occasionally they will get angry and puff up their lower chins, and if they do bite they are reluctant to release.

The really prized pet was the nagapie (Afrikaans for night-ape). These are nocturnal small primates, which come in two varieties, large and small. We preferred the small ones, as they fitted well in our shirt pockets. They had beautiful large brown eyes and soft grey fur, with four hands like a miniature monkey. They ate fruit and insects at night and slept by day. They were incredible jumpers and could move from object to object at lightning speed. We kept them in our pockets and took them to school with us. The larger ones were seldom kept as pets because of their size and proclivity for biting.

The other favorite pastime we had was tree-climbing. Although most African trees do not grow to tremendous height, they have smooth bark and many limbs. Our property had jacaranda, syringa, mulberry, eucalyptus and msasa trees. We climbed the trees like monkeys and had chases up and down. From time to time someone would push his luck a bit too far and slip and fall. Mostly this resulted in bruised limbs and honor, but occasionally a bone would get broken. The jacaranda, a native of Brazil, is a very attractive tree with small, delicate leaves and purple blossoms. The founding fathers in the various towns had the foresight to plant these trees along many of the wide avenues, providing shade and beauty for the future. The syringa was a similar tree but with yellow blossoms, larger leaves and berries. The mulberry was a favorite because of both shade and the tasty mulberries it yielded. The msasa is the ubiquitous African highveld tree and is native to Africa. Its leaves turn various shades of red and orange in spring and provide quite a spectacle for a few weeks.

The mulberry tree not only offered excellent fruit, climbing and shade, but it also provided the staple diet of the silkworm. We kids had an impressive collection of silkworms which fed voraciously on the dark-green mulberry leaves. The silkworm is a good-looking white caterpillar with black markings around the body. It grows to about three inches long and then starts weaving its cocoon out of pure silk, light yellow in color. We kept the caterpillars in boxes in the house, and provided various cardboard cutouts for them to cover with the silk thread.

Some caterpillars did not take to the forced pattern and got right on with the cocoon. After the cocoon was complete we waited about three weeks for the moth to gnaw its way out and then start laying the eggs for the next cycle.

Dad had four to five servants on the property most of the time. These were a cook, a houseboy, a nanny and two gardeners. When the whites took control of the country, in the English tradition, they immediately imposed a head tax on every black adult, to be collected by the chief in each area. The reasons were twofold. Firstly, as the blacks were beneficiaries of the peace, the medical facilities, the improved roads and farming techniques and other facets of European civilizations, it was felt that they should also contribute according to means. Secondly, the whites needed labor in their mines and on their farms, so a tax would encourage the blacks to get jobs, something quite unknown to them heretofore. The original head tax was a modest two English pounds per year.

Notwithstanding the benefits the whites had provided, the head tax was a source of strong resentment amongst the blacks. They considered it meddling in their private affairs, but more importantly, it lured many young blacks to the cities, farms and mines and left the villages without their normal quota of men. The elders considered this a travesty because from time immemorial a self-respecting male would never deign to do anything which could be considered work. Work was the exclusive duty of the 'mfazi's, the strong and willing wives and daughters. To further rub salt in this wound, male household servants were expected to obey their white mistresses and often even white children.

The servants lived rent-free in rooms on our property known as kias. At Hillside they had no electricity or running water but did have a separate bucket latrine. We supplied them with their traditional food of ground corn meal and meat and uniforms to wear while they were on the job. If they needed medical attention our mother would be the first to see them, and if she could not handle the situation we would take them to a doctor at our expense. They were paid a small cash wage each month to purchase luxuries. It was felt that this system made sense because all necessities were provided and there was no possibility that poor cash management could lead to deprivation. Of course those coming straight from the villages in the bush had no European skills at all and little concept of money and had to be instructed on every task.

One had to think carefully before giving instructions and asking questions. Not only was the language an issue, but even those servants who spoke reasonably good English used a different logic from us. This logic was quite understandable, as English is a language fraught with expressions that do not follow logic. One had to be very careful using the negative. Upon asking a servant "Did you not do the laundry today?" he may answer "Yes". To him, that meant yes, he did not do it. To you it meant he did do it. When directing a helper to turn a wrench to tighten a bolt, one had to be sure to explain that when a certain resistance was felt he should stop, otherwise he would continue until the bolt was sheared or the threads stripped. In the latter case, if alone, he may go on tightening the same bolt for hours. These are just a couple of many issues each race had to contend with in everyday life together, but most of the time misunderstandings were dealt with in good humor.

We were taught to treat everyone kindly, respectfully and considerately and the servants were no exception. We kids genuinely liked the servants and although we learned only "kitchen kaffir" and they spoke limited English, we communicated quite well. In many ways they were like children, curious, uninhibited and eager to learn. Our nanny Edith took very good care of us when we were very small, and as each child was born she took on the added load with great enthusiasm. Salisbury had a cool winter and the old house was draughty so perhaps for this reason we got every childhood disease possible. Mum and Edith did their best, but when the fevers got too high Mum would call in the family doctor, Dr. Ritchken. Dr. Ritchken was a small Jewish man who seemed happy to answer Mum's calls regardless of the time of day or night. He always drove the latest model Chevrolet which we held in great awe. We all had a great respect for his medical talents and he was a close family friend. In those days all the doctors made house-calls because few others had transportation readily available.

Our cookboy was named Herbert. He had previously been trained as cook for one of the consulates and could offer a very fine menu. He was a fairly young fellow when he came to work for us, and had a radiant smile which portrayed his congenial disposition. The flaw in the domestic laborer system was that whereas homeowners in the cities normally housed their servants on their properties, they did not necessarily house the servants' families. Sometimes the families would reside in the black township adjacent to each white city or town, but more often the family would be further away in the native reserve assigned to that tribe. This made family life for the blacks difficult, as they only saw their wives and children once a month at best when they had a free weekend. Sadly for us, after a few years Herbert got offered a post at Inyanga, close to his family, and he left. He was replaced by Joseph, who remained with the family for many years.

The black townships were set up by the whites to house black families and single workers. The township of Harare served the city of Salisbury. It was sited a few miles from Salisbury beyond the industrial area, close enough for the residents to ride bicycles or take buses to work but far enough to give privacy to both groups. The brick dwellings were solid and weatherproof and in later years had electrical service and waterborne sanitation. They were arguably more luxurious than the traditional tribal thatched hut, but grouped closely together without any trees or other vegetation they could not be described as model neighborhoods. They had bus service to town, schools, a beerhall, cinema and laundry facilities. Law and order was enforced by black policemen, part of the British South Africa Police force. These policemen were trained well and issued with smart khaki uniforms, caps and nightsticks. They wore beautiful leather belts, puttees and shining boots and each had a bicycle for transport.

On their epaulettes were the emblems BSAP in brass, for British South Africa Police. We liked these, for not knowing the translation of the acronym, we took it to be the Afrikaans word pasop, which means watch out.

These police patrolled both black and white areas and did an excellent job. They were supervised by a much smaller white force dressed similarly but with access to motorbikes and patrol cars. The Justice Department also had a criminal investigation arm, the CID and a Special Branch for more complex cases. The court system was staffed with well qualified lawyers and judges and the courthouse conducted its affairs just like the English, wigs and all. Although petty theft occurred, serious crime was very low.

Many private industries and government departments also housed their employees, with single and married quarters and most amenities. There was some crime and the inevitable drunken brawling after long nights at the beerhalls, but by and large the blacks led safe lives. There were difficulties applying white laws to black problems. In cases of adultery for instance, under black tradition, the husband of the adulteress was expected and entitled to kill both his wife and her lover. This did not apply in the reverse however, when the husband took an unmarried lover. White law considered any taking of life murder, with the penalty of death by hanging. Unfortunately a number of indignant black men went to the gallows after simply performing what they considered to be their duties. This and many other cultural differences were causes for strong resentment in the black communities.

To keep crime low in the white cities and towns, blacks were not permitted to move around in them during the hours of darkness without a "pass". A pass was a letter signed by the white employer granting the black permission to be on the streets for a specific time and for a specific purpose. To the uninformed, this would appear to be flagrant transgression of individual rights. To the white city dweller it was a necessary and effective means of preventing wholesale pilfering and loitering. Loitering was also considered a crime. It was assumed if a person was doing so and had no reason to be in that place he was up to no good.

Blacks were not obliged to leave their reservations or work for whites. Those who preferred to retain their traditional lifestyles were at liberty to do so, but they had to find a means of paying the head tax. After he retired from the Civil Service, Dad worked with the blacks in the reserves to set up agricultural co-operatives. These pooled resources to get advantageous pricing for seed and fertilizer and also provided favorable mass-marketing of the crops to ensure fair sales. In this way farmers could not only feed their families but also generate cash for taxes and personal needs. The white Department of Agriculture also provided black farmers with trained white agronomists and livestock experts to educate them on the best agronomic practices. This was ironically another major cause of resentment because these advisors stipulated the number of cattle that could effectively be grazed per acre in each climatic area. To the blacks, a thin cow was just as valuable as a fat one when transacting traditional business such as the lobola used for purchasing a wife. If left unrestricted, with the rapidly increasing population, each desiring the maximum number of cattle, the reserves would soon have become overgrazed and subject to severe soil erosion. The blacks did not understand this.

Each reserve was assigned a Native Commissioner who lived within the reserve and was responsible for its smooth operation. These men spoke Shona or N'debele fluently and understood the blacks well. For the most part they were very decent and dedicated men who effectively devoted their lives to the well-being of the blacks. Working with the chiefs, they settled petty disputes and acted as trusted advisors to the blacks in many respects. Often their wives ran clinics for the black mothers and their children. The reserves had schools staffed with black teachers well trained at the Teachers Training College in Umtali.

Because of the prospects of money, shelter and manufactured goods, tribesmen came to work in Rhodesia from far and wide. The different tribes had different characters and one had to be careful not to employ a mixture of tribesmen who were traditional enemies. There were few pure Zulus in Rhodesia, but the Matabele, although quite interbred by this time, were still the top dogs. Matabele were normally employed as crew-bosses on the mines because they were fearless and all the other tribes feared them. They did little to conceal their contempt for all other tribes, and heaped incredible insults upon them constantly. We did not employ any Matabele for this reason, but we did have servants from various tribes from both within and outside Rhodesia. The tribesmen from Nyasaland (Malawi) were highly sought after as they had pleasant dispositions and were generally good workers. Notwithstanding our care in hiring, we occasionally had intertribal fights in the kias which usually ended with someone leaving because he could not live with the other tribesman.

All the blacks whom we encountered were very good with children. They are by nature patient people, and seldom strike their own children. They live for the moment and depending on circumstances are either very happy or very unhappy. When we were very small we had nannies who took care of us while Mum was teaching piano in the house. We were very fond of these nannies and they were excellent babysitters. They were talented story-tellers and singers and they gave us almost maternal love and attention. We also made good friends with the male members of the staff and they taught us many things about the nature all around us. They showed us how to make traps for small birds and how to flush the field mice out of the long grass. They enjoyed grilling these birds and field mice on long sticks, like a shish kebab.

The blacks are natural musicians and love to sing. When alone, they sing to themselves softly as they work and when in groups they harmonize beautifully. If the work is onerous like digging a ditch, the tempo of the song matches the actions of the picks and shovels, everyone working in time with the beat. The drum was their main instrument in their kraals but they also had crude stringed instruments and a type of mini xylophone made from different lengths of beaten iron which they plucked with their fingers. The nannies sang to us kids frequently as they took care of us in the garden.

After a good rain at certain times of year, the flying ants would emerge from their nests. These were big, fat, termites with wings and the blacks looked forward to these occasions eagerly. They would station themselves at the mouths of the holes in the ground and catch the ants as they emerged. They would be stripped of their wings and lightly fried to a delicious, crunchy appetizer. Another seasonal favorite was the orange caterpillars which came in spring and feasted on the leaves of the Mahobohobo tree. These were nice, hairy, fat caterpillars about 2-3 inches long and were fried into a gooey mess. We never did feel tempted to try this delicacy.

Beer drinking had been a respected pastime in Africa for centuries. As the traditional habits of consumption did not honor time of day nor day of week, one of the most difficult adjustments for the blacks was to confine beer-drinking to Saturday nights. Like most beer-drinkers, they had various recipes and types of beer they enjoyed. Most were made from millet, the small, maize type plant indigenous to Africa. Like most good beverages, the quality was related to the time and care devoted to preparation. The chibuku was almost an instant beer, where water was added to a pre-fermented dry mixture. The result was an opaque, grey/white suspension which continued to ferment after consumption. Only real men could handle large quantities of this, but there were many real men. On the other end of the spectrum there was skokiaan, a wicked mixture of anything that added taste or alcohol content. This took time and skill, and the results were spectacular, sometimes resulting in blindness or even death. Traditionally, the objective of beer drinking was to enhance the singing and storytelling skills and to eventually render the drinker absolutely and completely drunk. There was no point in half-measures. Sundays were therefore days of recuperation and no work was expected.

Dad was a great politician at heart, but because he was afflicted with a serious stammer, he was reluctant to speak in public. He felt a strong empathy with King George VI, who had a similar problem. Dad listened to the news with great interest and discussed it at length with Mum afterwards. I first started paying attention to this in about 1950, when I was five years old. It was very plain that Dad was unhappy with the way things were going in England and Rhodesia. He was convinced (probably correctly) that two major wars had effectively killed off the cream of British manhood and that the current British government were a bunch of sissies. With the huge debt incurred by Britain to the USA, Dad felt that USA financial leverage was influencing British policy. He was convinced that Stalin and Roosevelt had ganged up against Churchill at the Yalta conference and the result was that Britain had been forced to agree to divest itself of its colonies in order to open these up to American and Russian trade.

To add to Dad's frustrations, Rhodesia was being flooded with English immigrants, many of whom had trained there during the war and had fallen in love with the country. These were known as Pongos to those old Rhodesians whose fathers and grandfathers had settled the country originally. The Pongos came from all walks of life, from the aristocratic to the slum dwellers. Most "old Rhodesians" were descendants of tough, adventurous pioneering stock who worked hard and set high standards. They were very critical of the immigrants who did not uphold these and did not understand the demographics of the country. The other issue was that the new immigrants did not regard Rhodesia as home and therefore tended to have a shortsighted view of issues affecting the long-term prospects for the country.

Chapter 4:
FIRST TRIP TO SOUTH AFRICA

The civil service in the colonies was structured to accommodate Englishmen and it was assumed that every good Englishman would naturally want to go "home" as often as he could regardless of where he had been born. For this reason, the vacation program was a three-month paid leave every two years. Both my parents had spent time in England prior to marriage, and so they preferred to take their vacations in South Africa. Mum had her family there and Dad loved the South African coast where he could swim and fish. The first trip I remember well was in 1950, when I was five. As Mum had the new baby, she and the baby went by train. Dad, my elder sister Jennifer and I went by car. We took our nanny Edith with us so that she would be available to look after the baby once we arrived.

Dad had a 1939 Chevrolet and we loaded this up with our luggage, food and spare parts. The country roads in

Rhodesia at that time were either gravel or gravel with two 18" strips of asphalt spaced to accommodate the average vehicle. Our car was known as S44 for the simple reason that this was its registration number, S standing for Salisbury. Old S44 was quite spacious and comfortable, riding about 12" off the ground to handle the large undulations and inconsistencies in the roads. Because of road conditions, we averaged about 45 mph, which was pretty normal. This meant that the 1600 mile trip would take us about 35 hours. However, with three months of vacation, there was no need to hurry.

Road travel was still quite an adventure. We left in early December, at the height of the rainy season, so the first excitement was crossing the swollen rivers. At this time the bridges were very low concrete structures or one simply crossed at a "drift" which was no more than a shallow part of the river with a bed of gravel or concrete. Water flow in Rhodesia could vary from zero in the dry season to a rushing torrent immediately after heavy rain. The first heavy rain could literally cause a wall of water to come rushing down a dry riverbed, so one had to be alert. The first swollen river we encountered was the Sebakwe, which had a drift crossing. Dad stopped the car at the water's edge and then removed his shoes and started wading across to check the depth. It came up to his knees, so he decided that the passengers must walk across to let the car ride a little higher. Whereas Jennifer and I did not weigh much, Edith was a different story. Nannies, almost by definition, had to be well fleshed out. Edith went beyond this point and obese would have been a kind description.

Jennifer and I started wading across, but as soon as the nanny's toes touched the muddy water she recoiled in horror and refused to budge another step. Most likely childhood experiences with crocodiles had given her a strong aversion to water any deeper than six inches. Edith was not to be persuaded, and so finally Dad capitulated and she climbed back into the car, the rear springs compressing a good two inches as she settled her weight onto the seat. We crossed without further incident.

The first night was spent with mum's sister Dorothy at their house in Shabani, an asbestos mining town. Dorothy's husband Bob was a manager at the mine, and went deep down into the earth every day. Uncle Bob was a great favorite as he had a wicked sense of humor and loved to play all kinds of tricks on us. He was also an amateur magician, and pulled coins out of our ears and performed numerous other feats of magic. No-one thought anything of contact with asbestos and we kids played with the raw ore which he brought us, plucking off the long green fibers. I don't know anyone who worked on those mines who died or became ill from asbestos. Uncle Bob eventually died in a car accident while still very healthy.

From Shabani we went on south to the Limpopo river, which marked the border between Rhodesia and South Africa. In normal conditions it is not a very impressive river, and at certain times of year it degenerates to a series of pools. The last part of the trip to the border takes one through the lowveld where, if lucky, one might see various species of wild game. The road went through the huge Nuanetsi ranch where Dad had friends who invited him to hunt periodically. In December the bush is green and it is difficult to see game, but we kept our eyes skinned anyway. The border crossing was quite an affair, with Rhodesian customs and immigration on the north side of the river and South African on the south. After seemingly endless queues and form-filling we were on our way, and soon arrived at the small copper-mining town of Messina. Despite the fact that it was in the height of the rainy season, Messina was hot and dry. Very hot, like 120F in the shade. After filling the car with petrol we set off for the ascent of the Soutpansberg via Whiley's Poort. Poort is Afrikaans for pass, and even though Whiley was an Englishman, everyone used the Afrikaans version.

The road passed over the summit of the mountains, and right there we stopped at the Mountain Inn for the night. The Mountain Inn was an attractive assortment of rondavels, chalets and main structure housing the lounge, bar and dining room. The front lawn looked out over the plains to the south, and one could see the main south highway going as straight as an arrow for fifty miles. The air on top of the mountain was clear and cool, and after moving into our rooms we took a welcome swim in the pool and prepared for dinner.

At that time pretty much all the hotels offered an all-inclusive rate which covered the room and three excellent meals per day. However, private bathrooms were not yet the norm, and most rooms did not have them. There were usually one or two communal bathrooms for each group of rooms, so guests had to be flexible, polite and leave the bathrooms clean after use. There was usually a tin basin with a water jug in each room for minor ablutions.

The Mountain Inn dining-room looked out over the plains below. The dinners were table d'hote which included ors d'oeuvres, soup, fish, main course, dessert and a selection of fruits, cheeses and biscuits. Considering the price at the time, the meals were real bargains. We all looked forward to these meals for two reasons. Firstly, it was a real treat to have such a selection of good dishes served by immaculate waiters. Secondly, as everyone ate at about the same time, this was an opportunity to meet other kids our ages and for our parents to meet other parents. The atmosphere was very colloquial and after dinner there would be numerous groups pursuing various activities.

The next day involved a long drive to Johannesburg, passing through numerous small Afrikaans towns. As Johannesburg is at about 6,600 feet elevation, the vegetation changes radically as one progresses from the lowveld to the highveld. Interestingly, although the lowveld looks uninviting, sparse and dry, the game prefers the grasses there as they are "sweeter". As the ecosystem depends on the grazers and browsers, most of the game is found in the lowveld except in times of drought.

Dad was not a crowd man. He detested a concentration of more than ten humans in one place, and when we went on family picnics in the bush he got very annoyed if any other picnickers had the poor manners to picnic within sight or earshot. He would walk over to them sternly and advise them of their lapse in bush etiquette. This had varied results and sometimes Dad elected to move. For this reason Dad absolutely hated Johannesburg. The only reason to go there was because that's where the road led and to visit our aunt Stella and her son Patrick. Stella's husband, Mum's brother, had been killed in the war and had never got to see his son. We loved staying with Stella and Patrick and Jo'burg was full of novelties for us. Notwithstanding this, Dad would pack everyone up early in the morning to get far out of town before the traffic built up.

From Jo'burg we headed south into the Orange Free State. We crossed the Vaal river at Parys, which the original Boer settlers had optimistically named after Paris. There was very little similarity now or then except that both have rivers running through them. Having never seen Paris, we were oblivious to the shortcomings of Parys and the Vaal was the first big river we had seen. It was named Vaal because of its permanent beige color, vaal being Afrikaans for beige. It was here that we saw our first oak trees and we gathered a fine collection of acorns to show to our friends back home.

The next night was spent in Bloemfontein, the capital of the Orange Free State. Having no family here, we stayed at a hotel. As we arrived fairly early in the afternoon, Dad took us to the zoo. We were astounded by the vast collection of animals from all over the world, and especially impressed by the liger, a cross between lion and tiger. He was a large animal with very faint stripes and no mane. Bloemfontein (flower spring) is a pretty town with a nice stream on the southern side. This was the center of the Afrikaans culture and Afrikaans was the predominant language spoken. The Boer pioneers had founded the town at the time of the Great Trek of 1836. They had judged it far enough from the meddling hands of the English to be able to live their lives as they wished, but of course the discovery of gold on the Witwatersrand had changed all that. Now very much part of South Africa, Bloemfontein was a prosperous farming center.

Next stop was Graff Reinett, in the middle of the Karroo. The Karroo is a vast area of semi-desert high on the South African plateau. The moisture-laden air from the coast is forced upwards by the Outeniqua mountains and dumps all its rain on the coastal side, which is lush and green. The other side is a complete contrast, brown and arid. The Karroo bush is the main vegetation, which has adapted to the desert environment. It is a small bush, not very attractive except to sheep, who can survive on it. Notwithstanding the heat and aridity, the Karroo has a charm of its own. The air is very clear, and visibility is excellent. The land is undulating, so there are magnificent views. The farms here are huge because each animal requires many acres of grazing. Graff Reinett is a small farming town with its own charm. It has an excellent museum depicting the lives of the Voortrekkers, where Dad took us to appreciate a little history.

Our first holiday destination was the town of George, named after King George V. We had accommodations in a nice boarding house on the main street, which had been recommended by Dad's brother Rufus. We arrived there on the evening of the sixth day of our journey and then went to the station to meet Mum and our baby sister

Eveleigh. George was an English town and had its own charm despite being slightly inland. It was backed by the Outeniqua mountains on the north and green fields on the south. Mum's cousin, aunt Betty, farmed here with her husband Quilla. Their small farm had cattle and sheep, and some nice ponds where I fished for bluegill.

Dad lost no time in preparing his fishing gear. The first step was the selection of two nice bamboo poles, a fourteen foot one for him and a twelve foot one for me. He then purchased rolls of black twine, eyelets, reel brackets, rope and varnish. First the poles were smoothed and varnished. He then bound each eyelet to the pole with the black twine, teaching me to do the same. The ends of the twine were cunningly pulled under the binding by a loop left for that purpose, so the finished job looked neat and professional. Next came the reel bracket. This was attached using the heavier rope, and this rope continued a foot either side of the bracket to supply a good gripping surface. The twine at the eyelets was then varnished again to seal and protect it. The finishing touch was a rubber cap to fit the stock of each rod. Dad had a huge wooden reel for himself which he had purchased on a prior trip, and he bought a smaller plastic reel for me. These were no fancy affairs with gears and levers, just simple spools with two handles spinning on a central axis.

The final trip to the tackle shop got us nylon line (just introduced), hooks, sinkers, tracer wire and swivels. By this time our stay in George was over, and we moved down the coast to Plettenberg Bay. This had been a small whaling station in the lee of a long promontory named

Robberg, or seal mountain in English. Plett had been Dad's favorite vacation place as a child and it was ideal for family holidays. We stayed at the Lookout hotel, just a few hundred yards from the main beach and the fishing rocks.

Dad & I on the rocks at Lookout Beach

The Lookout beach began next to the hotel with a large outcrop of rocks, convenient for sitting on to dry off after a good swim. The beach was long and flat with large, uniform lines of breakers. The water was crystal clear and the backline of breakers broke in ten feet of water so body and board surfing were excellent. At that time the big surfboards were not known in South Africa, so we used small belly boards made of wood. Dad and his friends fought their way out to the backline to ride the large breakers while the rest of the family rode belly-boards on the broken waves further in. After a good swim in the morning it was customary to sun-dry on the rocks and then walk along the beach looking for shells. At that time the Keurbooms river flowed into the ocean about a mile from the hotel and sometimes we would walk to the mouth. Behind the dunes the Keurbooms formed a large tidal lagoon with the brownish colored water commonly found in rivers on the southern coast. This river mouth was an excellent fishing spot on the incoming tide when large ocean fish would swim into the lagoon to feed off the smaller fish which made the lagoon their habitat.

The lagoon was home to various creatures and Dad taught me to get different types of bait there. The most fun was catching mud-prawns. When the tide went out, large mud flats were exposed, with thousands of small holes in which the prawns took refuge at low water. Applying basic physics, each of us took an empty jam tin and forced it down through the mud over a promising-looking hole. More often than not a startled prawn would be blasted out of a connecting hole and land helplessly on the mud where we snatched him up. We stored the cap-tive prawns in wet sea-grass where they could live unhap-pily for several days. Pencil-bait was another inhabitant of the lagoon. These were cylindrical clams about the size of a cheap cigar. We pulled these out of their holes using a long wire with a hook at the end. Another option was catching harders, a small sardine size fish that swam in shoals of fifty to a hundred. These had to be hunted in shallow water. We ran behind the shoal and struck the wa-ter with a long piece of barbed wire. Usually each strike yielded five to ten fish.

The rocks below the hotel also had a selection of baits. The most common was red bait, a guava colored flesh that could be found in oyster-type shells clinging to the rocks. These were only exposed at low tide and the best opportunity was at spring tide when the water was unusually low. It could be a dangerous business clambering down steep encrusted rocks and watching for the odd large wave that could sweep you off. The red-bait betrayed its presence by ejecting streams of water from the cap of the shell. A sharp knife sliced the cap off, and the red flesh was pulled loose and placed in a bucket. There were also normal black mussels which were easy to get but not as attractive to the fish.

Early each weekday morning the colored fishermen would launch their boats from the Beacon Island beach. Beacon Island had been the original whaling station, but at this time a long, rambling hotel had been built on the rocks protruding into the bay. The only evidence of whaling was the old cast-iron cauldron used for melting down the whale blubber, which was preserved on the front lawn of the hotel. The Beacon Island beach was sheltered from the big rollers by the rocky outcrops on each side, so it was the easiest place to launch boats from. The fishing boats were locally built clinker design with both oars and sail. The coloreds fished with handlines and returned each afternoon at about 2pm. My job was to scramble from the Lookout hotel along a narrow footpath and over the rocks to meet the boats and purchase four mackerel for one shilling. These mackerel were our favorite bait.

We usually fished early in the morning and in the evening. Early morning fishing was always at the point of the Beacon Island rocks at sunrise. We rigged our lines with bright silver "spoons" with a triple hook on one end and about two feet of steel trace on the other, attached with a swivel. Dad could cast a long way with his longer rod and I had to content myself with a few yards. My efforts were also limited by lack of skill, for casting with a simple reel required a lot of practice. One had to leave just the right amount of overhang from the tip of the rod, swing with well controlled precision and brake the reel with one's left thumb just enough to stop the line from over-running and creating a massive tangle. We fished for elf, a good fighting fish generally about two pounds in weight and delicious to eat. They ran in shoals off the point at sunrise, and each morning Dad would get at least one or two. I seldom got anything but a tangle, but this did not detract from the pleasure.

The evening fishing was from the Lookout rocks right below the hotel. Here we both used the mackerel, cut into strips, or red bait. The mackerel were for the big cob and the red bait for the smaller galhoen, blacktail and stripers. One time Dad cast out with a large piece of mackerel on the hook and before it could sink, a seagull had dived upon it and hooked itself in the beak. Dad reeled the angry bird in and we cut the hook to remove it painlessly, but just as he prepared to release the bird, it bit Dad viciously on the hand to register its displeasure.

From time to time our family would get together with other families at the hotel and in the village and go on a communal picnic. The entire southern coast of South Africa was a paradise of beautiful beaches and rock formations so we had a wide selection. For serious fishing the adult men preferred Robberg, so the families would set up on the beach at the bottom while the men hiked out to the point. This was a four mile walk on a narrow path so no kids were invited. On later vacations I went to the point and was entranced by the splendor of the large flat rock sloping gently down to the water and the huge waves crashing down upon it. Fishing from here was a dangerous business because one had to judge the waves carefully to avoid getting swept away. Each year several fishermen would get swept off and occasionally one would drown. The fishing was usually excellent here because Robberg was a long, narrow promontory extending far out into the ocean to form one arm of the bay. Some really big fish were caught here, over one hundred pounds sometimes and also many sharks.

On the beach we swam, climbed the rocks and dug for shellfish. In the evening we would gather a bunch of driftwood and the wives would make a fire to cook mussels, oysters and hopefully fish when the men returned. The meals were very basic, just slices of whole-wheat bread, seafood and vinegar. They were always delicious. We did similar outings to other favorite spots, among them Nature's Valley and Keurbooms Strand to the east of Plett and Knoetze and Knysna to the west. Most of these beaches had no amenities at all and we enjoyed them in their natural state. Usually on our vacations there were several families from Rhodesia whom we knew and we also made good friends with other guests staying in our hotel. Most families stayed two to four weeks at the same hotel so everyone got to know one another. It was a good system and lots of fun for all of us.

Too soon the holiday was over, and all of us headed home together in old S44. Dad and Mum liked to vary their routes home, so this time we headed east to the town of Port Elizabeth where Mum had spent some of her childhood and where her father, stepmother and aunt remained. Port Elizabeth was on Algoa Bay, first visited by the Portuguese captain Vasco da Gama on his trip in 1497. In 1820 a group of English arrived here to set up a British colony on the southern African continent east of Cape Town. Shortly after this the Philips family arrived, Mum's great grandparents. Port Elizabeth was a pretty town with mountains behind it and nice beaches either side of the port. Mum's mother had passed away when I was one year old, so I have no memories of her. Old Jack had married her cousin Minnie and we spent several days visiting them and aunt Mary Philips.

The trip home was five days of slow driving. The South African national road system was still under construction in various sections, so at these we were diverted on to temporary "deviations" which were very corrugated dirt roads. Old S44 juddered and shook and dust roiled in the windows and worked its way inside the trunk lid on to all our luggage. At that time, both in the house and in the car, it was firmly believed that all the windows must be open all the time in order to get sufficient "fresh" air. We did close the car windows briefly if following or passing another car on the dirt roads, but that was the only exception. At the end of each day we could literally scrape the layers of dust off ourselves.

At night we stopped in various small hotels in small Afrikaans towns. The Afrikaans were very hospitable people and the whole family was always made very welcome by the hotel owners. Most hotels in the small towns were family-operated and one got a clean room with a washstand, basin and jug of water. The separate bathrooms and toilets were shared by all guests but everyone was considerate and the system worked well. All the hotels provided three full meals a day included in the room price and we ate very well. In the evenings after dinner we kids would play with the other kids while the adults had a few drinks and played cards or board games. If there was a piano at the hotel, Mum would play for the guests or conduct sing-alongs, depending on the amount of alcohol consumed. Safety was never an issue and apart from the odd petty theft there was little crime.

Dad liked to check his car after each day's run because the wicked corrugations could play havoc with exhausts and suspension parts. I eagerly joined him in this ritual and we usually found something that required attention. Dad always carried a comprehensive set of tools and spare parts, so we were well equipped. Because of the low volume of traffic and long distances between towns, most travelers stopped to help another who had broken down. I suspect Dad really enjoyed doing this because apart from the human aspect, he loved fixing problems of any kind. He would pull over behind the unfortunate travelers and virtually push everyone else out of the way while he proudly lugged his impressive tool kit to the scene and started to address the problem. With the lack of parts or facilities one had to be right resourceful in adapting the material at hand to get the vehicle mobile again. Broken springs were reinforced with tree limbs bound with wet bark or wire and one time we stuffed a blown tire with hard-packed grass to get the car to the next town. Dad was very ingenious with his solutions and it was a rare occurrence for him to leave defeated. The repairs could take anything from a few minutes to many hours, but everyone took it well and cooked up meals or tea and made the most of the involuntary gathering. There was never any payment involved, just a good handshake at the end.

When we got back into Rhodesia we planned to spend the night with auntie Dorothy and Uncle Bob again. When we arrived at the Shabi river just outside town we found it in full flood, with the water about four feet above the low bridge, flowing strongly. Uncle Bob was on the other side waving to encourage us, but there was nothing to do but wait for the water to subside. We settled down to cook dinner on the river bank with all the other stranded travelers, and after a few hours the level dropped to about a foot over the bridge. The water was not the only impediment however. When African rivers flood it is a rapid and turbulent avalanche of water which rushes down, sometimes four feet high. It carries away anything in its path, including animals and trees. The first task was to cut away all the trees and limbs caught in the bridge railing. Dad called up all able-bodied men and boys and equipped with a variety of axes, picks and shovels, they waded out and set to work clearing the bridge. Often there were snakes, mice and monkeys clinging to the branches so one had to be alert. As it was now dark the only available light was from the few torches available and car headlights. All went well and after a few hours the water had dropped to a few inches and the debris was clear. Dad was very upset because a few families (who he was sure were Pongos) did not help in the cleanup and were first to cross the bridge without even a word of thanks. He and uncle Bob spent the rest of the evening lamenting the unwelcome influx of uneducated Pongos who had dragged down the standards of the country.

Chapter 5:
SCHOOL

When I was about three years' old Mum felt it was time for me to go to nursery school. I was duly enrolled at Mrs. Briggs' school which was in her house about half a mile away. Most of the time was spent outdoors on the swings, jungle-jim, roundabout and seesaw but we had indoor activities as well. One morning I was playing with tool set outside when I was confronted with the tightly stretched pants of a colleague half-way up the monkey bars. The temptation was too great, and I could not restrain myself from giving him a nice blow with the hammer right where the fabric was stretched the tightest. He didn't like this at all, and fell to the ground howling. Dad and Mum had to do a lot of negotiating to keep me at the school, with strong threats from Dad that this kind of behavior would be punished severely.

Having noted my proclivity for tools and machines, at my fourth birthday my uncle gave me a small tool-set of my own. As the adults were chatting over cups of tea, I took my tools under Mum's large grand piano and proceeded to remove one of the legs. These were attached with large wooden thumbscrews and my new wrench gave me good purchase. I had removed two of the three screws when Dad spotted what I was doing, and he dived to get me out from under the piano before it collapsed on me. Thinking this was an isolated incident, everyone went back to tea-drinking. The next thing they knew, all the lights went out and I was thrown across the room after having opened up one of the 220-volt receptacles and sticking my new screwdriver into the wiring. The tool set was confiscated for a year and strictly supervised for a while after that.

This same year my younger sister Eveleigh was born. Thinking I would be happier staying at the nursery school for a few days while Mum was in the hospital, I was dropped off there without explanation. After I realized that I was not going to be picked up as usual, I began to wonder if my parents had given me to the Briggs permanently. I didn't say much, but Mrs. Briggs noted that I had become extremely sad, and suggested that Dad should come and get me. He and Mum immediately explained the rationale, but this was a tough sell and I secretly suspected that they had intended to trade me in for the new sister. For this reason, when I first saw my new sister, instead of being delighted I was resentful. After she had been home few days and was the focus of all the attention, I proclaimed to both parents that "I hate this damned baby!" This language was guaranteed to get some kind of major reaction, and it did. Fortunately both parents realized my natural reactions to not being the youngest any longer and they worked hard to win back my confidence. My young sister turned out to be a delightful baby and person and we have remained very close.

In 1951 it was time for me to start kindergarten. Hillside school was not on the side but at the top of the hill to the east of our house. It was a small school handling only kindergarten through standard two. The main building housed two classrooms, standards one and two and a separate building housed the two kindergarten classes, KG1 and KG2. Sister Jennifer had already been attending the school the previous two years, so at 7.00am the two of us and neighbor JD walked the half mile from our house up Hillside Road to the school. There was no question of any soft-spoken welcome or introductions. Mrs. Green lined up the children, boys on one side, girls on the other and made it abundantly clear that she was equivalent to God and should be instantly and unquestioningly obeyed in every respect. There was not a peep from anyone and our education started off in a most efficient manner.

JD was in KG2 but as both classes were in the same room, whenever the Mrs. Green left the room for a few minutes, JD and I teamed up to play what pranks we could on the other kids, or even throw a few punches if any resistance was offered. We took the best places, hogged the best equipment and educational aides and generally behaved like bullies. The first time we realized that this was not acceptable was when Dad and JD's dad got home from work and gave us respective applications of the walking sticks on our rears, followed by a brief explanation of the offense and a strong admonition to correct our behavior. We realized immediately that we would have to be more circumspect in our efforts to live well, so we devised various other means of accomplishing our objectives.

Kindergarten was from eight until twelve each weekday and standards one and two until one o'clock, so all of us had afternoons free. Our parents were friends with a couple who both worked all day, so their daughter Julia came home with Jennifer and spent the afternoons with us until her parents picked her up at five thirty. Julia was technically a Pongo, but we forgave her for this because our parents obviously liked her parents and we liked her. So it was that after lunch every weekday the four of us would roam the property looking for entertainment. Mostly it was harmless fun, climbing the trees and eating the mulberries, playing with our various pets and exploring the immediate neighborhood.

Then one day JD's parents had a dinner party where they had Christmas crackers to help celebrate something. These crackers had paper hats rolled up inside them which table guests were supposed to wear. JD salvaged a few of these which we took to be king's crowns, so the next afternoon we donned these and started playing the role of kings. At first this took limited form, strutting and giving orders to anyone in earshot, but after a while the

74

role began to grow on us and we decided that it was clearly in our powers to change certain aspects of our lives which needed improvement. We did not like the fences on the property because they impeded our free progress from field to field, so with the aid of pick-axes the two of proceeded to tear down the wires on our preferred routes. When Dad got home he was surprised to see the cattle grazing hungrily on the front lawn. It did not take him long to discover the two of us still busily creating more damage, and I must say, the ensuing confrontation was ugly. Dad was a small man in stature but a giant in presence, and our knees began to tremble as his flashing grey eyes locked in on us. Not one to procrastinate, he seized one of the uprooted fence-poles and commanded us to prepare for punishment. We adopted the appropriate position and the sentence was duly administered. The royal disposition evaporated instantaneously.

Saturday mornings involved a certain ritual for most of the kids in Salisbury. This was the time that we all went to one of the cinemas downtown. There were two at that time, the Palace and the Princess on First Street. At ten o'clock we watched the Movietone News, a short documentary in black-and-white showing world events that had occurred at least a few weeks previously. This was followed by a cartoon, usually Tom and Jerry or the like. Then came the interval, which was the highlight of the morning because this was comic swap time. All of us had collections of comic-books involving Superman, Spiderman, Batman, the Lone Ranger etc. We brought the ones we had read to swap for ones we had not, and a thriving business ensued. After interval we watched the feature film, occasionally even in Technicolor.

While at Hillside, our aunt Isabelle died of cancer, leaving Mum's brother Jack with their four-year-old daughter Erika. It was decided that the decent and most practical course of action was to ask JD's family to vacate the rental house so that uncle Jack and Erika could be close by. They did this with good grace and everyone remained friends from a slightly longer distance. Isabelle was from a wealthy Polish family which had lost everything with the Nazi and Russian invasions of Poland in 1939, so she had no relatives close by. She was staunchly Catholic and her wish was for Erika to be brought up as a Catholic despite the fact that Mum's family was Anglican. Erika lived with us during the day and returned to her father at night when he returned from work, so effectively became our sister. As soon as she was eligible she attended the Catholic convent downtown but came back to our house after lunch each day.

While my paternal grandparents were alive it was customary for all their offspring to assemble with families for Sunday lunch at Copshore, their small holding south of town. This made for quite a gathering but Granny took it in her stride. Grandad was a small fellow, always immaculately dressed, who liked to see each of his grandchildren for a maximum of five minutes per visit. Granny was more tolerant and loved to spend time with each of us. Both of them were in their late 70's by this time and we were intrigued by the way Granny's hand shook with every movement. Granny looked very old, with wrinkled skin and wire-frame glasses, her hair always in a neat bun. She dressed in long, dark clothing and stooped with osteoporosis but we loved her and she loved us. Granddad was better preserved and dressed in light-colored suits, complete with jacket and tie, regardless of the occasion. Dad advised us that Grandad, although obviously old and frail, was not to be provoked. Apparently he had a wild temper, as Dad recounted, evidenced by the stories of his chess matches. Granddad loved to play, but hated to lose. On the rare occasions that he did, as his opponent proclaimed check-mate, Granddad would seize the board and all the remaining chess pieces and hurl them across the room. He would then storm out and refuse to speak to anyone for up to three weeks. This had the desired effect, and pretty soon all his opponents learned that the only way to enjoy the game was to make sure Granddad won.

Two of our aunties lived in rondavels close to the house. Madge, the eldest, had gone to work at sixteen to help support the family and had never married. Helen, one above Dad, had been fortunate to get a scholarship to Rhodes University in South Africa. However, after six months at Rhodes she fell in love and got married, abandoning her studies. The marriage lasted long enough to produce a son, our cousin Christopher, who lived with his mum at Copshore. Now, at a weak moment when he was about six years old, Christopher had allowed himself to be photographed front-on wearing only a large pumpkin leaf in the appropriate location. His mother insisted on displaying this photo on her dresser in their rondavel. Each Sunday our arrival prompted a race to the dresser between Jennifer and I to laugh at the photo and Christopher to hide it. Helen steadfastly refused to pack the embarrassing photo away so Chris had to endure the ridicule for several years until he prevailed.

Copshore was an intriguing place for small kids and we roamed the extents as a large group of cousins, normally causing no damage other than the occasional trampling of granny's flowers or setting an accidental bush fire. The terrain was flat with sandy soil and plenty of large trees for climbing. As cousin Christopher was somewhat remote from other young kids most of the week, after school his mother employed a servant to take care of him and keep him company. This servant was from Nyasaland (now Malawi) and was blessed with a most accommodating disposition. His name was Joffat, but we called him Joffe. Now Joffe was a most accomplished fellow in many important areas of African life. He taught us all about the bush and African folklore. He had an impressive capacity for beer consumption and routinely drank all his competitors under the table. We kids loved Joffe and he accompanied us during our excursions on Copshore, keeping us out of major trouble and killing the occasional snake which crossed our paths. Joffe remained with Madge and Helen until his death in the 1990's.

After I had completed my three years at the Hillside school I moved to Nettleton school in Cranbourne which was a full junior school going through standard five. Cranbourne had been a Royal Air Force pilot training base during the Second World War and many of the houses used to accommodate pilots were now sold or leased to lower-income families. These structures were known as pises, a French word used to audibly soften the visual affront of the square concrete structures totally devoid of any architectural appeal. Among these new-comers were many English immigrants who had trained here and then returned to live. The Pongo children attended school with us. They were different and so it was natural that they would have to undergo some kind of assimilation process before being entirely acceptable to us locals. In thinking back, I wonder how much our attitudes were affected by our parents' comments and how much they were instinctive. In all fairness, the numbers of immigrants and locals were about equal, so they had no numerical disadvantage. Fighting at school was considered part of the curriculum and basically a healthy method of dispute resolution. Every break-time would afford an opportunity for several fights, which were watched eagerly by the non-participants who cheered on their favorite. In high schools one was required to request a formal fight and wear gloves, but in the junior schools fights were spontaneous. The fights were not necessarily restricted to Queen Anne boxing rules, and most were simply no-holds-barred brawls. They seldom lasted more than a few minutes and no serious harm was done. The girls had even more flexibility in defending themselves, with hair-pulling and biting considered quite acceptable.

The Pongo kids had to earn their acceptance the old-fashioned way, so as a welcoming gesture, each was invited to fight. Some took this in good spirit and others took it rather poorly, but after a few weeks of each new term everyone had won acceptance and we all got on well. I was not a very good fighter, lacking the killer instinct and co-ordination, so I got my share of whippings. Regardless of the outcome, if we were caught fighting, both participants were required to visit the headmaster to receive the decreed six strikes of the cane on the naked backside. The pain of the cane was minor compared to the embarrassment of dropping one's pants in the headmaster's office. To further strengthen the message, most of us received another application of the cane, stick or belt when we got home for having disgraced the family at school.

At that time Dad bought me a used 20" bicycle so that I could ride it to school. Nettleton was about two miles from our house, across the Makabuzi river. I was a bit concerned about the purchase because I knew this bike had belonged to schoolmate Fatty, and at about 200 lb he had certainly outgrown its capacity. I checked it over carefully before registering the expected gratitude, and from that moment on it became a prized possession. A bike was a big deal at school and after the normal polishing and shining I spent every cent of my pocket money on little enhancements. Jen and I rode our bikes to school every day and kept pretty fit. In the afternoons I would meet my buddies and ride far into the veldt on the smooth paths known as kaffirpaths. We did a lot of exploring and got to know the whole area well.

Life was not without its perils. From a very young age I had loved everything mechanical and so I was very pleased when one afternoon a truck arrived carrying an old car similar to our S44. The car had been in an accident and was without drivetrain but still had many parts intact. As soon as it had been unloaded in the back field, JD and I got our tool kits and set to work. After a short time we got impatient using the wrenches, so switched to the hammer. Our enthusiasm increased rapidly, and before long the car was reduced to a beaten mess, with not one piece of glass or instrument left intact. When Dad arrived home he eagerly set out to admire his new purchase, which was for the purpose of supplying spare parts for S44. His smile of anticipation instantly changed to snarl of rage as he beheld the total demolition we had wrought. He did not need to enquire as to the identity of the perpetrators, but grabbed JD and I by the scruffs of our necks and marched us to the nearest mulberry tree where he ripped off a suitable branch and swiftly administered punishment.

Actually I think he was quite proud of us because later that evening I overheard him describing the incident to friends with much laughter. Dad was not destined for a life of boredom and this was one of many things we demolished in good faith, but once the beatings were over everything reverted to normal very quickly.

When I turned six Dad borrowed an old BSA pellet-gun from cousin Lauchie and set about instructing me in the art of marksmanship. Although propelled by compressed air, the small lead pellets could easily kill small birds, and quickly growing bored with target-practice, JD and I turned our sights on to these unfortunate creatures. It was not long before the area around our houses became eerily quiet, with not a dove or any other bird calling in the mornings. At school we were taught the tale of William Tell who was forced to split an apple balanced on his son's head using his bow and arrow. We decided this was an honorable challenge and took turns in shooting tin cans off each other's heads with the pellet gun. Fortunately my sister reported this to Dad and the gun was confiscated, a great benefit to the bird life in the region and perhaps saving our eyes..

In 1951 our brother David was born. Dad took us all to the nursing home to admire him and we were very impressed with his size and bountiful red hair. This completed the family and the four of us grew up very happily together. I was delighted to have a brother and although six years apart, we did many things together until I left home.

Every year Boswell's Circus came to town and set up on the vacant land just across Widdicombe Road, several hundred yards from our house. Dad could not afford to take us all every year, but he did take us once. This was a great thrill and we marveled at the acrobats, clowns and animal stunts. After lunch we were free and spent our time among the circus people, watching them practice and feed the animals. We were particularly impressed with the lions and elephants. During the day, the Indian elephants, which are more docile, roamed the area with hobbles on their front legs so we got very close and fed them oranges. The circus had one African elephant but it was kept in a strong enclosure.

Dad's elder sister Bell, her husband Tucker and their three children David, Audrey and Zilla lived on a small farm beyond the Hillside school within easy walking distance of our house. We lived in awe of David who was ten years older than Jennifer and was considered an adult by us young kids. Because of the age difference, we did not spend much time with him but we saw a lot of the girls because Audrey was close to Jen's age and Zilla close to mine. Tucker and Bell lived in a house formed by joining two rondavels together with a central living area in the interconnecting section. Rondavel is Afrikaans for round-dwelling. The concept followed the traditional African hut in that it was circular with a thatched roof and simple to lay out and construct. Whereas the African huts were normally constructed of tree limbs with thatch or mud between for the vertical wall, the European version was more likely to have a brick wall and a cement floor. African huts had no windows and just a simple aperture for a doorway. The floor was beaten earth often coated with dried cow-dung to keep dust from forming.

Bell's rondavels were nicely decorated and very comfortable and we enjoyed visiting and roaming the farm with our cousins. Dad and Tucker were both mechanically inclined and Tucker invariably had several old cars and bits of farm machinery in various states of repair for the two to discuss. At one point a light aircraft crashed on his property and after the owners had salvaged what they wanted, Tucker dragged the wreck to his front yard as a source of aluminium. Of course this was most attractive to us kids and we enjoyed sitting inside the plane and fantasizing.

Dad followed local politics very closely and was getting very anxious about the future of the country. In 1952 the British government came up with a grand plan to create a Central African Federation out of the countries of Southern and Northern Rhodesia and Nyasaland. In 1953 this plan was voted on by means of a referendum of all the registered voters in each country. Dad and most Rhodesian-born whites were vehemently opposed to this plan because they correctly saw it as a prelude to black rule. Northern Rhodesia and Nyasaland were not colonies, but British Protectorates. They had small white populations and these whites had never been led to expect that they would have perpetual rights to the land. For this reason the development and infrastructure were far inferior to those in Southern Rhodesia. Also, from the economic standpoint, Nyasaland was without valuable minerals or major agricultural output and so would be a drag on the economies of the other two countries.

In the short term the plan appeared to have certain attractions to the naïve voter. It promised economies in government and a larger trading block. Southern Rhodesia became bitterly divided, with the "old Rhodesians" opposed and the new immigrants in favor. Unfortunately the new outnumbered the old, and the referendum passed. Had it not passed, the alternative, on paper at least, was complete independence for each country. Dad was furious that this opportunity had been foolishly squandered. The Central African Federation formally came into being on August 1st, 1953.

In July 1953 there was great excitement because the Queen Mother and Princess Margaret visited Salisbury. Dad did not think much of the Royal Family, regarding it as an anachronism whose time had passed. On the other hand, Mum was entranced and followed all the royal news avidly. Part of their route would take them along the new Widdecome road close to our house. All we school kids were provided with little Union Jacks and special mugs commemorating the coronation of Queen Elizabeth. I still have the mug. On the appointed afternoon buses took us to line the route and we waited patiently for the royal entourage to appear. Sure enough, right on time, the open Rolls Royce drove slowly by with the Queen Mother and Margaret sitting side-by-side and giving us all the royal waves. We followed instructions and waved our flags vigorously, cheering loudly. We were all staunch Englishmen on that day and believed our future in Southern Rhodesia to be rosy.

This same year, in commemoration of the centenary of Rhodes' birth, a great exhibition was held in Bulawayo to celebrate the progress made in all the British possessions in Central Africa and showcase the products produced there. The countries represented were Uganda, Kenya, Tanganika, Zanzibar, Nyasaland, Northern and Southern Rhodesia. Mum had a favorite cousin Jim and an aunt Dora in Bulawayo, so we set off in our red Dodge to visit them and attend the exhibition. The road south led through the towns of Gatooma, Que Que, and Gwelo and the 300 mile trip

took the whole day. We stayed with Aunt Dora in town
and visited the show each day. This was a new experience for us and we marveled at all the products and
displays of agricultural and mining equipment. Many
of the stalls offered samples of their wares and we
collected all we could. There were processed foods,
textiles, tobacco products, mining exhibits, building
materials and machinery. As part of the show there
was a complete Matabele village set up as it had been
when the Pioneer Column arrived, complete with
Chief, Indunas, witch-doctor and womenfolk. The
warriors performed impressive dances, clothed in
animal-skin loin-cloths and armed with spears and
shields. They leapt high in the air and stamped their
feet loudly in time to a drum beat. The young maidens
danced bare-breasted clad only in short skirts and sang
traditional songs. The witch-doctor painted himself
white and clad only in the skin of a hyena, wailed and
moaned as he cast a variety of small bones on the
ground and gave dire predictions in Sindebele. We
were most impressed.

After several days at the show we drove out to the
Matopos, a series of huge granite formations south of
town where Rhodes, Beit and Jameson were buried. There
was also a large monument with murals in bronze depicting the massacre of Alan Wilson and his 33 troopers who
were scouting the retreating Matabele after the 1893 uprising when their retreat was cut off by the rising waters
of the Shangani river. They fought bravely to the last man
and the Matabele showed respect for their courage by not

mutilating the bodies as was their normal custom. Their remains are buried within the monument. The Matopos are said to have been one of Rhodes' favorite places, with a long view in all directions from the top.

Chapter 6:
4 MONTAGUE AVENUE

After only a year at Nettleton Dad was offered a beautiful house on Montague Avenue at a very reasonable rent which was owned by the government. Under a strange arrangement, Dad owned the two Hillside houses but the 14-acre plot on which they sat was leased from the municipality. This plot had been earmarked for a new development, so the municipality bought out Dad's interests and we moved. The cows had to go, but we brought the chickens and ducks to the new house. Number 4 Montague Avenue was a five-bedroom, three bathroom mansion on a three-quarter acre lot. The "avenues" in Salisbury were nicely laid out wide streets flanked by Jacarandas on both sides. No. 4 was right at the entrance to Prince Edward high school which was most convenient for my future. The Girls' High was a few blocks down the road so the family was well positioned. Uncle Jack and Erika moved in with us, occupying one wing of the house with a private bathroom. We brought our cook boy Joseph and uncle Jack brought his houseboy Charlie. Whereas Joseph was probably in his fifties and very even-tempered, Charlie was younger and excitable, but most of the time the two worked well together.

I was in standard two at the time, so I had to attend Blakiston junior school, about a mile north. Blakiston was one of the heroes of the Mazoe massacre which had occurred shortly after the settlement of Mashonaland. The school kids were divided into four "houses", each named after a local hero. I was assigned to Pascoe house, with the identifying color green. The objective of the house system was to promote healthy competition in sports and academics. Each house had its own flag according to color, red, green, blue and yellow. Each sport had its inter-house competitions, and once a year an official Sports Day was held. This was a major event when the entire school participated and all the families attended to cheer their members on. It was a whole-day affair and every type of sport was involved, almost like a mini Olympics. Events were arranged by age so that everyone competed with his or her peers. All public junior schools in Rhodesia were mixed boys and girls, but in sports we were separated. There were no blacks in the white schools and no whites in the black schools. Other races had to figure out their own systems for education.

My first day at Blakiston set the tone for the year ahead. Our assigned teacher for standard 2b was a Mr. Williams. Each year was divided into three classes, a, b and c according to academic abilty. I was summarily placed in b because I had moved from another school and had to prove myself. It was a good system, allowing the teachers to tailor the lessons according to the average IQ of each class. If a pupil in the b class excelled, he moved to the a, and vice versa.

Mr. Williams believed that good pedagogy required strict discipline. By way of introduction, upon entering his class the first morning, he instructed all the boys to line up with their faces to the blackboard and adopt a bent-over position. He then moved down the line with the short baton used in relay-races and gave each boy a sharp strike on the backside. Whereas the girls did not benefit directly from this initial instruction, the message was communicated effectively to them too.

Despite this experience, we all liked Mr. Williams as he was a confident and engaging teacher who loved his profession. All teachers had to also manage a sport, and Mr. Williams coached soccer in the afternoons. He had the welfare of each student at heart, and would not tolerate any bullying or poor behavior. At break time it was customary for the boys to play games of marbles, where the more skillful players won marbles from the weaker. Accordingly, after break, Mr. Williams would instruct all the players to place their marbles in separate piles on his desk, whereupon he would go through a redistribution process to make sure the games could resume on an equitable basis the next day. This was my first experience of socialism and because I was reasonably adept at marbles I resented my winnings being distributed to those less

skillful. Furthermore, I had gone to great trouble to acquire a fine selection of "goens", the steel balls from used
ball-bearings. These varied in size from pea-size to golf-
ball size, the latter being devastating to the common glass
marbles. Mr. Williams regarded these giant "goens" as an
unfair advantage and regularly confiscated them.

Life was simple in those days and there was no question as to anyone's identity. Rhodesia was a British colony
which gave allegiance to the Queen of England. The official and only language was English and the religion was
Anglican. People were free to practice whatever religion
they liked and speak whatever language they preferred in
private, but in public schools the Lord's prayer was recited every morning and Anglican hymns were sung. The
blacks were called various names, but usually munt, which
is an abbreviation of the Shona word muntu, meaning
man. The Jews were called Jews and the Greeks Greeks.
Jokes were told involving all nationalities and few took offense. The few Jews at school took their traditional Jewish
holidays and during our scripture lessons they sat aside
and studied their scriptures. Nobody thought much of it.

As the school was about a mile from our house, I
rode to and from on my bicycle. The 20" starter bike
purchased used from Fatty had been replaced on my 9th
birthday with a splendid new Raleigh 26". This was my
pride and joy, and I kept it shining and well lubricated.
A buddy down the street, Ewart Sorrel, had a very fancy
racing bike with drop-handlebars and a "fix" which meant
the rear sprocket had no freewheel mechanism. This had
its pros and cons. It meant one could never rest with the

pedals stationary when going downhill, but it gave very good control for fancy maneuvering and allowed Ewart to perform all kinds of fancy tricks. We rode to and from school together, always stopping mid way along Blakiston Street to admire the full-grown male baboon that one of the residents kept chained in his front yard.

Baboons are most amusing animals, very close to humans in many respects. Whereas humans try to conceal most of their less admirable feelings, baboons do not worry about such things. They show anger, greed, jealousy and downright meanness at the slightest provocation. They detest being teased in any way, and their perception is such that I became convinced that this old baboon could read my thoughts and knew before any overt sign that I was planning to tease him. He was a splendid specimen, with huge canine teeth and an impressive red behind. As we approached the fence each morning he would strut up and down the range of his chain and try to figure out what form the day's teasing would take. As soon as the challenge was revealed, he would flex the skin on his forehead to lift his eyebrows, giving a menacing glare with his bright brown eyes. Depending on the occasion, he would poke his head forward in a threatening manner and throw twigs and small stones at us.

When Ewart was not available to ride with me I faced another challenge. There were two fat twin brothers in my class. They could not move very swiftly on foot, but on their bikes they were fast. If they saw me riding alone, they would exert all their energy to catch me, pull me off and basically beat me up a little. Thus the rides home alone were always a stressful ordeal, watching over my shoulder and trying to out-ride them. Sometimes I got away, but frequently I did not. Dad was not very sympathetic to my plight, he believed a little fighting was healthy and would teach me to defend myself.

On the other hand, there were certain attractions to the ride home. Half-way along my route lived two beautiful sisters, one of whom was in my class. If I could get behind them on their walk home, there were certain rewards that even a 9-year-old boy could appreciate.

On Tuesdays and Thursdays after school everyone had to participate in one of the sports offered at the school. In the cooler months this was soccer, and in the warmer months cricket for the boys. Girls had rounders and hockey. My two close friends at this school were Richard Dennison and John Mosely. On the days we didn't have mandatory sports we would gather at one of our houses and kick the soccer ball between us or roam the countryside exploring the small streams and bush. Even though Salisbury was quite a large town by then, open countryside was very close to our residential area so we rode our bikes or walked. The blacks always walked through the bush in single file and in doing so created many smooth narrow paths which were perfect for cycling.

Dad had very strict rules regarding homework which have stood me in good stead ever since. His principle was work before play, so we kids had to sit down right after lunch each day and complete the day's assignments. Dad also believed that each member of the family should do his share of family chores, so each lunchtime he would give instructions on these. When he returned at about 4.30 he would check to see that all had been completed to his satisfaction.

On weekends there were many options for entertainment. One of my favorites was visiting the Hargreaves, family friends, on a large farm just the other side of the Warren hills. The farm was a short drive or one hour walk. The old farmhouse was built on wooden pilings on the west side of the hill with a nice view over the fields. Uncle Bernard managed the farm for the Pascoes and raised crops of maize, beans and other vegetables. He also ran a small herd of cattle and a few sheep. The Hargreaves had three children, interspersed between us in ages and we all got on well. Keith was a little older and Stuart a little younger than me, but we roamed the farm together. I would frequently sleep over with them and other friends would join us.

In September the surrounding bush got very dry before the start of the rains in October. From time to time fires would break out in the long natural grasses and it wouldn't take long before large areas had been scorched. To limit the damage, the farm crews were sent out with pieces of sacking to beat out the flames. We enjoyed participating in this and deluded ourselves that we made significant contributions. One year for some reason there were very few fires, so we took it upon ourselves to start our own. The results exceeded our expectations and pretty soon we had a roaring blaze completely out of control, progressing at alarming speed towards the farmhouse. Fortunately the crews moved in fast and extinguished the blaze. Afterwards the boss-boy confided to us that he knew we had started it but that he would not reveal this information to Uncle Bernard. We lived in fear for a few days as Uncle Bernard was a pretty good disciplinarian, but the boss-boy kept his word.

During this period the city constructed three large reservoirs on top of the hill behind the farmhouse to supply pressure to the new city water supply from Lake McLewaine, formed by damming the Hunyani river. During construction we were kept at a distance by the work crews, but soon after completion we climbed over the fence to conduct our own inspection. We were delighted to discover that each large concrete reservoir had a very convenient ladder built into the sidewall. We climbed on to the top of the tank and opened the trapdoor to behold our new private swimming pool. We stripped off and enjoyed the cool water and returned frequently when the weather was hot. It seems the good residents of Salisbury never did suffer any ill effects from drinking the water after three dirty small boys had swum in it.

Swimming was a popular sport and the Salisbury public park incorporated a large swimming pool adjacent to Kingsway. This pool was distinguished by the fact that it had a 10 meter diving board where the more courageous could test their skills. I must confess that I never became seized with the urge to leap from there, as the view from the board was spectacular and the pool appeared as a small postage-stamp far below. During the Christmas holidays the pool was a favorite hang-out for all the kids and we became very good swimmers at a young age. The trip to the pool had its dangers for me because a couple of the older boys enjoyed ambushing the smaller fellows en route. I always had to be alert and ready to put on a sudden spurt of speed on my bicycle, but periodically I was caught and beaten up a little.

While we were living at Montague Avenue Granny died and Copshore was sold. The two sisters, aunts Madge and Helen, moved into town and bought a large old rambling house on Greendale Avenue. They also took in their old maiden aunt Lizzie, Granny's twin. To make sure no-one troubled the three ladies, John Bainbridge, a bachelor who had rented a cottage at Copshore, moved into a separate flat close to the main house at Greendale. The two favorite black retainers, Joffe and Cabula, also made the move.

The advantage of this move to me was that my cousin Christopher was now close by and we could visit each other by bicycle. Both of us loved the outdoors and machinery of every kind and we spent many enjoyable weekends together at Greendale. We had started the hobby of building model aeroplanes and for my 10th birthday my parents had bought me my first small diesel engine, a 1cc ED Bee. These little diesels were temperamental engines and difficult to start, so we spent endless hours in the workshop patiently flicking the propeller to get this one to run. We mounted it in a balsa-wood model kit which was suitable for this size engine. The plane was controlled by two long lines which operated the tail flaps. We needed a large clear space to fly it, so we walked down to the drill-field a few blocks away on Rhodes Avenue. Without any prior experience, the first flight was very short. The plane took off nicely, rose steeply as it headed into the wind and then dove rapidly into the ground as it got downwind. We picked up the pieces and dug the engine out of the mud and went home to lament the disappointing culmination of all our hard effort. Surprisingly this engine survived for many years and successfully powered many more planes.

At this time Christopher's mother Helen had an old Fiat 500 car. Before long it started making ominous noises and Dad ventured the opinion that the engine was worn out and with the expected cost to rebuild the engine it would be wiser to junk the car and get another. This was officially the strategy, but instead of having it hauled to the junkyard, Christopher and I volunteered to fix it. The car was very small and light so we tipped it on its side and removed the tiny engine. We dismantled it completely and found the worn crank bushings. After much persuasive talk we finally convinced auntie Helen that if she would just buy us the required parts, we would reassemble the engine and it would be as good as new. Flying by the seats of our pants and seeking advice from Dad periodically, we put everything together and were soon driving triumphantly around the yard. Helen however was not entirely convinced of our mechanical abilities and wisely sold the car while it was still running.

At Copshore granddad had had a delivery bicycle so that one of his servants could ride around the neighborhood selling the vegetables he grew. This was moved to Greendale with the rest of Granddad's possessions. Chris and I took a fancy to it, and we started on excursions with the very suitable arrangement of Chris doing the pedaling and me riding in the basket frame. The frame was not particularly comfortable, consisting of 1" round steel bars, but nonetheless it was a very favorable tradeoff for me. We named the bike Kaffirpath, after most of the routes we took.

To start with we did short trips around the neighborhood, but pretty soon our range extended to twenty miles or more. Chris was an enthusiastic pedaler but when he needed help I ran my feet along the ground to give a little extra push. We decided that a little music would be welcome during our trips, so we fitted a crystal set with two headphones and a long antenna to the bike. The problem was getting a continuous ground. We tried various lengths of dog-chain and arrays of wires, but with bouncing and variable terrain we never accomplished complete success. Nevertheless, we got snatches of music and if we really liked the piece we would stop to listen.

We did have one injury because of Kaffirpath. One afternoon we were doing laps around the servant quarters, much to the amusement of the servants. They could not understand why we enjoyed riding a delivery bicycle when we had perfectly good 3-speed bicycles of our own. Attentive to the growing applause, Chris ramped the speed up higher and higher. Eventually the front tire skidded on a freshly fallen guava and the bike slid into the barbed-wire fence which surrounded the compound.

As my knees protruded from the front of the frame, one barb ripped deeply into my leg just below the kneecap, neatly removing a piece of flesh one inch long and about a quarter inch wide.

This was obviously a candidate for several stitches, but if we reported the wound and its cause we were sure that our Kaffirpathing days would be over. As luck would have it, Helen worked for the Red Cross and in this capacity kept a very impressive first-aid kit in the house. Chris had observed the treatment of many injuries, and so he happily took on the role of doctor. We cleaned and disinfected the wound and bound it up very neatly. When the bandage drew enquiries, we said it was a minor scratch caused by falling on to a sharp stone. We had cunningly selected the perfect stone and placed it under our favorite climbing tree to provide evidence for this story. The servants were sworn to silence, as they knew that we had certain information that would be harmful to them.

I don't think any of the adults were ever fully satisfied with this explanation, but they could not break our story even when they enquired again years later. The wound did well under Dr. Chris's professional care and after several weeks the bandage was removed to reveal an impressive scar.

The next challenge for our parents was the smoking issue. Dad had made it clear that if he ever caught either of us smoking there would be a price to pay. We took this as a personal challenge, and immediately went down to the local kaffir store where awful unfiltered cheap cigarettes were sold in packs of eight for 10 pennies. In looking back I suspect that the main ingredients for these cigarettes were tobacco stems and floor-sweepings from the processing plant, but the price was unbeatable. They were called Star, and we lit up as soon as we got out of the store and into the large field behind the Greendale house. Not being connoisseurs in the smoking business, we were quite happy with what must have been a very harsh taste, but as we did not inhale the smoke, only our tongues suffered. We became more and more bold, and before long we began arriving back at the house without having chewed gum or eaten toothpaste. The aunties sniffed suspiciously and old auntie Lizzie glared at us accusingly, but we explained brazenly that for there to be a prosecution, the deal was that Dad must catch us in the act. That did not sit well with the aunties, and after a few phonecalls Dad apparently delegated this responsibilty to John Bainbridge without our knowledge.

We had now reached the point where we thought it would be nice to have a couple of puffs before going to sleep, so we switched off the lights in our room and lit up. The next night we had just settled down to a comfortable and relaxed series of satisfying draws when the door was thrown open and the light rudely switched on by John Bainbridge, with all the aunties lined up behind him as witnesses. Their triumphant leers were met with strong protestations from us that this uninvited intrusion of our privacy contravened the normal and accepted rules of civility and that furthermore, the rules we had accepted were that Dad himself had to catch us. Regrettably Dad did not back us up on this one, and after submitting to due process our visitation rights were suspended for three months.

During all this time Joffe played a significant part in Chris's and my lives. He was technically a garden-boy, but had absolutely no interest or talent in this field. If there was no other possible way of spending his time he would half-heartedly cut the lawn or weed the flowerbeds, but as soon as he was sure nobody was watching him he would turn to more enjoyable pursuits. As he was a respected family retainer he fooled nobody but was seldom reproached for his indolence.

Joffe was in his element in the "city". Not only did he have a much broader selection of goods to steal, but Salisbury was full of good looking young African maidens and matrons who served as domestic servants and nannies. It was difficult for us to see a real Don Juan in Joffe. His countenance was remarkable only for its lack of any kind of beauty, his eyes were perpetually bloodshot and his frequent and radiant smile exposed his only two yellowed teeth. His physique, although robust, was verging on primal and he could comfortably stand erect and pat his kneecaps with his hands. Notwithstanding these apparent handicaps, he was clearly irresistible to all the womenfolk between the ages of twelve and eighty. From his perspective he found this entire age-group most attractive as well, so all were winners except the frequent irate husband or father of one of his conquests.

Joffe did not believe in any preliminary courting or conversation when presenting himself to the ladies. After a lecherous leer that left no misconceptions regarding his intentions, he would reinforce the offer with graphic hand signals. The time and place played no part in his decision-making, and many a young maiden found herself enjoying Joffe's favors in most inappropriate locations before she knew what had happened. These favors must have been very pleasing to the majority of his conquests because many became regular recipients.

Like most Africans of his era, Joffe loved having his photo taken. When Christopher and I were in our teens, I received Kodak Brownie box-camera as a gift. While displaying it at Christopher's home Joffe expressed a desire to have his photo taken. I did not have any film in the camera, but made a big show of taking the photo as a full portrait. Christopher and I then cut out a full-face picture of a male gorilla from a wildlife book he had. We mounted it in an old frame and presented it to Joffe. Initially his thanks were effusive, with handclapping and small bows. He took it to his hut for further examination, and after an hour or so returned to the house apologetically. He wished to convey to us that although the photo was undoubtedly magnificent in its color and detail, its resemblance to him was questionable. He pointed out that the man in the photo had many teeth, whereas he had only two. He attributed this to poor technology and lost his respect for photography in general.

To Joffe, stealing was a fine sport which required stealth, subterfuge and good planning. His principal victims were other blacks, but occasionally he would bend the rules and steal something particularly attractive from whites. His favorite ploy was to steal something, sell it and steal it again to be sold again, often for several cycles. If he liked the particular merchandise, after the final sale he would steal it back and retain it for himself.

Auntie Lizzie, our parents' maiden aunt, was another interesting character. I only got to know her well after the family moved to Greendale, as she was allocated a nice room in the house and usually ate meals with Madge, Helen and Christopher. At this point she must have been in her late seventies and was beginning to show signs of dementia. Whereas Chris and I were always polite in her presence, we derived great amusement from observing her and occasionally setting little traps. She was not so far gone that she didn't realize the evil within us, and one day after breakfast observing Chris pass by outside the dining-room window, she confided to his mother Helen "Beast of a boy that, I don't know why they keep him here!" During winter she spent her days heating water on the wood stove and pouring it into old jam tins which she then placed beneath her bed. This was a continuous operation, for as the water cooled she took the tins back to the stove for re-heating. Fortunately the water never got too hot and she never burned herself. In retrospect Madge and Helen were most kind and patient with the old lady and she was indeed fortunate to have two caring nieces to live with in her old age.

Madge and Helen loved all animals, but dogs particularly. Being both kindly souls, they could not bear to see suffering and so many an abandoned animal was rescued and brought to Greendale. Madge was somewhat selective and preferred spaniels, but Helen had quite a wide variety of mongrels over the years. These served both as pets and to a lesser degree discouraged potential intruders. Most of the time there were three to four dogs and a few cats roaming the property. Our favorite was a rangy mongrel named Barbara who was good-natured and playful. She was a medium sized dog with light-brown short hair and a long, sharp snout. Helen's favorite was a small, long-haired Pekinese-type mongrel named Binky which Chris and I detested. Binky was ill-tempered and cantankerous, conditions which were not alleviated by our teasing him. For this reason he stayed close to Helen and went everywhere with her.

The Greendale house was close to Coronation Park, a kidney-shaped dirt racetrack named after the coronation of Queen Elizabeth. It was set in a flat area of Msasa near the Makabusi river and within easy walking or cycling distance from the house. The surface of the track had been enhanced by saturating it with old engine-oil which also eliminated the dust which would have otherwise emanated from the fine red soil. On Saturday afternoons local race enthusiasts would bring an impressive assortment of cars and motorbikes to compete in the scheduled races. Chris and I could not afford the price of admission, but we took advantage of several good-sized Msasas close to the fence to climb and from this height we could actually see more of the track than the paying spectators. One had to stake one's claim to the choice branches early in the day because there was hot competition from other kids and all the blacks.

The contestants were a fairly regular bunch and we all had our favorites which we supported vigorously with loud cheers as they came around. Being of solid pioneer stock the driving was aggressive and there were no safety measures at all. The cars were an assortment of Triumphs, MG's, Jaguars and various home-made open-wheelers. Several prominent racers emerged from this track including world-champion motorcycle racer Errol Amm and car driver John Love. Regrettably Errol was killed while racing in Europe and a monument to him was erected close to Coro Park alongside the main Umtali road. We were saddened one afternoon when Chris's neighbor Butler was killed before our eyes as his open wheeler hit the tire of the car ahead and flipped high in the air before coming to rest upside down. Without a roll-bar Butler had no chance.

Dad's cousin Lauchie lived on a huge farm named Stapleford about thirteen miles north of town. Lauchie's mother Adelaide was the sister of Dad's mother Ada, and Dad was very fond of her. He had spent many enjoyable weekends with Lauchie at Stapleford during his childhood and youth, and we kids always enjoyed a visit to Uncle Lauchie, his wife Leslie and their two children Glen and Virginia. Lauchie's dad had immigrated to Southern Rhodesia from Scotland in the late 1800's together with others of the his family. Hard work and shrewd judgment had paid off and he had accumulated about 10,000 acres of good farmland dotted with the ubiquitous granite rock "kopjes". The Stapleford house was a spacious, rambling brick structure with wide verandahs on three sides. All the farm families were accustomed to getting together for tennis days and so most farms including Stapleford had a tennis court as well.

A visit to Stapleford usually involved a picnic and braaivleis at the base of one of the kopjes. Uncle Lauchie always kept five or six pointer dogs for hunting, and these dogs loved nothing better than a good braaivleis. They could discern our intentions even before any overt preparations were made, and gathered around Lauchie's pickup truck in anticipation, yapping excitedly. When Lauchie eventually got ready to leave, he would open the tailgate and the dogs would fall over themselves jumping in the truck bed. Once in, they would jockey for the prime positions and all end up with their front paws on the sides and their snouts extended as far as possible. Despite long experience in the truck, every time Lauchie hit the brakes or went over a bump in the track, they would all lose balance and be left in a rolling, yapping tangle on the bed floor.

The Salisbury area is termed "highveld" for the logical reason that it is a high plateau, around 4,800 feet above sea level. There are no large mountains close by, but there are some small hills and many "kopjes." "Kopje" is the Afrikaans diminutive for head but in this context it is used to describe small outbreaks of large rocks, geologically termed igneous intrusions. These were formed when molten lava was forced close to the surface and then eventually exposed after the softer surface around had been eroded away. The results can be spectacular, with huge boulders precariously balanced one upon another.

The picnics at Stapleford invariably occurred at the base of one of the farm's kopjes. The adults would make a fire with deadwood and start cooking the meat and drinking beer while we kids climbed the kopje. We liked to imagine that leopards still lurked in the many caves, and exploration was always an exciting affair. We scaled the smooth granite surfaces and watched the rockrabbits and gogomannetjies scamper in and out of the crevices. There were some really splendid gogomannetjies, with bright blue crests and orange heads, resembling miniature dragons.

In some of the caves, crude Bushman paintings were still discernable. The Bushmen had been the original inhabitants of most of the lower part of Africa, but had been displaced by more advanced Bantu tribes moving down from the north. Their paintings in orange ochre depicted stick animals and men, normally hunting scenes. Only small groups survive today, living in the remote reaches of the Kalahari desert in Botswana and Namibia. They have largely resisted civilization and live their traditional lives hunting and gathering.

In the evening Lauchie and Dad would take the dogs and a selection of rifles and shotguns and go out to look for pheasant or guinea-fowl. The dogs were well-trained and would point perfectly when they spotted game of any kind. Guinea-fowl were the favorite quarry and they could usually be found feeding in the big fields at sunset and in the early morning. When left undisturbed the birds make a distinctive noise like two rocks being banged together, but when separated they have a different call easily recognizable. There are various varieties of African guinea-fowl but around Salisbury the common bird was about the size of a domestic chicken with black and white plumage and a hard blue crest on the head. In my opinion the meat is rather tough, but tasty. To display the correct sportsmanship the guinea-fowl were normally chased to flight by the dogs and then shot on the wing. Dad used number 6 birdshot and a 20-bore single-barrel shotgun, whereas Lauchie used a 12-bore double barrel. Most trips were successful and the two usually returned with a few birds to be eaten the next weekend.

On one of these trips Dad was walking through fairly long grass when he spied a thick, black/grey object in his path. His first thought was that it was a discarded tractor tire, but as he came closer it was clear that the tire was starting to move and was in fact a sixteen-foot python. He was now too close for both his and the snake's comfort, so to protect himself and the ranging dogs he shot the unfortunate reptile. He had it neatly skinned and cured the skin by pegging it out in the sun, his intention being to have a nice pair of shoes made for Mum. Mum could never work up much enthusiasm for this plan, and the skin remained rolled in Dad's wardrobe until he passed away.

Stapleford had quite a large population of black workers who lived in a village of their own a few hundred yards from the main house. They grew crops of their own, tended by the womenfolk, and the kids attended the farm school. Lauchie was the undisputed chief, and as such, commanded high respect. Blacks were required to dismount from their bicycles in the proximity of the farmhouse and remove their hats when addressing the Master or the Madam. They lived generally happy and healthy lives and minor disputes were settled equitably by judge Lauchie.

Dad's eldest brother Rufus had graduated in French from Rhodes University and taught school in Umtali, living in the original family home downtown. Rufus was happy with his nickname owing to fact that he had been Christened Percival Joseph. He was a small red-headed fellow, a talented sportsman with a flair for poetry and sharp humor.

According to Dad, this Umtali property had originally had a very nice Msasa tree in the back yard, which provided good shade. Grandad, after enduring many years of deprivation in the transport department with only a motorbike and sidecar to haul the family, finally saved enough to acquire an old 1929 Dodge automobile appropriately named Vesuvius. Granddad was an accomplished mathematician and calculated that when reversing the car, the steering-wheel should be turned in the opposite direction to when going forwards to make the same turn. Holding to his theory, each day he backed the car out of the garage and hit the Msasa tree. Not one to admit fault, after several such encounters and increasing damage to the car and tree, he solved the problem by cutting the tree down despite strong protestations from the rest of the family. He never did figure out how to handle backing out of a diagonal parking space in town, so settled for holding the wheel straight and backing across both lanes of traffic.

Rufus was a talented sportsman and loved the bush-veltd. His teaching job merely served to fund his frequent

excursions into the bush where he derived his true enjoyment. After teaching in Umtali he was transferred
to Guineafowl school in Gwelo where he purchased
a small-holding of a few hundred acres of bush. Here
he erected a simple block shed and dug a well for water
which was all the family needed for the perfect vacation.
Dad, Jen and I spent a week there one September and we
had a fine time. Rufus' eldest son John was a professional
hunter and joined us there for a few days between trips.
John loved a healthy challenge and spent his time crawling into dark caves in search of leopard. The tracks were
plain but the wily beast successfully eluded John. Rufus'
younger son Tim and I spent our time hunting gogomannetjies in the numerous rock kopjies on the farm. One
had to be fast and accurate to hit them because they stuck
their blue heads out of crevices for a few seconds before
withdrawing hastily after seeing us. We became adept at
quick aim and fire and pretty soon the gogomannetjie
population had been decimated.

Each evening we would build a huge campfire next
to a large granite rock in an area close to the shed which
Rufus had built a grass fence around to provide shelter
from the wind. The evening meal was cooked over this
fire, various game birds and occasionally some duiker that
John had shot. There were few large antelope left in the
area, these had been shot out many years previously, but
occasionally a kudu would wander through. The blacks
that Rufus employed to take care of the farm ate with
us and formed part of the campfire group, enjoying the
lively conversation and banter as much as their command

of English permitted.   We all slept on camp-beds outside if the weather was fine and inside the shed if not.

Although wild game had been in abundance during Dad's childhood, by the 1950's it had been severely depleted. Some of this was due to hunting and for preservation of crops but the main reason was a policy the government adopted to eradicate the tsetse fly. This fly is harmless to wild animals but lethal to cattle and humans. The government determined that if the wild game was eradicated, the fly's life-cycle would be interrupted and it would eventually die out. Accordingly, government marksmen were sent into affected areas with instructions to eliminate the game. This they did and in fact the fly was largely wiped out, but at a high cost to the country's wildlife. Rufus's farm had a few kudu, impala, duiker and bushbuck left but we did not hunt them.

Chapter 7:
NORTHERN RHODESIA

In 1954, Mum decided it was time to visit her brother Jim who farmed in Northern Rhodesia. We had never met him or his wife Vi, so this was a big adventure. We set off in Dad's red Dodge station wagon and headed up the Great North Road, through Banket, Sinioa, Karoi and finally down the escarpment into the Zambezi valley to Chirundu. The huge suspension bridge over the Zambezi had been built in 1939 with funding from the Otto Beit foundation. We cleared immigration on the southern side and then walked to the center of the bridge to admire the mighty Zambezi. At this time the river had not been dammed at Kariba and was in full flow, an impressive sight.

After going through border formalities on the northern side, we continued through Lusaka to Jim's farm, about 20 miles south of the mining town of Broken Hill.

Jim and wife Vi had no children so they were very pleased to see us and treated us with great kindness. They lived in a rambling house which Jim had built in stages, making the bricks on the farm. The farm was about 2,000 acres and absolutely flat, covered with msasa trees. Jim had supervised the clearing of his fields, which was no mean task. In the absence of heavy equipment, his farm workers cut down the trees with axes. Useable lumber was accumulated for use in the tobacco barns and the remainder was stacked in piles. Once dry, these piles were set alight and burned for days. After that the really hard work began, digging out the stumps. This was all done by pick and shovel and was a time-consuming process. Once the stumps were loose, they were hooked by chain to the tractor and pulled out. The stumps were also burned. Only then could the tractors move in to plough the virgin soil and prepare it for planting.

Jim raised corn and tobacco and the soil and climate supported both well. Tobacco was the cash crop but it was labor intensive. The tobacco seed is minute, like a grain of dust, and cannot be planted directly in the field. Seedlings are raised in a nursery under carefully controlled conditions and when 4-6" tall they are transplanted to the field. Nowadays this is done using a mechanical planter, but in those days it was done by hand. As the seedlings grew into full plants they needed to be fertilized and sprayed to protect them from various diseases and pest attacks. At a certain point the plants had to be "topped" to prevent them going into flower, thus diverting all the energy into producing big leaves. The leaves ripened from the bottom up and timing was critical. As each layer started maturing it had to be "primed" which entailed going through the field with bent back and picking off individual ripe leaves. This process had to be repeated several times until the stalk was bare.

Jim had to build tobacco barns to cure the leaves. These were high brick structures with poles running across at different levels to support the tobacco sticks. On one side there was an external brick furnace which had its stack connected to a grid of metal flues on the barn floor. These flues delivered heated air into the barn. Vents at the top controlled the flow and temperature. The barns were fired using wood from the farm.

As the leaves came in from the fields they were stitched together and then draped over sticks about 6 feet long. These loaded sticks were then carried into the barns and placed across the support poles. Once the barn was full, the doors were closed and the fire started. The curing had to follow a precise cycle and farmers would need to check temperatures frequently around the clock. The curing cycle lasted about 4-5 days for each barn so a farmer like Jim with no skilled assistant got little sleep during the curing period. Once cured, the leaves were removed from the sticks, graded and then packed into bales for marketing.

We happened to visit Jim during curing time so we eagerly assisted in each process as best we could, mainly on the stitching line. In the evenings Dad, Jim and I would go out in Jim's truck to hunt for guinea fowl, a great treat for me. During the days I hunted doves with my pellet gun. Jim was a big, strong man with a quick temper and so his labor force treated him respectfully. Like most big men he was kind and considerate and loved nothing better than a good joke so we liked him a lot.

All the tobacco produced in the Rhodesias was sold at auction in Salisbury. This was the annual high-point in farmers' lives and they usually came to town with their entire families to accompany the sales. The auction floors were nicely set up with restaurants and bars ready to cater to the newly-rich farmers. The tobacco bales were set up in long rows and the auctioneers worked their way along these delivering an unintelligible stream of high-velocity gibberish which nobody but the buyers could understand. The buyers came from all over the world because Rhodesian tobacco was considered the closest to the original US quality. At its peak, Rhodesia was the third largest producer in the world after China and the USA.

Salisbury was home to tobacco processing plants owned by the big multinational tobacco dealers and these plants sent their trucks to the auction floors each day to collect their purchase. Once processed, the crop was shipped all over the world to be incorporated into cigarettes and other tobacco products. The tobacco industry provided good work for thousands of Rhodesians of all races.

Jim and Vi came to town to watch their tobacco being sold. This was an anxious time for the farmers because the price spread was great. Poor tobacco sold as low as six pennies per pound, whereas the best could fetch up to ten shillings. On top of this, like most farm commodities, there were years of over and under supply which affected prices significantly. On this occasion prices were good, and Jim was very happy, collecting a check for thousands of pounds at the end of the sale. We all helped him celebrate.

Auction time was eagerly anticipated by all the businesses in Salisbury. The farmers stayed in the best hotels, drank and ate heartily and bought their families new clothes and other gifts. The car, truck and farm-equipment businesses did very well and many a farmer drove home in his new Mercedes or Chevrolet. Jim settled for a Ford station-wagon. Tobacco also brought Rhodesia a huge infusion of foreign currencies which kept the country in good financial shape.

Chapter 8:
THE MOVE TO UMTALI

As part of the transition to Federation, certain civil servants were offered the choice of positions in the Federal government or early retirement with full pension. There was no way Dad was going to support the Federal government and so in 1955 he took the retirement option at the young age of forty three. He packed up the family and we moved back to his childhood town, Umtali. He rented a very spacious house in Fairbridge Park and Jennifer and I were enrolled in Chancellor Junior School.

This was a great adventure for us because our house was situated on the slopes of the mountain range encircling the town, backing up on Christmas Pass, the main road to Salisbury. We had virgin bush at our back door, and a little to the south we had Miekle's Jungle. The whole area had been Dad's old hunting grounds and he took great pleasure in introducing us to all his favorite haunts and flora and fauna. The town was still home to many of the pioneer families whom Dad had grown up with and the Miekles, Hulley's, Cripps and Coventries were great friends. Their fathers had been the first to settle this part of Rhodesia and the original homesteads were still intact.

Fairbridge Park house

The original site of Umtali had been further west on the Umtali river, the other side of the mountain range. Shortly after settlement the railway engineers determined that this site would be too costly to access with the new Beira railway and the town was moved to its present site. The old site was named Old Umtali and became a mission station. Missionaries were well respected in their quests to bring religion, education and medical assistance to the blacks but inevitably the missions were sowing discontent as well. Both Robert Mugabe and Joshua Nkomo, the two primary leaders of the black nationalist movements, were raised in missions.

We rode our bicycles the couple of miles to school each day and soon blended in with the other kids. Umtali was a little different demographically from Salisbury because there were many Afrikaans and some Portuguese kids in the schools. Chancellor was a boarding school, catering to kids whose parents farmed in the eastern part of the country. A large group of Afrikaners had trekked to this area directly after the Boer War and had acquired large farms in Rhodesia. Dad got on well with them as they shared his conservative values, and most of Umtali had been strongly opposed to Federation. There was one unfortunate fellow in my class who was foolish enough to admit that his father had voted in favor. He was immediately re-named Federation and was mocked mercilessly for his parents' unforgivable shortsightedness.

At break time I was introduced to a favorite Afrikaans game called bok-bok. There was little sophistication and not a lot of enjoyment to this game in my opinion, but in the absence of any alternative I participated. Two teams of six were selected each day. One team played the part of the horse, which meant that the number one man, usually the smallest, bent over and hugged the trunk of the bok-bok tree. The others formed a bent-over line behind him, each sticking his head between the legs of the fellow in front and locking his arms around the other fellow's legs. This had very little appeal for me and I tried to be the front guy as often as possible. This position also had the advantage of being the least loaded.

The opposing team would line up behind the "horse" and take running jumps on to its back, trying to get as far forward as possible by running with the hands across the backs of the opponents. Once all six were loaded, the challenge would chanted "Bok-bok staan styf, hoeveel vingers op jou lyf?" (Bok-bok stand stiff, how many fingers on your body)? One man would be selected to reply and he had to guess how many fingers the rider was holding up, based on the perceived load. If he was correct, the teams switched positions, if not, the horse remained in place for another round.

This game was an orthopedic surgeon's dream, as if the horse members did not arch their backs correctly to handle the shock of a heavy body landing suddenly, serious damage could occur. Of course nobody thought of this possibility and most of the boys were in good condition, so we played our game blissfully ignorant. In later years it was banned from all schools by some well-intentioned sissies.

Federation was a marked man and had to be punished daily by being allocated the center position of the horse line, this position taking the hardest hits. He was a good sport however and accepted his lot with good grace. The Afrikaans boys were generally good athletes and were very contemptuous of anyone who was not, I being one. I therefore empathized with Federation as I had to tolerate constant taunts and threats and occasionally defend myself in a fight or two, which

I generally lost. Despite the disgrace his parents had vested upon him, Federation and I became good friends and even more surprisingly, our parents did too! We could not do too well in sports involving hand/eye co-ordination but we were both good swimmers so we settled for that. Federation went on to be a first-class diver and represented Rhodesia at international competitions.

Federation lived in a nice house on Main Street about half a mile from the town center. Close by on Third Street was an abandoned house. This house had been constructed of wood, a rarity in Rhodesia because of the termite problem. To give the best protection, the house was built on brick foundations which were about four feet above ground level which meant it had a large space under the wooden floor divided into a series of tunnels matching the main divisions within the house. This house became contested property amongst the groups of boys in town. Our group had a definite advantage in that Federation's elder brother was in the police reserve and trained periodically with the regular police. Part of their training involved the use of tear gas. Some of the canisters did not ignite, and his brother brought them home. We found that by holding a lighted match to the aperture where the fuse had been, we could activate them. We would conceal ourselves under the house in one of the many tunnels and when a competing gang arrived to take possession we would emerge and set off the tear gas. This soon cleared the house and the battle would be over.

This house also happened to be at the starting line for the annual soap-box derby. Third Street was quite steep here and well suited for this race. My class mate Peter was an avid soap-box contender and together we constructed two impressive vehicles for the next event. Peter's dad was generous in allocating funds for the cables and pulleys used for the steering but we had to come up with the wheels and wood ourselves. By scavenging abandoned baby prams and getting discarded wood at building sites we managed to find everything we needed. After several weeks of sawing and nailing we were ready. There was a pretty good lineup of vehicles for the race and the heats were divided by age. Each heat had two soapboxes and the race was decided by a process of elimination. Peter had a distinct weight advantage over the rest of us and easily won.

After taking the time to do the necessary research, Dad bought a nice half-acre plot on the Circular Drive overlooking the Boys' High School and selected a suitable contractor to build a new house for us there. This was a great location, facing south-east with a magnificent view of Cross Kopje and the Vumba mountains. In 1957 we moved into our new house and the whole family had to pitch in to get the yard in shape. Dad and Mum had laid out the floorplan of the house as a long, single-story brick structure with dining-room and lounge at one end, kitchen in the center and four bedrooms at the other. Jennifer and I got bedrooms to ourselves and Eveleigh and David shared a large bedroom.

Everyone loved the new house. It was uplifting to wake up in the morning and look out over the valley and Cross Kopje to the mountains beyond. We could predict the weather pretty well just feeling the wind. An east wind brought in warm air from the Indian Ocean and rain. In September, when the countryside was at its driest, at times the whole valley was ringed by veld-fires. From our back yard we could hike up the hill behind us for a beautiful view of the town, or climb the firebreak up Cecil Kop for a view of the whole valley. It was a short distance to the center of town on wide avenues lined with flamboyant trees. In springtime these had bright red flowers which lit up the town. In spring as well the msasa trees got their new leaves which were brilliant shades of red and orange for a few weeks.

As in most Rhodesian towns, milk, bread and meat were delivered to the residents each day by bicycle. As our house was on the outskirts of town at the top of a long hill, the delivery men kept in good shape. Fresh vegetables were offered early each morning by a group of 'mfazis who balanced large baskets on their heads and journeyed from their small gardens in Mozambique to sell in town. They would lay the baskets down on the ground at our kitchen door and sit beside them patiently while Mum selected the day's purchase. They usually had several infants with them which travelled strapped to their backs. During the selection process these infants would crawl around like tortoises and every few minutes one would have to be gently redirected back to the group.

Our cook Joseph had elected to return to Salisbury to be closer to his family, so we hired two new servants. Robson, the cook, was a diminutive Shona with a very sunny disposition. Our garden-boy was a Manica from Mozambique known to us as Ruweesh. Only years later did we discover that it was his pronunciation of the Portuguese name Luiz. Although from different tribes, they spoke very similar dialects and got along well. They shared a kia at the back of the property and were given food, clothing and a salary by Dad. We liked both of them as family members and they took very good care of us when our parents were absent. Robson was a talented cook and we ate well. Dad held them both to a high standard but they respected him for his kindness and honesty. All the blacks trusted Dad implicitly and he never exploited or deceived them.

Umtali was a picturesque town of about 8,000 whites, nestled in a valley surrounded by mountains. It had been tastefully laid out by the original pioneers and the main street was built wide enough to turn around a wagon and full span of oxen. The settlers planted flamboyant trees along the streets and avenues and by the time we moved there they were all mature and a wonderful sight when in flower. All the city streets were paved and lighted and downtown had a good selection of offices, shops and hotels. The two original schools were also downtown and it was these that Dad and family had attended. We had one traffic light at the intersection of Main Street and Victory Avenue, strategically placed at the intersection next to the police station and another in the center of town.

Main Street ran the full length of the valley but the shopping and business area occupied about ten blocks. The Cecil Hotel, Meikles department store, Mitchell's chemist and the two main banks were on Main Street. On Saturday mornings a treat was to go to Meikles upstairs lounge and order a Knickerbocker Glory, a sumptuous combination of fruit and ice cream in a tall glass. It cost half a crown. The Cecil Hotel had a spacious veranda where uniformed waiters served tea and cocktails and the dining room served a five-course dinner for ten shillings.

In the early days Umtali had been the location of the main railway workshops which provided maintenance for the Rhodesian Railways. The workshops were located at the lower end of town and had attracted many good technical artisans, some of whom set up their own mechanical service shops in town. The town was blessed with a diverse range of inhabitants and catered to the interests of agriculture, commerce, industry, sports and the arts. It was the center of a vast farming area with production of tobacco, corn, citrus and all the vegetables.

Main Street Umtali 1900

In the early days gold had been discovered in the
small village of Penhalonga, just the other side of the
mountain. The Rezende mine had yielded quite well but at
my time the output was small and the mine was operated
by one family on a modest basis. Their son was at school
with us. Incongruously, Penhalonga had been selected by
the wealthy Courtauld family as the most desirable location in the world. The Courtaulds had made a fortune in
the textile business and producers of the synthetic material Rayon, used widely in the manufacture of ladys' stock-
ings and other fabrics. Sir Stephen and Lady Courtauld
were childless and fell in love with Penhalonga while touring Rhodesia. They constructed an impressive residence

named La Rochelle after their English estate. They were great patrons of the arts and graciously donated the funds to build two beautiful halls in Umtali to promote drama and music. The Courtauld Theater was for drama and the Queen's Hall for music. Both were first-class and fully equipped. Because of her involvement in the local music club, Mum became a great friend of Lady Courtauld and the two collaborated on various musical productions. We had some budding playwrights in the community who wrote and produced comic musicals. They could sing the songs but relied on Mum to write the music and provide the musicians, which she did with great pleasure. The actors and actresses were selected from an enthusiastic group of townspeople and most of us participated in at least one production. Mum also participated in most of the musical productions in the Queen's Hall. These varied from small quartet and quintet to full orchestra, most of the musicians coming down from Salisbury for the occasion. At Christmas time we had Carols by Candlelight in which all the schoolchildren participated.

When we first moved there, Umtali had an old public swimming pool downtown in the city park. Swimming and diving were popular sports and we trained vigorously. In the late 50's the town constructed a new complex on a large tract of land. This was a big improvement as the new pool was Olympic sized and had a complete infrastructure with secure changing-rooms, cafeteria and ample lawn and spectator space. It became the focal point for all the youngsters during summer and was well attended by all on weekends. The town also had two nice golf-clubs with their own pools, tennis courts, restaurants and bars. Club life was popular and for some the club was a second home. Umtali fielded several rugby and cricket teams and these trained and drank enthusiastically at the sports clubs.

The white population in Umtali was probably 80% English. Most of the Afrikaners lived on farms in the surrounding areas and their children were boarders at school. We had two Jewish families and several Greek families who owned various businesses. The Greeks provided an excellent service on weekends because they were the only ones prepared to keep their small grocery stores open. The town had a prominent Indian family who ran a store on Main Street. The blacks who worked in town were housed on the properties of their employers or in the township of Sukubva, about two miles south of town.

The town had all the amenities of a good English town. The main religion was Anglican and we had a nice church where Mum played the organ on Sundays. Other religions had their own churches. Marymount girls' school at the base of Cross Kopje was run by Carmelite nuns from the USA. In later years a private boys' school run by Carmelite monks was built next to it. Up in the Vumba mountains close by was a junior boys school named Eagle. All these were boarding schools.

As part of the English tradition Jennifer and Eveleigh became Brownies and I became a Boy Scout. Our scoutmaster was the father of one of the boys in my class, a good Englishman dedicated to the cause. On Friday nights I rode my bicycle down town to the Drill Hall where our meetings were held. At ten o'clock I rode home alone and was completely safe even though our house was outside the main town. The scouts held regular camps in the bush nearby and we learned all the essentials of survival and bushcraft. In one summer vacation we all went to Beira and camped on the beach for two weeks, enjoying the Portuguese food and wine and all the pretty Rhodesian girls.

Chapter 9:
HIGH SCHOOL

In January of 1958 I made the major transition from junior to high school. In Dad's time there had only been one co-ed high school downtown, but a few years before we arrived in Umtali a new boys' high school had been built on fifty six acres in Tiger Kloof north-east of town just below our new house. The girls continued to attend the old school. Each school had about 500 pupils divided into classes of about 30 for forms 1-4. Forms 5 and six were for university aspirants and were smaller. Everyone entering high school had to write preliminary examinations to determine which level of tuition they were best suited to. The classes ranged from A to D, with A to C being the academic streams and D being the trades stream. I was happy to get into the A class with my buddy Federation and other close friends from Chancellor school.

Umtali Boys' High was a beautiful school with spacious playing-fields, tennis courts and large swimming pool. The headmaster, Coney Fleming, was a real character who understood boys perfectly and reveled in his job. He instituted a novel form of punishment for the new school which allowed the errant pupils to contribute materially to the school's improvement. Instead of caning or demerit points, transgressions were punished with hours of "manual labor." Depending on the severity of the transgression, hours could range from one to ten. Each afternoon after school the offenders had to report to the daily taskmaster, who assigned them various tasks on the school grounds. In this way the boys built fine athletic facilities at minimal cost.

For each new intake of boys, Coney assigned everyone 50 hours of "voluntary" manual labor. Voluntary was not really a true description because there was no choice at all, but it sounded good to the parents. For the first five weeks of school, each new boy had to contribute two hours a day to grounds improvement. Not only did this accelerate the progress, but as Coney patiently explained to dissenting parents, when humans are all complaining together they find common interest and make friends quickly. This was indeed true, and after the five weeks we all knew one another very well.

Coney and all the schoolmasters were avid sportsmen in the true Rhodesian tradition. Whereas the academic instruction was excellent, there was no doubt that the true mission of the school was to develop the best sports teams in the country. Our manual labor crews built a professional cinder running-track, first-class playing-fields and various shelters and enhancements which made the school a showplace. When no major project was in progress, manual-labor crews did weeding, grass-planting and other beautification work. Our teams trained hard and competed against other school teams around the country every weekend. When the games were at home, the entire town turned out to cheer the teams on. We had strong competition from some of the other government schools but the private schools were generally soundly whipped.

Most of our teachers were real characters. The headmaster Coney and his wife Ellie were much loved and respected by all the boys. For them it was clearly a labor of love and being childless, they regarded the schoolboys as their family. Coney could apparently see clearly into each boy's mind for he was able to predict behavior with uncanny accuracy. He tolerated no impertinence or insubordination and although physically a short man, no boy ever dreamed of disobeying him.

Dad was very clear on his expectations for his children's education. He demanded what he considered to be maximum efforts on our behalves, which was not unreasonable. His first requirement for me was that I enroll in the Afrikaans class for boys whose home-language was Afrikaans. The rationale for this was that I would learn faster and better if surrounded by Afrikaners, notwithstanding the fact that I could only understand a few words. He purchased an assortment of Afrikaans novels which I was required to read and understand in order to catch up. Dad perused each school report carefully and although I generally was in the top 3 in each subject, he saw no reason why I should not be consistently first. With this compassionate encouragement I did succeed in getting the First Prize for three of my four years leading to the Cambridge exam. This was also due to the excellence and enthusiasm of our teachers.

Pete, our English teacher, was very lively in class and liked to roam up and down the aisles as he spoke, giving light smacks to the backs of the heads of any boy he suspected of drifting off to sleep or failing to concentrate. If anyone had inadvertently left his satchel even slightly obstructing the corridors between desks, Pete would advance on the offending obstacle like a rugby player converting a try, and the satchel would fly across the room and hit either the blackboard or the rear wall. Those who had stored their sandwiches in their satchels soon learned to store them elsewhere.

Then there was Spike, a colleague of Pete, both having attended Plumtree High School in the southwest of the country. Spike taught history with great enthusiasm and became highly offended if he suspected any pupil of not sharing in this enthusiasm. These offenders were subjected to two remedial routines, one a rapid circular manipulation of the short hairs on the back of the head, the other a sharp twist of the ear. Like Pete, Spike disliked obstructions in the aisles, but he would pick up the offending satchel and execute a neat drop-kick to send it straight out of the window. As his class was on the second story, it was a long walk to retrieve the satchel after class from the field below.

JJ was our Afrikaans teacher. Being from the Orange Free State he had never really accepted the outcome of the Boer War and regarded all Englishmen as pansies. However, being possessed of a magnanimous disposition, he did his best to toughen us up. Daily he lamented the infrequency of good fights at break time, reminding us that in his day most boys were expected to fight on a daily basis. He also made it plain that the mandatory use of boxing gloves subverted the primary objective of the fight, which was to maim and bloody one's opponent. Notwithstanding these objections, he did condescend to act as referee at the official fights which were held in the prefects' study. If the participants lacked the necessary zeal, he would stop the fight and instruct them how to inflict more damage. JJ spoke the English language as a direct translation of the Afrikaans, one of his favorite requests being "wipe me off the blackboard, please Jones!"

Our Latin teacher was also our rugby coach. He did not enjoy running, and so rode a small motorbike around the field to accompany the game. As an added encouragement to those who he felt were flagging, he applied several strokes to the rear with the sjambok he carried with him as he rode by. The sjambok is a short whip made of rhinoceros hide. The hide is about 2cm thick, and the whip is made by cutting a strip about 1m long and then shaving it from full thickness at the butt down to about 5mm diameter at the tip. It was used by the boers as an effective riding crop and when used on the buttocks of a schoolboy it generally produced good results. As I was one of the worst runners in the team I received more than my share of whippings.

Form 1 maths was taught by Silky, a talented and demanding teacher who also coached rugby. Maths was my strong suite and at end-of-year exams I was confident of having scored 100%. Silky awarded only 98%, having subtracted 2% for imperfect writing and to impress upon me that perfection was unattainable. Our science master was an Englishman by the name of Brewer, instantly nicknamed Bill. He was very dedicated and was more than happy to assist us all in our various hobbies when scientific input or materials were involved. At that time I was passionate about radios, and he contributed many surplus "valves" to resurrect old sets I had acquired.

Geography was taught by JB, a muscular South African whose main passion was rugby. Nobody talked back to JB, just his presence was enough to maintain strict discipline. JB was head of Palmer House and lived there with his pretty wife Mary. We boys were very happy that Mary took a great interest in the school gardens and could be frequently admired as she pruned and cultivated in the many flower beds surrounding the school. JB's buddy was Tiggs, another ex-rugby player who taught French. The two of them coached the First Team with great passion.

Art was not a talent that I possessed but inasmuch as every pupil was required to take the classes, our art teacher Jock was obliged to try to improve my renderings. My natural tendency was to have everything straight or with a fixed radius and symmetrical which did not lend itself well to most people's ideas of art. Jock was a fiery

Scotsman who believed that every student was a potential da Vinci and my efforts to accommodate him met with swift and unequivocal derision. In the four years I had to take these classes he never gave up hope, despite the complete lack of progress.

In my last year the school hired a Russian teacher by the name of Bogamos. His ostensible purpose was to teach French but it was widely and probably correctly suspected that he was a Soviet spy. He drove a forbidding black Daimler which only added to the theory. A few years later two Americans moved to town, one renting the same Fairbridge Park house that we had lived in. These were found to be CIA agents and were subsequently deported by Ian Smith. The townspeople were very indignant that these two and their families had accepted their friendship and hospitality under false pretenses.

Our Rhodesian education department correctly believed that despite academic intellect or lack thereof, every boy must leave school with some useful skill. Accordingly, our school was equipped with very fine workshops for carpentry and metalwork. All students were required to take these classes, with the D-stream spending more hours. We were taught by professionals and created a fine selection of artifacts over the years. Our woodwork master was affectionately nicknamed Monkey for the excellent reason that his countenance bore a remarkable resemblance to the primates. The metalwork instructor was a Welshman appropriately nicknamed Taffy. Rhodesia also offered the apprentice system whereby pupils who did not aspire to a university education could leave school at sixteen and enroll as apprentices in various honorable and vital skills. They worked alongside experienced journeymen and quickly became competent and productive.

One of our students was an avid astronomer, a science he had learned from his father. In a most charitable gesture, his father donated a 7" refracting telescope to the school which was duly erected on the roof of the science laboratories. Whereas there were some members of the newly-formed astronomy club who studied celestial bodies, most of the members preferred to focus on the dormitory windows of Marymount girls' school across the valley, where truly heavenly bodies occasionally presented themselves for study.

Our school was right next to the eastern border of Rhodesia with Mozambique. Not long after the school opened, the boys in the school hostels discovered that a hike of a few miles would place them in the small Portuguese town of Machipanda. The Portuguese had few laws of any kind and paid little attention to those that they did have, and so alcohol was sold happily to anyone who had the money to pay for it. For a while those who wanted to make the journey did so reasonably responsibly and by the time they returned were none the worse for wear. One Sunday evening however, an overzealous imbiber decided that the trip home over the mountains would be made infinitely more endurable if he carried with him a demijohn of the cheap wine. No-one knows exactly the sequence of events, but when the fellow failed to appear for evening roll-call a search-party was dispatched. He was discovered asleep in the bush, totally drunk and stark naked with the empty demijohn hooked in his small finger. Coney decreed that the weekend drinking sessions must cease forthwith.

The next challenge that Coney had to deal with was the snake epidemic. One brave fellow brought a non-poisonous grass-snake to school one day in his pocket. Naturally this snake was brought out for display at every available opportunity, and that same afternoon after school the surrounding bush was filled with boys searching for snakes of their own. Snakes are hard to find and harder to catch, but thereafter each day the collection of snakes at school increased, each boy searching for a bigger and better specimen. The intention was to confine the catches to non-poisonous varieties, but most of us were not well educated on the differentiating markings between these and similar looking poisonous snakes. Of course it did not take long until someone was bitten and a teacher had to be summoned. Some of these snakes are extremely poisonous and the victim had to be rushed to the hospital. There and then the entire school was assembled and everyone was instructed to empty his pockets into one of several large sacks. The resulting reptilian exposition would have put the country's pre-eminent snake-park to shame, but the snakes were unceremoniously hauled off for release far away from the school.

The following year Coney was again put to the test following a visit to the town of a world-famous hypnotist. Everyone in town attended his show with great interest, and he put on an impressive performance. The next day the boys tried his techniques on their friends, and whereas they had paid close attention on how to induce the trance, they obviously had not learned the secrets of ending it. In the hostels that evening the staff were confronted with several cases of boys who could not be woken up, and the hypnotist had to be called for instructions. Once again at morning assembly Coney had to impress upon us that certain pastimes were prohibited henceforth.

The first years in high school passed rapidly. The school week was classes from 8 in the morning until 1 in the afternoon except Wednesdays, when for some reason understood by none, we had afternoon school from two until four. Tuesdays and Thursdays we had sport from three thirty until five thirty and on Fridays we had Cadets from two until five. Each day began at seven thirty am with everyone assembled on the lawn at the front doors of the school. A hymn was sung, we all recited the Lord's Prayer and Coney gave us the news of the day and any special instructions. In my last two years a fine assembly hall was built which also served as a the-atre and once this had been completed, assembly took place there.

Sports and Cadets were mandatory for everyone ex-cept those with crippling disabilities, of whom the school declared there was none. In the summer the sport choices were cricket, tennis or swimming and in winter every-one played rugby. The teams were ranked by age-group except for the first team. Sports were not my forte but I played anyway much to the disgust of the better play-ers. Everyone had to participate in physical training (PT) and athletics. PT was a normal forty-minute class twice a week, instructed enthusiastically by the Scottish PT master Jordie Brown. Jordie was short and stocky and full of energy. We did PT in an open field regardless of weather conditions and over time Jordie prevailed upon Coney to allot him sufficient funds to purchase an impressive array of PT equipment. We had vaulting bucks, parallel bars and various other devices to put our muscles and brains to the test. In Jordi's mind every single student was a potential star gymnast, and those whose natural abilities did not allow them to meet their predicted potential were loudly excoriated by Jordie to encourage them to greater efforts. At the end of each PT session teams were picked to play each other at basketball or baseball. Two "captains" were randomly appointed by Jordie and these alternated in selecting players. I became accustomed to being one of the last to be picked each time.

As part of the great sports culture of Rhodesia, athletics (field and track) were paramount. With the help of numerous hours of voluntary manual labor from the students, the school built a very fine athletics field complete with cinder track. In the spring of each year everyone trained hard for the great Sports Day. This was an occasion attended by the whole town and all the farm parents came for the weekend to cheer on their sons. Each age-group had the full range of events including the classical Greek discus, shot-put and javelin. It was a mini-Olympics and culminated in a full-scale decathlon. At the closing ceremonies prize cups were awarded by a suitable prominent citizen and a Victor Ludorum was declared who thenceforth for one year was equivalent to Jesus.

Cadets had been established in the early days of the occupation as a backup force in case of massive insurrection. It involved military training and we had to don khaki outfits with appropriate webbing belt, boots and puttees. We were issued with old 0.303 rifles and were marched around the school grounds and periodically went to the rifle-range for practice. We learned all the military commands, navigation, weapons mechanics and strategy. Once a year we attended a bivouac in the bush nearby where we camped for a two weeks in the open without bathing. Here we did marksmanship, map-reading, automatic weapon practice and learned all the dirty songs the British Army had to offer. Normally these camps were attended by a professional staff sergeant from one of the army bases whose IQ squared was below 50. The camps were great fun for all including the teachers, who enjoyed the freedom of the bush and the unrestricted nightly beer-drinking and story-telling.

The beer-drinking was not confined to the teachers and experienced pupils took care to conceal large quantities of beer in their kit-bags before leaving for the camp. Whereas legally minors under the age of eighteen could not purchase alcohol in any form, there was a convenient method of circumventing this law. As a driving license could be obtained at age sixteen, those who had access to cars would take orders from their friends and then drive slowly by one of the open verandahs of the various hotels in town. The black waiters were alert and picked up the hand signals to meet the car around the corner. Here they willingly took orders for beer and delivered it to the car unopened in return for a handsome tip with no questions asked. Of course nobody was fooled but it was a simple means of thwarting an unpopular law and the hotel proprietor, the waiters and the boys all benefitted.

Each evening after dinner in the bush the bedrolls would be carefully unrolled to reveal the beer bottles and each "company" would start drinking with great gusto. Juniors were posted as sentries to warn of the approach of any of the schoolmasters, but generally they had the good manners to stay in their own camp. Fortunately the bedrolls could only handle a limited number of bottles which had to last for two weeks, so no serious drinking occurred except for those improvident fellows who drank their full supply the first night. After one or two beers the singing would begin and we considered ourselves very fortunate to have been blessed with a vast repertoire of filthy songs handed down from two world wars. The English language is very rich in vocabulary and the songs were cleverly composed to have catching melodies and graphic lyrics.

Rhodesia was very cognizant of the role of Britain in the two world wars. Armistice day, the 11th of November, was a big deal in the country. At 11am each year the students assembled and conducted a serious service of thanks to all those who gave their lives in protecting our culture and way of life. Moving hymns were sung, our honor roll was called and the service ended with the best of our cadet buglers playing the Last Post. It was a time of reflection of all that is precious in life and the price that our families and friends had paid to preserve these privileges. It brought home to each of us the fact that life is tough and we must be prepared to work hard and overcome hardships if we are to prevail. Although all of us were too young to have fought, our fathers, uncles and friends had stepped up to the plate and the stark reality of personal courage and sacrifice brought tears to many eyes.

There was a definite hierarchy amongst the pupils. The seniors were all-powerful and treated the juniors as miserable dogs. The top sportsmen, regardless of academic abilities, were considered gods. In the hostels, each senior was assigned a "fag" whose duty it became to attend to the senior's every need from polishing his shoes to warming the toilet seat in winter. This was an accepted system because each junior could be assured that his day would come. The "day-boys" were exempt from this but needed to be respectful of seniors unless they were prepared to take a few punches and insults.

All the academic classes wrote the English Cambridge University O-level exams at the age of sixteen. These involved eight subjects, and if successful, the pupil could leave school at that point. If aspiring to attend university, the pupil could elect to continue a further one or two years to pass the South African M-level or Cambridge A-level. Those doing this had to share classes with the girls' school in order to make the best use of available resources. Our school had a 5-ton Thames truck and the girls' school had an old bus, and each day we traveled back and forth between schools depending on our particular classes. We rode in the bed of the truck, hanging on to the wooden side-frames.

This program introduced previously unknown contact with the girls which was good for the pretty ones and bad for those not so blessed. We soon invented nicknames for all the girls, some less complimentary than others. One of the girls had bright red hair and a profusion of orange freckles upon a very white skin. She was immediately christened Termite, which did little for her self-esteem. Our star rugby player fell in love with one of the prettiest girls and began a hot relationship with her which detracted from his passion for the game. After a few ignominious losses, his team-mates prevailed upon him to confine his dating to days without important games.

The Girls' School was the original co-educational Umtali High School down town which Dad and all his family had attended. It was also a boarding school with two hostels, Tulloch and Eickhoff. The headmistress was an intrepid spinster who was justifiably proud of her nickname Dracula. We took ballroom dancing lessons in the large assembly hall and awkwardly maneuvered our partners around the floor with varying degrees of enjoyment and success. Mum taught music there for several years and both Jennifer and Eveleigh completed high school there.

Mum played an important role in the Boys' School life because she played the piano for the hymn each morning and she also produced very fine musicals using the pupils from both schools. As our house was a few yards from our beautiful new hall, she generally just walked the distance. Mum adored her music and did a very professional job of the musical productions. Together with the staffs of both high schools she put on one or two shows a year, usually Gilbert & Sullivan or Rogers & Hammerstein and the whole town enjoyed them. She also put on concerts and sing-alongs in the magnificent Queen's Hall downtown. From time to time she would invite her musical friends from Salisbury to perform with her and the little town was treated to first-class classics. One night a week Mum invited seniors from both schools to glee-club sessions at our house. I suspect most of the male participants and some of the girls were not really there for the music, but they sang enthusiastically and enjoyed the evenings. Dad really enjoyed them as well and it was his pleasure to serve everyone with coffee and cookies mid-way through the evening.

Chapter 10:
LIFE IN UMTALI

Mum had a small Jack Russell terrier we named Pog. Whereas Mum had never laid any personal claims to this dog, the dog laid claim to Mum and kept as close to her as he could. Like most Jack Russells, he had no fear and a very short fuse. This temperament was not mellowed by the fact that all us kids loved to tease Pog and he never failed to rise to the occasion, bearing his teeth, growling and snapping like a caged lion. He had a generic hatred of all blacks except for our own servants. Our other dog was named Scamp. He was a cross between a bull-terrier and a ridgeback, an interesting fellow with half a ridge down his back and a long, broad snout. Scamp and Pog got along fine except at mealtimes, when each would wolf down his food as rapidly as possible and then attack the other if there was any food remaining. Scamp was by nature a docile animal, but when together in the presence of other dogs, Pog would attack regardless of any size disadvantage. Scamp was obliged to come to the rescue, and once involved he was a vicious fighter whose long powerful jaws gave him a distinct edge. He would lock these on the other dog's throat and it was all we could do to pry him loose.

Scamp loved to hunt in the surrounding bush. The problem was that the small game trails were set up with snare traps by the local blacks and if Scamp failed to come home at night it was certain that he had been caught in one. He was not a random barker, so it fell to me to roam the surrounding bush whistling at intervals until he would bark a greeting and I could locate him and free him. He was always cheerful and seemed to accept his predicament with great equanimity. Luckily he never struggled in the snare and suffered no injuries. The snares normally caught rabbits and small antelope and some of these victims suffered for days until the trapper returned to his catch.

One morning during our school vacation a young baboon wandered into our yard. It had obviously been captive or caught in a snare as its abdomen was raw and bleeding. We cleaned and dressed the wounds and waited for Dad to come home to see how best to handle the situation. Even young baboons have long, sharp teeth and can inflict serious injury if provoked or frightened, so after tending to the wounds and feeding the young fellow some bananas, we kept a respectful distance. Having had a monkey as a pet in his childhood, Dad assured us that if we treated the baboon well and did not tease him, no harm would come to us. We named him Benji and set him up in one of our sister's doll's cradles complete with bedding and the little fellow went off happily to sleep. Dad made a nice house for him behind our house and set him up with a collar and chain and he seemed to be very content. During the day we let him loose to play and he rode on our shoulders and scampered about the bush, but always returned to us.

One night we were awakened by a terrible screaming and Dad rushed outside to find a large dog had Benji in its mouth. Dad never ventured outside without his stick, and after applying it liberally to the dog, Benji broke loose and jumped on Dad's shoulder. Feeling sorry for the youngster, Dad placed him in a cardboard box next to his own bed and both of them went back to sleep. At daylight Dad was awakened by small black fingers prying his eyes open, revealing a pair of bright brown baboon eyes peering anxiously into his. That weekend we made Benji a nice house high up in the large Msasa tree by the swimming pool, and gave him access to the ground via a long metal pole which his chain could slide along.

Young baboons make wonderful pets and are very human in many ways. Benji was small enough that he could be controlled and he actually never tried to bite us. He and brother Butch enjoyed many a good wrestling match and despite his small size, Benji always put up a good performance. He was somewhat uncertain about approaching the dogs, being curious but cautious. He would manage to unclip his chain from time to time, and on these occasions he took the opportunity of examining the dogs more closely if he thought they were asleep. He soon learned that Pog was unapproachable and could not be snuck up upon, but Scamp allowed Benji to examine him as long as he didn't push his luck too far. Scamp liked to settle himself in the cool sand under the shelter of the garage roof, and here Benji would sneak up quietly and begin his discovery process. Firstly he would gently lift Scamp's cheek to expose his teeth, and then with the other hand, probe the teeth and feel the tongue. If Scamp accepted this, Ben then grabbed the eyelashes and pulled one eye open, peering intently into it. Usually this was the last straw and Scamp would slowly get up, sending Ben screeching away.

If the house was open, which was usually the case, Ben's next stop was the dining room where Mum kept bowls of fruit on the sideboard. Not knowing how much time he had before being caught and chained again, Ben would run down the sideboard and take one bite out of every piece of fruit. If no-one approached, he would re-peat this until his belly and pouches were full. He would then wander through the house examining anything that interested him but he seldom did any damage. He never left the yard when he was loose and definitely considered it home.

Most evenings we would take the dogs and Ben for a walk in the bush behind our house or at the high-school across the road. The dogs roamed freely, but Ben would ride on my shoulder until he saw something that justi-fied his exerting himself. Baboons are very fond of ants' eggs, and when we came to promising large stones I would turn them over for him. Sometimes they yielded a nice nest of white eggs and occasionally a tasty scorpion. The ants did not take kindly to this invasion, so Ben had a cunning technique of brushing them away with rapid hand-movements while he stuck his snout into the pile and sucked up the eggs. Inevitably his lips got some ant-bites, but he accepted this as the price of a good meal. He was a little more careful with the scorpions. They have a powerful sting, so speed was of the essence. As soon as the scorpion raised its stinger, Ben would strike like lightning and break it off before the scorpion knew what had happened. Ben then seated himself comfortably on his hard red behind and proceeded to dismember and eat the scorpion at his own pace.

Ben liked to run off and play in the trees and sometimes when he went out of our sight we would run away and hide. As soon as he realized he was alone, Ben would commence a terrible screaming and come running at full speed to where he last saw us and finally discover us, leaping on to my back and gripping me tightly with all four hands. On one occasion he was riding on my shoulder, grasping my ears when I felt him suddenly tense up and apply severe pressure. I looked down to see a large cobra right in front which I was just about to step on. Ben also liked to go for bicycle rides, sitting on my shoulder and holding on to my ears or hair. However, after a short distance he got restless and proceeded to clamber all over the bike, shaking the frame and making a nuisance of himself.   Unfortunately baboons are dangerous pets when full grown, so when Ben reached adolescence we gave him away to a farmer who had no small children. Some years later we got a baby monkey that some blacks were selling on the roadside. We didn't use a lot of imagination and named him Monk. He was a great pet too but when he reached a certain size we gave him away to the local zoo.

Dad loved projects, and after getting the main house, garage, workshop and landscaping to his liking he decided it was time to build a swimming-pool. The Umtali climate was such that a pool could be enjoyed from September to April and of course we kids were filled with excitement at the prospect of our own pool. The new Umtali municipal pool was great but having our own pool was the epitome of luxury.

Dad was not one to follow accepted design parameters so he managed the pool project himself. The first step was a large hole in the ground, so to accomplish this he called his buddy at the jail and arranged for six sturdy convicts to be delivered to the house on Saturday, complete with picks, shovels and an armed guard. This was an accepted system for which one paid which helped defray the prison costs. Dad marked out a rectangle on the ground behind the house and instructed the convicts to start digging. With careful coaching in a matter of hours we had a perfect hole 34 feet long, 14 feet wide with a an 8- foot deep-end and 4-foot shallow-end. He then hired a bricklayer to build the walls and pour the slabs for the bottom. Not being a swimming-pool expert, when pouring the floor, the bricklayer left expansion slots all around the perimeter and across the center in two places. The theory was that these would be filled with bitumen which would allow the concrete to expand and contract.

Dad decided that he and I would handle the bitumen, so one Saturday he arrived home with a 44-gallon drum of it which we proceeded to heat over an open fire. We then used jam-tin ladles to scoop liquid bitumen out of the barrel and pour it into the expansion joints. Bitumen does not break cleanly, so with each ladleful we got long tendrils which got on our hands, legs and clothing. Finally the job was done and Dad and I had to figure out how to get the bitumen off our bodies. After trying various detergents we realized that the only solution was a good solvent, so we filled the bathtub with a few inches of gasoline and scrubbed ourselves off with this. It took a few cycles to get ourselves and the tub clean again, after which we took hot showers with soap. The clothing had to be discarded.

The next task was to paint the pool. As a combination sealer and paint, Dad selected aluminium bituminized paint and gave me the privilege of painting. It was now January and still school holidays but one of the hottest months of the year. I soon discovered that the combination of heat, concrete and paint-fumes made my head spin from time to time, but after a couple of days the job was done. We then started the filling process with great excitement. After about 24 hours the pool was full and we all jumped in and had a great time. Our joy was short-lived however, for the following day we noticed that the level had dropped considerably more than could be accounted for by evaporation. After three days the pool was almost empty, so there was no question but that we had a major leak. We pumped out the remaining water and immediately discovered that the water-pressure had forced all the bitumen through the expansion joints. My next task was to chisel out all the remaining bitumen, which was no small undertaking. Once this was done, Dad bought a suitable length of 1" manila rope and we hammered this into the joints, pouring new bitumen on top of it. Experience paid off here and we took great care not to get the bitumen on ourselves.

This strategy was no more successful, the pressure forced the rope and the bitumen out of the joints as before, so now I had to chisel out the remaining bitumen and rope. At this point, under strong pressure from me and the rest of the family, Dad broke down and sought professional advice. This involved re-pouring the floor with expansion joints only going partially through the concrete, allowing the remaining concrete to crack slightly as the slabs dried. For the third time we poured the bitumen and finally had success.

Leaks were not the only issue with the pool. As package filtration systems were not available then, Dad came up with his own scheme. Our house level was considerably below pool level, so Dad decided that he would use this fall to siphon water from the pool to a gravity sand-filter and then pump it back. A siphon relies on an absolutely tight piping system so no air can enter, but we never accomplished this. After dismantling and doping all the piping joints several times we decided to give in and move the filter to a position above the pool, using the pump to suck water from the pool and deliver it to the filter. We relied on gravity to get the water through the filter and back to the pool. This worked when the sand was absolutely clean, but as it became clogged the flow got progressively less. The solution to this was that every week one of us had to climb inside the 500-gallon tank and skim off the top layer of sand with a shovel. The system worked, but was certainly not maintenance-free. However, the pool was a great attraction to all of us and our neighbors and we had many a good time around it.

As an added bonus, my friends and I discovered that when our sisters' friends came around to use the pool, they left their clothing neatly folded in our bathroom. We had long known that by carefully scraping the dry leaves from the bamboo plants, fine fibers could be accumulated which caused serious itching if applied to the skin. We therefore took considerable pleasure in sprinkling these fibers inside the bras of the girls and then waiting expectantly to assess the reaction when they got dressed again. Most girls are reluctant to violently scratch their breasts in front of men or boys, so it was always rewarding to see how each one handled the challenge. Of course after a few cycles our plot was discovered and Dad was informed. Whereas he probably secretly enjoyed the joke, this did not stop him from bringing out the stick and taking appropriate disciplinary action.

Umtali was conveniently situated close to several attractions. The Vumba mountains lay to the east and offered welcome respite from the heat in summer. We knew several families who farmed there and there were two very nice hotels near the top, Mountain Lodge and Leopard Rock. There were also many excellent spots to picnic. Most of the area was readily accessible and if Dad fancied a location he would simply pull off the road and set up. A favorite spot was at the base of a large rock mountain named Castle Beacon. A footpath led to the summit and on a clear day one had a fifty-mile view in all directions.

To the north lay the mountains of Inyanga ('Nyanga, Shona for moon). The highest, Inyangani, reaches 8,800 feet at the summit. Family friends lived in Juliasdale and we visited them frequently. They had two sons who were contemporaries and often I would spend a week with them during school holidays. We loved roving the hills, fishing and swimming in the clear pools in the trout streams and hunting dassie in the many rock out-crops. There were two nice rock outcrops near Juliasdale. Banganiti was a huge, dome-shaped mountain of solid granite. This was a tough climb as the rock surface was steep and smooth so we had to search for foot and hand holds. The other, Manyoli, was more broken and had many small caves and burrows where the dassie lived. These dassie or rockrabbits were actually rodents but as large as rabbits, with absolutely no tails. We indulged in rock-rolling when we discovered suitable round boulders perched precariously on the mountainsides. This involved a certain amount of excavation at the base of the boulder to remove the earth and small rocks holding it in place. The last few handfuls had to be removed with care be-cause some of these boulders were several tons and could break loose suddenly. We also had to predict the route of the boulder as it descended to make sure no structure or picnickers were at risk. There were some very spectacular descents with these large boulders gaining huge momentum, leaping into the air over obstacles and finally coming to rest in a shower of sparks and fragments at the bottom of the valley.

To the north of Juliasdale lay various other attractions; the Honde valley, the Troutbeck Inn, World's View lookout point at the top of a large rocky outcrop, Rhodes' Hotel and the Inyangombe Falls. The Troutbeck was a positively elite hotel in the true Scottish style, complete with golf course, horse-riding and good trout fishing. It was too expensive for our family so we had to content ourselves with just looking. Cecil Rhodes had stayed at the Rhodes Hotel, a rambling structure like spacious house with wide verandahs and a rocking chair reputedly used by Rhodes. Dad and Mum had spent their honeymoon there and it had not changed much. From here one could take a dirt road and descend into the Pungwe gorge. The river was crossed with a "drift" which was merely a bed of stones laid in the river bed which the water flowed over. These had been very common when we were young, but most had since been replaced with bridges. The water depth over the drift varied according to season and recent rainfall and at times it was impassable.

The Pungwe drift was a favorite picnic spot because the bed of stones created a nice pool upstream where we could swim. The water was quite cold, but very invigorating. We also could hike a mile upstream to another natural pool where we could ride a small waterfall. We had many good picnics here with family and friends, and would usually have the pool all to ourselves.

The road beyond the drift was not maintained and was quite rough, but Dad had no problem taking his old Dodge station-wagon slowly over the deep ruts and washes to get to the base of Inyangani. From here we hiked up a path to the summit where a small beacon had been erected by the surveyors. On a clear day the view was magnificent. Further along the main road were the 'Mterazi Falls where a small stream flowed over a sheer cliff about 3,000 feet down into the Honde valley below. By lying on one's stomach on the flat rock at the edge of the cliff, one could get a clear view of the falls cascading down the cliff face. Inyanga was a marvelous mountain playground where nature could be enjoyed to the fullest in cool, invigorating temperatures.

In winter we could always get warmer by heading south towards Fort Victoria through various Tribal Trustlands. This road was still the 9 foot strip of tar with gravel shoulders because traffic was fairly light. When approaching another vehicle the theory was that one kept the right wheels on the tar and had the left wheels on the gravel, thus maintaining reasonable grip and control. Of course this sometimes led to a game of chicken, each driver wanting to be the last to move over. The more cautious drivers would then get off the tar altogether and the winner would stay in the center, very rude and dangerous but not uncommon. About 60 miles from Umtali was the resort of Hot Springs where hot, sulphurous springs bubbled out of the ground and had been piped to one large swimming pool and a series of smaller private baths. There was nothing better than leaving the cold and immersing oneself in this warm water, notwithstanding the heavy aroma of sulphur. Of course the complex included a hotel, private cabins with baths and a popular bar.

A little further down the road one had a choice of continuing south to the mountainous areas of Melsetter and Chipinga or heading a little west over the Sabi river. Dad had spent many of his school holidays with a friend whose family farmed in Melsetter and he knew the area well. The road followed the Umvumvumvu river up into the mountains and the little village of Melsetter consisted of a hotel, a few stores and a petrol station. This area was mainly a farming community growing coffee and some other crops suited to the undulating terrain. Our cousin David managed a large farm here and we enjoyed visiting there, hiking and swimming in the cold streams. On one trip there I was driving Dad's Chevy and was rounding a curve in the road when a huge python started to cross right in front of me. I had no choice and ran over it, but we stopped to see how badly it had suffered. Snakes are actually quite fragile reptiles and very subject to spinal damage. This snake was about 16 feet long and 4-5 inches in diameter. Dad wanted to get it to move off the road so approached it with his faithful walking stick. It was clearly quite seriously hurt, but nevertheless raised its head to strike at Dad. He persisted however and eventually the snake managed to escape into the brush, probably to die later unfortunately.

The western fork led to the Sabi river. This was one of the largest rivers in the east, but like most Rhodesian rivers could be a raging torrent in the wet season and a miserable trickle in winter. The government had developed quite an extensive irrigation scheme to draw water from the Sabi and pump it to the tribal areas to enhance the crop production of the blacks. We sometimes picnicked along the banks of the river or lunched at the old Birchenough Hotel on the far side of the impressive high-arched Birchenough Bridge. The hotel had been a favorite spot for hunters in the early days as the lowveld regions had most of the game, but this had been largely shot out and in our time there was not much going on at the hotel except a few diners and drinkers.

The arch of the bridge was an impressive steel structure rising high above the veld and visible from miles away, the sun reflecting off its silver paint. The story goes that during construction when only the arch had been completed without the suspended roadway below, an old farmer approached with his ox-wagon. Before crossing at the original drift he took a while and inspected the new construction with great interest. After contemplating for a while, he felt it his duty to inform the foreman that even with a double team of oxen the slope of the arch was far too steep to get his wagon over and even if he could, the descent would be far too much for his crude brakes!

From the Sabi the road led to Fort Victoria, a small farming and mining community. About thirty miles from the town was an impressive chain of stone ruins, the largest of which was named Zimbabwe. Without any written records, no-one is sure who built the original structures but the best guess is that they dated from around the 13th century, long before the current tribes had occupied this area. Whereas they are not sophisticated in the absolute sense, they are far advanced from the structures of the current tribes and there is speculation that slave-labor was used. The stones are rough-hewn and stacked without mortar, with the main peripheral walls of the "temple" about 8 feet thick at the bottom and rising to about 20 feet in height. The walls do not form a precise circle or oval so little actual design work seems to have been done. Within the walls are various passages and divisions and also a solid stone conical tower, perhaps related to some deity.

On the hill beside the temple there is another structure, named by the whites the Acropolis. It was clearly a fortification used by the inhabitants of the plains during times of attack by other tribes. There is evidence of crude smelting furnaces probably for weapons and tools and perhaps for gold to trade. Zimbabwe ruins was a popular tourist destination and we visited on several occasions, sometimes camping and sometimes staying at the rustic Zimbabwe Hotel. Although the Temple and Acropolis are the most famous, in fact these ruins stretch for about twenty miles and must have comprised quite a large settlement in their time. When the first hunters discovered these ruins in the mid 19th century, the top of the temple wall was adorned with a number of soapstone carvings depicting what appeared to be the head of a predatory bird. This became known as the Zimbabwe Bird and some of the originals are preserved in various museums. On one face of the wall there is a chevron pattern worked into the stones but no-one knows what significance this had other than decorative.

Although the family preferred to vacation on the beaches in South Africa, this meant a 1600 mile road trip and in order to justify the expense we stayed at least six weeks. For shorter and cheaper beach trips we settled for the Portuguese port of Beira, about 200 miles east of Umtali. The road was reasonable and depending on delays at immigration and customs, the trip took four to five hours. Beira was an old town settled by the Portuguese as a supply station on their voyages to the east. It was a good safe port and the town was typically Portuguese with attractive structures and good restaurants and clubs. The Portuguese had a more liberal disposition than the English and alcohol could be easily procured and consumed any time of day or night without restriction. The Manica beer and the many good wines from Portugal were very popular with Rhodesians. Beira had a direct rail link to Umtali and the port served Rhodesia for many of its imports and exports.

Mindful of the potential for the increasing number of Rhodesian visitors, an enterprising local businessman named Brito constructed a large complex of crude asbestos-cement cottages along the beach which he optimistically named Estoril after the famed beach resort close to Lisbon. The only resemblance was that both were on the ocean. The cottages were about 20' x 30' rectangles spaced closely together on a vast stretch of level sand just over the dunes. There was no vegetation of any kind. To add a little variety they were painted in different bright colors. There was no air-conditioning and no ceiling so the asbestos-cement walls and roof radiated the summer heat very effectively to the interior. The centerpiece of Estoril was a large cafeteria right on the beach which served food and drink at reasonable prices. These could be freely consumed on the beach and in the ocean and in fact this custom was strongly encouraged. The first trips I took were with the family and the boy scouts and a certain amount of supervision was involved. Once I had my driving license, notwithstanding strong reservations, Dad lent me Mum's Opel station wagon and a buddy and I set off on our own trip.

The first stop was in town at Duly's garage where we stocked up on several cartons of First Lord cigarettes. After lighting up, we made the trip to Beira by nightfall and drove out to Estoril. Not having the funds for a cottage, we had brought a small tent and set this up in the camping area. As soon as the sun set we realized that we had picked a poor location on the land side of the dunes as thousands of hungry mosquitoes descended upon us. We closed the tent flaps and smoked prodigiously but to no avail. There was nothing for it but to abandon the tent and sleep on the beach at the high-water mark where a stiff breeze kept the mosquitoes away. For two 16-year-olds the unrestricted life of Beira was heaven. We visited all the bars and nightclubs and stretched our meager funds to the limit. Beira had one particularly nice restaurant, the Oceana, which literally had the outside tables in the ocean for those who wanted to cool their feet while drinking. We soon figured out that as long as we ordered beer, each order was accompanied by a variety of small snacks including seafood, meat and chickpeas. All were heavily spiced with the Portuguese peri-peri which created fire in the mouth and raised the body temperature by about 5 degrees. This had the intended effect of increasing the thirst. On this basis it was unnecessary to buy food.

The Estoril beach was long and straight and to prevent the ocean from eroding it the city fathers had placed wrecks at intervals at right angles to the beach. Just south of the cafeteria there was a fairly large vessel with its prow out in the waves at high tide. Some of our more adventurous classmates figured out that if timed precisely, one could dive off the prow into the top of a swell and have enough water depth to survive. This was a tricky business as the prow was about 30' above the waves and the speed of the swells had to be factored in. I knew this was not for me and watched my buddies enjoy it.

The Portuguese had been in Africa for centuries and indeed had penetrated into Manicaland but never set up any permanent settlement there. They had a different approach to the local tribes, basically leaving them to their own devices and not attempting to educate them. They intermingled quite freely and in some cases intermarried. This seemed to work quite well but gave the natives little prospect for advancement. Portugal used its African colonies to train its military and the army personnel were in evidence everywhere. The young conscripts seemed to be attracted to every member of the female species and roamed the beaches in their leisure time looking for company. As they spoke no English their technique was simply to sit down next to a prospective conquest and stare at her unabashedly until she made some kind of move. Mum was quite encouraged when she was approached one evening while quietly enjoying the sunset.

Mozambique had a beautiful game reserve, Gorongoza, in the center of the country. We visited this one winter with friends and stayed at the main camp in one of the chalets. To reach the camp we had to cross the Pungwe river by pontoon, which was pulled back and forth by the operators using a cable strung across the river. Gorongoza was flat with abundant water and grassland, ideal for all the grazers and browsers. Big herds of zebra and wildebeest were in abundance and to keep the balance correct there were plenty of the big cats. In winter the grass is low and dry and visibility is good so we got excellent viewing of all the animals. Sadly the long civil war in Mozambique after independence in 1975 decimated this fine park.

Mozambique also honored the traditional Portuguese sport of bullfighting. The Portuguese do not kill the bulls so that one good bull may participate in many fights and become more formidable with each. Once a year the small town of Macequece held a bullfight which was easily accessible from Umtali. This was eagerly anticipated by the young bucks and they crossed the border in groups to drink the beer and cheer on the bull. I never made the trip because while I was still at school the Rhodesians had rendered themselves personae non grata

at these fights. The story goes that one year the fight
was progressing rather slowly with little excitement and
the audience became bored. To spice things up a bit, a
group of Rhodesians took to the ring and grabbing the
bull by the tail, secured it for long enough for others to
mount it. The surprised beast pranced around the ring
bucking and lunging but the odds were too high and he
finally had to lie down and rest. To proclaim their victory
the Rhodesians then made the insulting move of tearing
down the Portuguese flag and hoisting the Rhodesian flag
in its place. The Portuguese took this with poor grace and
arrested the culprits. After suitable negotiations involving
exchanges of cash, they were released with instructions
never to return.

In 1960 politics was driving Dad nuts again. In
February, the British Prime Minister, Harold MacMillan,
visited Africa and made his infamous "Wind of Change"
speech to the South African parliament. *The wind of
change is blowing through this continent, and whether we like it or
not, this growth of national consciousness is a political fact. We
must all accept it as a fact, and our national policies must take account of it.*

There was no mistaking the portent of this message,
all the more surprising coming from the leader of the
British Conservative Party. South Africa reacted swiftly
and held a referendum on becoming an independent
republic in October 1960. This referendum passed and
South Africa left the Commonwealth, becoming the
Republic of South Africa in October 1961 under the
direction of Prime Minister Hendrik Verwoerd. This

same year Britain granted independence to the former Protectorate of Tanganika. Of equal or more importance, in the 1960 US elections, Democrat John Kennedy narrowly defeated Republican Richard Nixon. None of these events bode well for Southern Rhodesia.

Chapter 11:
THE UPPER ZAMBEZI TRIP

In 1960, when I was fifteen, Dad decided to visit his brother Rufus who operated a barge service on the upper reaches of the Zambezi river. Rufus was the second oldest in the family and had been the accepted leader of the three brothers. Rufus had been a bright student and had won a scholarship to attend Rhodes University in Grahamstown, South Africa. He had an illustrious tenure there, being a great prankster and leader. During one vacation, lacking the funds to travel home, he lived in a cave on the beach at Port Alfred and survived on pilfered fruit and fish which he caught. He majored in French and returned to Rhodesia to teach this language in high-schools until he retired in 1956. He was a great lover of the African bush and so the opportunity to live on the Zambezi river was welcome as a retirement option.

The barge service ran from Mumva just above the Victoria Falls to Katima M'lilo in the Caprivi Strip. The transport consisted of the main powered barge and a dumb-barge lashed to each side of it, each craft about 40 feet in length and 8 feet in beam. The cabin and galley were on the main barge. It transported manufactured goods and foodstuffs upstream and returned with animal skins, artifacts and other assorted goods. The trip took four days upstream and three days downstream unless the river was in flood. Rufus was accompanied by his wife May and sometimes by his two sons, John and Tim. John came to shoot crocodiles and Tim came for the good fishing. Rufus's daughter Linda was married to Cecil, who ran the sister barges operating in the other direction.

The Zambezi was totally unspoiled along most of this route, but there were a few villages where we stopped to deliver or pick up goods. The Zambezi has many tributaries and blind lagoons and so the black captain had to know the river and its channels well. The surrounding area is flat and the river meanders slowly through wide channels with reeds and low trees on both sides. At night we tied up to the bank because navigation was tricky unless there was a full moon. Rufus and May slept in the cabin and the rest of us slept on deck under mosquito nets.

During the day Tim and I ran lines over the stern to catch Tiger fish. These are great fighting fish with long, sharp teeth and grow up to 20 lb or so. They get their name from the golden stripes that run vertically down each side. The normal speed of the barge was faster than ideal for trolling, but the fish were fast and took the shiny spinners well. If we hooked large ones we would shout to the captain to slow down so we could enjoy the fight and bring them in. He was very patient and never complained about the disruption of progress. Tiger are not good eating in our judgment, but the blacks enjoyed all we gave them. At night we would use bait to catch the delicious Zambezi bream and May cooked up fine meals of these.

There was plenty of game along the banks and we frequently saw elephants and hippos enjoying the cool water. The lechwe is an antelope found in this area and from time to time we spotted these coming down to drink. The bush was fairly dense all along the banks so it was difficult to see smaller game unless it came into the open. The river was teeming with crocodiles which cousin John would shoot from the barge for their skins. Crocodile meat is not bad eating and has become quite popular as "bush" meat but at that time we never considered eating any.

The Zambezi also served as a conduit and recruiting route for WNLA, the Witwatersrand Native Labor Association. They ran passenger boats up and down the river picking up and returning laborers for the gold-mines of the Witwatersrand. Laborers were signed up for contract periods on the mines which they could renew or return home. They liked this, as it gave them exposure to all the attractions of the Johannesburg area and earned them hard cash which they used to buy all the things not available to them in the bush.

After four days we arrived in Katima M'lilo, a tiny trading post on the small strip of South West Africa (Namibia) known as the Caprivi Strip formed at the junction with Angola, Bechuanaland (Botswana) and Northern Rhodesia (Zambia). At that time Katima consisted of the Native Commissioner's residence, a few huts and a general store. There was no real dock and we tied up to some pilings with a crude wooden ramp and porters unloaded the goods by handcart. Because of the relatively rapid flow of water, the Zambezi has no Bilharzia, so not having bathed for four days, we availed ourselves of the opportunity for a swim. There was a small stretch of sand beach next to the dock and we stripped off and entered the water with great relish. Because of the multitude of crocodiles we had to be very watchful and not venture deeper than our wastes. The water was clear, but crocodiles can strike at lightning speed and even pursue their prey on to the land. Dad and Rufus stood guard with their shotguns but fortunately everything remained calm and we soaped ourselves up and emerged feeling wonderful.

The main cargo for the trip back was a family on safari with a long-wheelbase Land Rover. The barges had no means for loading or storing a vehicle but this did not deter anyone. A crude ramp was made of long tree-trunks and stout planks were placed across the three hulls to suit the track of the Land Rover. With much revving of the engine, pushing and shoving, the vehicle made it up the steep ramp and came to rest against the chocks the owner had taken the precaution of nailing to the planks. Rufus,

Cecil and the captain had judged the position very well and the barges rode level in the water.

We had an uneventful trip downstream and joined the rest of the family for a few days at the Victoria Falls. This was our first trip to the Falls and we stayed at some chalets on the Northern Rhodesia side. The spectacle of the wide Zambezi falling four hundred feet into the gorge below was absolutely breathtaking. We were there in the month of September when the flow is the least, but this the best time to see the falls themselves because at high-water there is so much spray one can just see a white haze. In the early part of the century Mum's aunt Una had been admiring the falls from the edge on the Southern Rhodesian side when a deranged black ran up behind her and pushed her over into the maelstrom below. Needless to say, she did not survive.

From here we drove down south to the huge Wanki game reserve. We stayed the first night in Robin's Camp in a comfortable rondavel. The next day we drove slowly through the park, seeing almost all the species of game and ended up at Main Camp where we spent the next night. Wanki is famous for its elephant herds and indeed all along the way we saw many elephant and much of the bush had been devastated by their browsing. The Game Department had to manage the population scientifically because the terrain can only sustain a certain amount of damage. Elephants rip off large branches and push over whole trees in order to get the tasty leaves they like so from time to time culling had to take place.

As part of the plan for the new Federation, the Federal Government decided to proceed with an ambitious project to dam the mighty Zambezi river and vastly expand the power supply for the region. The Copperbelt in Northern Rhodesia had been clamoring for hydro power to feed its vast mines and smelters and had originally submitted a plan to dam the Kafue river, a tributary of the Zambezi. Southern Rhodesia had objected to this because it also had increasing power needs so in 1955 the Italian civil engineering company Impresit was contracted to design and build the dam downstream from the Victoria Falls in a suitable gorge between two rock formations. The project was completed in 1959.

The resulting lake was 140 miles long and 20 miles wide and covered an area of 2150 square miles. It was and still is the greatest body of water by volume created by man, with a mean depth of 95 feet and a maximum depth of 320 feet. The first stage power station on the Southern Rhodesia side produces 705 MW. A second stage was added in 1976 on the northern side, increasing the output to 1266 MW. More capacity is being added on the northern side for completion in 2012.

The project involved the relocation of the Tonga tribe and thousands of wild animals who made their homes in the area to be flooded. This was a sore point for the Tonga, who, not unreasonably, resented their tribal land being expropriated. Although every effort was made to accommodate them in adjacent areas, it was not "home" and they felt their lives had been diminished and their gods offended. The animals were dealt with in Operation

Noah, in which the Game Department relocated about 5000 animals of all species to safe ground. There were many volunteers and some experiences were priceless, chasing petrified monkeys up trees and manhandling tranquilized rhinos on to transports. Even snakes were rounded up and placed in sacks, a dangerous job. When all the animals were out of the area, huge steel balls were towed by large bulldozers to clear the trees and brush. They rolled indiscriminately and did a fine job. The resulting debris was then burned, leaving a fairly clear area to be flooded.

Most Rhodesians were nature lovers and accompanied the project with great interest and we kids were especially intrigued. After going through Wanki, Dad decided it would be the perfect time to visit the new project, so we deviated from the main Bulawayo road and drove to the dam. It was indeed spectacular, a huge, curved mass of concrete bridging the gorge. At that time the dam was still filling and only one gate was open to supply the river downstream. It was a challenging engineering feat and Impresit had some unforeseen difficulties dealing with a large fissure in the rock of the north bank. We toured the site with great excitement and then continued our journey, crossing the Zambezi over the new dam.

About this same time, black-and-white television was introduced to Salisbury and a budding new industry emerged around it. The mother of our good childhood companion Julia found a new calling in life and became deeply involved in several productions. "Aunt" Lale was a vivacious English lady who reveled in the new medium and we watched with great pride when she made her appearances. In Umtali we could not receive any signal because of the mountain range behind the town, but a grainy picture could be watched by driving over the Christmas Pass and having a few drinks at the Christmas Pass hotel. We seldom did this and did not miss having TV at all.

In this same year our Uncle Ken built a house next to ours and moved in with his wife Chris and two children Susan and David. Ken had flown bombers for the RAF during the war and all Chris's family except her had been killed during the Blitz. Ken worked for the Rhodesian government in the soil conservation department. Soil erosion was a major problem in the black farming areas because of overgrazing and poor agricultural practices. The blacks clung to their traditional beliefs and cattle were an important part of their lives, the more the better. Ken had a difficult task convincing them that fifty fat cows are preferable to a hundred emaciated beasts and they strongly resisted all efforts to limit their herds to the available grazing. If left to themselves, the grass would disappear, the goats would then devour any remaining vegetation and the first heavy rain would wash away the topsoil. In the more undulating areas Ken had to convince the farmers to plough across the slope and build contour ridges to deflect the rainwater sideways and conserve the soil. The conservation department was quite large and its officers had an ongoing battle to prevent the country from becoming a desert.

Amongst Ken's possessions was an old Skoda convertible car which no longer ran. As he had no use for it and he knew I loved tinkering, he donated it to me. I summoned my friends and with great excitement we pushed the dilapidated vehicle from Ken's yard to ours. A quick evaluation revealed that the car needed a battery and a thorough cleaning of the fuel system. Dad had a fine workshop and so with a little financial assistance for the purchase of the new battery, we soon had the engine running. At fifteen I could not drive legally on public roads, so I drove across the Circular Drive to the school grounds and put the car through its paces there.

The Skoda was not in the upper league of automotive engineering and had several major deficiencies, but these were of little consequence considering my total investment.

As soon as I turned sixteen I rushed down to the licensing office and with great confidence, proceeded to take the test. The licensing officer must have thought I was a little too cocky and to bring me back to earth he failed me. I returned two weeks' later much humiliated and this time passed. The Skoda then became my main form of transport, its use limited only by my ability to buy petrol. Shortly after I got my license the school held a parade through town with various floats and music. The convertible top had long since crumbled to dust and Ken had discarded the framework so my buddies and I fashioned a very neat thatched roof for the car, with the ridge running down the center, and we joined the parade. At parade speed this roof performed well and afforded us the necessary shade, but on the way home we went up to the speed-limit of thirty miles per hour and the poor aerodynamics of the roof soon became apparent. After fluttering a little, it broke loose from its wooden mountings and floated right off the car. Fortunately there was nothing right behind us so we picked up the remains and returned them to the bush from whence they came. After this Dad and I fashioned a new frame out of conduit piping and used Mum's sewing-machine to sew a new vinyl top. It did not precisely conform to the sleek lines expected on a convertible, but it kept out the sun and the rain.

During my school years I performed several major maintenance jobs on this Skoda and also repainted it by hand, a duplicate of the rather uninteresting light brown that Ken had previously painted it. It was much loved by all my school buddies but I rather suspect that girlfriend Pam preferred to drive in Dad's Chevy. In 1964 I drove it the thousand odd miles from Umtali to Kitwe and it did yeoman service there for a year before I drove it home and sold it for thirty pounds.

Chapter 12:
FIRST LOVE

1 961 was an eventful year for me for two reasons. The first was that my first bona fide girlfriend found me and the second was that at sixteen all students in academic classes had to write the Cambridge exams. The girlfriend situation was not initiated by me, for I was very shy with girls outside the family. Our kindly neighbor took pity on me and suggested to her friend down the street that her daughter Pam should invite me to the annual dance at the private Marymount school beneath Cross Kopje. It seems Pam was not entirely opposed to the idea and the formal invitation was duly proffered and accepted. I had one pair of long trousers and this was sent off for dry-cleaning as it had not seen much use. The stock uniform for boys at these occasions was a green school blazer, grey flannel trousers, white shirt and school tie. This was for the very good reason that few boys had

any other clothes except the khaki shorts and shirts worn daily. As all the boys in town went to the same school, everyone at the dance had the same attire. The girls were a different story and dolled themselves up in the latest fashion with great color and variety.

Pam was a sweet girl with fair hair and green eyes. We had a wonderful time at the dance and I drove her home in Mum's Vauxhall. This model had a wide, unobstructed front bench seat, ideal for the serious petting couple. Pam snuggled up close to me and I thought I had gone to heaven. As the direct route home was about five minutes, we decided to prolong the ecstasy and stop a little before dropping her off. Knowing the area well, I pulled into a small track leading to a water reservoir on the mountain behind our houses. Wondering exactly how to proceed without giving offense, Pam sensed my dilemma and threw her arms around my neck and proceeded with a long, delicious kiss. I suppose we all remember such occasions, but this kiss still ranks as the best of my life. I got goose-bumps and felt a tingling all over my body. She must have enjoyed it too, for we repeated the procedure many more times before prying ourselves loose and driving home. Pam and I dated until I left Umtali and enjoyed many good occasions together.

The eight subjects of the Cambridge exam were maths, science, history, geography, English grammar, English literature, Latin and (in my case) Afrikaans. The questions were prepared and graded in England. I was fortunate to be good at maths and science and my excellent short-term memory allowed me to study the other subjects a few hours before each exam with almost complete recall. Most of us in the A-class passed with good marks and this exam was considered a prelude to the real exam two years ahead, the Higher Schools Certificate which would gain us entrance to college. Many in the less academic classes left school at this point to pursue their careers. One thing must be said about our education system. Regardless of intellect, every pupil leaving a Rhodesian public school left able to speak and write his native language correctly. Interestingly, no African languages were taught in white schools, but English was taught in black schools. I suppose the theory was that eventually everyone would speak English and be equipped to communicate anywhere in the world. Initially of course the blacks had a multitude of dialects, no alphabet and no written languages so coming up with a practical means of writing a consolidated form of these was not simple.

Dad's vacation schedule was on a two-year basis because of cost, so in the interim years we stayed home. A year after the Cambridge exams was a home year and in order to fund my dating and transportation needs I took a vacation job with our neighbor, who administered the black township of Sakubva just south of town. Sakubva was a well laid-out township with good roads, power, water and sewage. There were blocks of flats for single persons and small houses for families. These were all of brick and concrete construction and were pretty rugged. Understanding that many of the residents had little or no experience with delicate appliances and devices, these were kept to a minimum. Sinks, handrails, steps etc. were all solid concrete. Windows were steel-framed. The township was self-sufficient with its own schools, clinics, movie-house and bars. It had its own police-force and maintenance department and a range of sporting fields. There were no squalid slums in Rhodesia. The townships were clean and orderly and in the tribal areas the traditional villages of grass huts were set out neatly on swept earth.

Our neighbor was the de-facto mayor of Sakubva. He had a small staff of whites to assist him and they oversaw the black staff who ran the township. My job was in the maintenance department where I could use my mechanical skills helping the black mechanics to keeps the township's vehicles and maintenance equipment running smoothly. The machines that required the most attention were the lawnmowers and I became an expert in overhauling the small engines.

On Saturday mornings at 10 am films would be shown for the children at the theater. They were very enthusiastic patrons and I remember during a showing of Elvis Presley in Jailhouse Rock the kids sang along with great gusto, creating a roar that could be heard for miles around.

Just south of Sakubva was a very nice teachers' training college for blacks, administered by an old friend of the family. His son Mike was in my class and a good friend so I spent many a good time at their house. Mike had a very impressive electric train set all nicely mounted on a large wooden platform and we spent many hours evaluating all the possible combinations of engines and carriages.

This training facility prepared teachers to staff the rapidly increasing number of black schools and the curriculum was similar to the Heany teachers' training college for whites which sister Jennifer attended. There were both black and white instructors and the level of education was the same Cambridge standard as our schools. The facility itself was first-class with spacious lecture rooms and on-site accommodation. Black children were thirsty for knowledge and were ideal pupils, perfectly behaved and they benefited greatly from the high standards set by teachers from this college.

Chapter 13:
THE BOTSWANA TRIP

Our school headmaster Coney was a great lover of the African bush and each year in the September school holiday he would invite boys sixteen and above to accompany him and his wife Ellie on a safari. In 1961 I joined a group of seventeen schoolboys, five staff and two black cooks on one of Coney and Ellie's famed trips. This year he had picked a route through south-western Rhodesia into Botswana and up to Maun in the Okavango. The school owned a five-ton Thames truck and two Land-Rover pick-ups and these were our transport. Each person was allowed one army kitbag of clothes and camping gear. There was also a large wooden box containing eating and cooking utensils and a very robust box for the liquor supplies of the staff. It was prudent to include someone with medical knowledge and so the local dentist joined the group. He was built like a wrestler and appeared to have a similar disposition but he was an excellent dentist and a great character. He was not one to pamper his patients and with his powerful hands and arms the drilling process was painful but very quick. Tooth extractions were effortless.

The staff drove the vehicles and rode in the cabs and the boys and cooks road in the beds, six in each Land Rover and the rest on top of the kit-bags in the Thames. September in Rhodesia is dry and clear, perfect for camping in the open. The first leg of the trip took us to Bulawayo where we set up camp in the yard of one of Coney's numerous friends. Coney liked to keep things simple and so tents were considered an unnecessary luxury. Everyone simply unrolled his sleeping-bag on the most level piece of ground he could find and went happily to sleep. Meals were prepared by the cooks over open fires and served military style in metal plates. After the meal the group filed by two basins of hot water, the first with detergent for washing the plates and the second for rinsing.

Traveling was surprisingly comfortable high up on the pile of kit-bags on the Thames and we amused ourselves telling stories and enjoying the countryside. The Land Rovers were not so comfortable and the view was very limited because of the canvas cover.

The next day we stopped for lunch at Plumtree school on the western border where Coney and two other staff had attended high school. Plumtree was very nicely set up with spacious grounds and buildings. The most impressive feature for us was the exclusive prefects' lounge, a separate rondavel complete with bar and smoking area. It seemed that the Plumtree boys were partial to pipes, as there was a large selection stacked neatly in a long pipe-rack. Pretty much all the pupils at Plumtree were boarders from the surrounding farm families and these work-hardened fellows usually fielded excellent sports teams.

We crossed the border with minimum formalities and then proceeded to Francistown in Botswana. Whereas the roads in Rhodesia had been wide tar or nine-foot strip type, in Botswana all the roads were dirt except for a few streets in Francistown. It was my misfortune to travel the Tuli-Francistown section in the back of one of the Land Rovers and when we arrived at our campsite we had accumulated about five millimeters of dust on our sweat-soaked skins. Water is a precious commodity in Francistown, so we scraped off most of the dirt with our fingernails before using our one-bucket allocation of water for the remainder.

Francistown was small, with a main street of stores and one hotel surrounded by residences. We set up camp on the shooting-range, having been assured that no practice was scheduled for that night. After dinner we made a bee-line for the local pub where we were greeted effusively by the local residents who hadn't seen a new face in months. After a few beers we were invited to a party at one of the residences where we found three girls enjoying the attention of about fifty young men. Notwithstanding the unfavorable odds, everyone had a great time.

The next morning we set off for Nata, which was little more than a name on a map. Once we left Francistown the road could be more accurately described as two ruts in the sand. The standard vehicle in Botswana was the Chevy or Ford pick-up truck and the ruts matched the track of these. Our Land Rovers had a narrower track and the Thames a wider and this proved to be a problem. Both vehicles had to travel with two wheels in the soft sand outside or inside the ruts and so going was very slow. As the veld had periodic small fields of majordas (a type of mellon) we found these ideal for games of bowls. We could jump off the vehicles, have a quick game and then run to catch up again. We finally reached Nata about sundown and set up camp. We were at first quite surprised and happy to see a small river with a series of pools, so having endured a hot, dusty trip, we stripped off and jumped in. Our joy soon evaporated as we realized that the water was stinking and foul and we had to use precious buckets from our fresh-water barrels to rinse off.

Our next leg of the trip was out into the middle of the Makgadikadi pans, a vast plain of short grass with occasional pans of water and groups of stunted trees. We drove over the virgin bush near Mumswe and set up camp amongst a thicket of trees quite close to quite a large pan, about fifty meters in diameter. We examined the water carefully before venturing in and once fully immersed we felt wonderful. It wasn't long however before one boy after another felt a sharp bite and emerged quite rapidly to find a nice fat leech sucking voraciously at his blood. These leeches were fat, slimy worms about 5cm long which grew rapidly fatter as they gorged on us. The staff assessed the situation quickly and determined that the prescribed method of dealing with leeches was to apply the hot tip of a cigarette to their heads. From nowhere suddenly each boy produced a cigarette and administered the remedy, taking care to enjoy the rest of the smoke once the leeches dropped off. Having accepted that swimming was not going to be enjoyable, we contented ourselves with filling buckets from the pan and throwing the contents over one another. We certainly scooped up some leeches but the rapid contact gave them no time to latch on.

Coney had somehow managed to obtain permission from the local chief for our party to hunt for the pot. There was plenty of game around us, predominantly wildebeest and springbok, but it was gun-shy and kept a long distance away. All the staff were excited at the prospect of a good hunt and drew lots to see who got the first shot. The imperturbable JJ drew the short straw and loaded up his 8mm rifle for a shot at a distant wildebeest. During the daytime on the pans the heat is formidable and this causes rising currents of air to distort vision over long distances. JJ was well aware of this but decided to fire anyway as there was nothing to lose. The range must have been over 500 meters which is not an impossible shot under good conditions, but four shots later the wildebeest was still ambling along happily enjoying the sweet grasses and JJ had to face the overt derision of the staff and covert derision of the boys, but he took it all in good humor and even cracked a wry smile. The fifth shot brought the unlucky beast down and when we inspected the carcass we discovered it had lost the left eye and was therefore blind to our party.

That night it was decided that due to necessity the finer points of sportsmanship could be stretched a little and two parties set out in Land Rovers equipped with shotguns and spotlights. One of the staff fancied his skills at astronomy and was appointed navigator as there were no discerning topographical features to landmark. I was in one Land Rover and before long we were hard on the chase after a small herd of springbok. The driver did a masterful job of closing in and the appointed shooter let loose at the rump of the closest animal with both barrels of his 12-bore shotgun. This took care of the hind legs but the unfortunate beast continued crawling along with its front legs, dragging its rear. I was dispatched with a rather blunt hunting knife to finish the job by cutting the throat. I did not think much about this until I grabbed the horns and stared into the soft purple eyes pleading with me for mercy. I hesitated a few seconds but the creature was obviously in great agony and so I finished the job as quickly as I could.

Aside from the transgressions from sportsmanship in shooting an animal in the rear with buckshot we discovered there were practical disadvantages as well. After skinning and hanging the carcass our cooks prepared a fine stew of springbok rump which was delicious in flavor but marred by the fact that every mouthful contained several pellets of solid lead which had to be separated by the tongue and duly spat out. In those days no-one even thought about lead-poisoning and I very much doubt that a few dozen pellets sucked for a few seconds do have any lasting damage. To my knowledge those of the group that have passed away did so from other causes.

The terrain became even more sandy as we progressed northwest and from time to time the vehicles got bogged down. Part of Coney's camping gear included a hundred foot long heavy manila rope. When the going got tough, this rope was attached to the tow hook on the front of the vehicle and everyone except Ellie and the driver manned the rope and pulled the vehicle along. Usually this was for short distances but occasionally we had to pull for a few hours until the terrain improved. The Land Rovers could generally slog along in low-range but the Thames with only rear-wheel drive and a full load was the major problem. Obviously the progress was slow under these conditions but no-one was in a hurry and we made what distance we could.

Once we went off the road to find a campsite we traveled over short grass which was quite firm. On one of the wide plains we spotted a flock of guinea-fowl and decided to chase it down. Guinea-fowl spend most of their time on the ground and only fly when necessary. They can run quite fast and initially they tried to flee on foot. When they realized this was not going to work they took to the air, but soon tired out and had to land again. We singled out one bird for final pursuit and finally it was exhausted and we simply walked up and caught it. Our initial intention had been to eat it, but it looked so pitiful we brought it back to camp and put a sock over its head, whereupon it went happily to sleep. The next morning bright and early we removed the sock and let it loose. It showed no more fear and strolled away casually, pecking the crumbs around the campsite.

On another occasion we came upon a honey-badger on the plain and chased after it with the truck. It was not intimidated at all and turned on the truck, biting viciously at the tires to the point that we had to stop and let it make a dignified retreat. We also saw several bat-eared foxes and other small game. The plains were surprisingly smooth and with good visibility we could drive at quite reasonable speeds, the only obstacles being ant-heaps and ant-bear burrows.

We finally reached our destination, Maun and set up camp on the banks of the Thalamakane river, a little southeast of Maun. Maun is the entry point to the Okavango, a vast area which is flooded by the Zambezi and its tributaries for several months each year. It is rich in wildlife and the lagoons left by the floods are crystal clear. Maun itself in 1961 was not impressive, a small, dusty ranching and hunting center with a few stores and the famous Riley's hotel on the banks of the river. Our camp was very pleasant, right at the water's edge under some large trees. The first night we realized that these trees were the roosting area for a local flock of guinea-fowl. Spike, being the proud owner of the 12-bore shotgun, placed it conveniently beside his sleeping-bag. At first light the next morning the guineas set up their normal calling and Spike laying flat on his back, raised the shotgun and blew a couple of birds out of the trees above him. The guineas were not too smart, for this routine continued for several days until the flock was severely depleted and sought out a safer place to roost.

The Thalamakane at that time of year was quite strong and we had a fine time swimming and fishing. The risk of crocodiles was always present but we believed that if we created enough commotion they would not approach. There were the usual tilapia and pike to be caught during daylight hours but at night the big vundu fed in the shallows. We baited handlines with small mice and cast our lines in one or two feet of water. The vundu is a scavenger which feeds on the bottom and grows to thirty kilos or more. It looks like an immense catfish, with long whiskers. Needless to say, like the African barble, it is not good to eat, so we donated our catches to the local tribesmen. Vundu fishing was not very exciting because once hooked, the huge fish put up no fight at all. After catching a few we left them alone.

The local tribesmen moved about the rivers in makoros, dug-outs made from large tree-trunks. These were heavy and unwieldy and very unstable. One afternoon a buddy and I discovered what we assumed to be an abandoned makoro stuck in the mud with its bow rotted away. We figured out that if we both sat in the stern, the bow would be clear of the water and so we made ourselves suitable poles and set off down river. It was quite a balancing-act but we managed to keep afloat and had a fine trip. We were amazed at the number of large snakes happily swimming along beside us and kept our distance. After the trip we abandoned the makoro, which proved to be a costly mistake. That night a full delegation consisting of the chief and elders of the local tribe and local Maun police visited our camp demanding payment for the "stolen" makoro. Not wishing to offend the locals, a purchase price of five pounds was agreed upon and duly paid and the chief left a very happy man.

At that time there was no development along the river and we could walk long distances along the banks in both directions. Spike was generous in loaning his shotgun and so we took turns hunting franklin, small partridge-type birds abundant in the region. They were good runners and could change direction at full speed so even though they were on the ground there was some skill required. They were good to eat and formed part of our menu for the days on the Thalamakane.

After a few days a trip to Maun was arranged to stock up with petrol, water and food. By unspoken agreement the staff went directly to the bar at Riley's and the boys went around the back and purchased beer at the "off-sales" counter. Lacking suitable cover to consume it without overt disobedience of the rules, we set ourselves up in the spacious men's room of the hotel and prayed that the staff would confine their ablutions to the toilet in the bar. This was not the case however and our drinking and smoking was rudely interrupted by the arrival of Pete, our English teacher. He summed up the situation instantly and excused himself for the intrusion and the issue was never mentioned again.

The trip home took a slightly different route to visit another of Coni's buddies who was in charge of the cattle disease control in Botswana at 'Mkalambedi.

Large herds of cattle passed through Botswana on their way to the markets in South Africa and disease control was an important issue. A large fenced area was set aside lower down on the Boteti river to quarantine transit cattle until they could be given clean bills of health. We set up a nice camp on the river close to the house of Coney's friend and that evening he and his wife joined us for dinner. He had a rich selection of hunting stories and informed us that just a week ago he had shot his one-hundreth lion!

The river was much smaller here and we found the sandy banks and shallows full of baby crocodiles just freshly hatched. These little fellows could be caught easily and despite their small size, latched on to our fingers with their long jaws. The franklin were also in great abundance here and we did not go short of fresh meat. We shot a couple more springbok on our way back through the pans and these lasted through the remainder of the trip, lead pellets and all. Upon arrival back in Francistown we could not wait to jump into the municipal swimming pool. Not having had access to water for several days it was wonderful to immerse our bodies completely. The residents of Francistown were not that enthusiastic about a group of dirty boys washing the dust off in their previously sparkling pool. We spent one more night at the Kyle lake near Fort Victoria. Here the last springbok was consumed. Having been in the hot sun for three days it was well aged and the skin came off very easily, exposing green flesh below. The skinners refused to partake of the meal, but the rest of us declared it the best meat we'd ever eaten.

After three very enjoyable weeks we arrived home safely and enjoyed hot baths with scrubbing brush and soap.

1961 saw another political milestone which incensed Dad. With the break up of the Central African Federation imminent, the British government submitted a"White Paper" to Southern Rhodesia in which it proposed a constitution which had two separate voter rolls, A and B, with the B-roll having lower requirements, allowing accelerated inclusion of blacks in the government. This was put to a national referendum which the blacks chose to boycott but was passed by the majority of whites with the conservative Dominion Party strongly opposing because this constitution had no guarantee of full independence in the event of the break-up. Under the new constitution the transition to black rule would have been made over a period of time but eventually there would be a large number of qualified black voters. It must be assumed that they would always vote for black candidates regardless of suitability, so at some point they would gain a majority in parliament. Dad calculated that this would occur within 20 years and again, he was correct but by a different mechanism.

Chapter 14:
LAST YEARS AT SCHOOL

1962 was my second last year at high-school and in December I was required to write the Cambridge Subsidiary exams in my chosen subjects of maths, physics and chemistry. English was a required subject for all, and to improve my Afrikaans further I elected to take this as well. Being a typical schoolboy I left study until the last moment and then spent long hours just before each exam poring over my notes. My short-term memory stood me in good stead once again and I came through with one of the best scores in the school.

The system after the mandatory Cambridge exam changed to be more of a university style, with each student responsible for his own diligence and conduct. Each class at this level had its own home-room to use during periods when there were no other scheduled classes. The year before I reached "subsid" the school had constructed two very nice new laboratories for the upper classes, one for chemistry and one for physics. The chemistry teacher "Happy" Crosse was an intrepid fellow with a sharp wit who did not suffer fools gladly at all. His only redeeming feature in our eyes was his surprising marriage to a very good-looking teacher at the girls' school. The surprise was rooted in the fact that Happy was considered one of the least-blessed staff appearance-wise and all of us wondered and publicly debated whether or not he possessed some concealed talents which could possibly justify the beauty having consented to marry him.

Happy was very serious about his chemistry and duly proud of his fine lab. He kept an impressive selection of every conceivable element and compound in his storeroom and I do believe we got an excellent education in his field. At that time no-one was very concerned about carcinogens or any other danger really and we dabbled and experimented in sublime ignorance. Our two favorite elements were sodium and potassium which Happy stored in tightly sealed jars in the form of small cubes. We would fill a large sink with water and carefully float a half-cube on the surface to watch it react violently with the water and race around the sink. Other favorites were phosphorous and magnesium which burned with an impressive output of smoke and light. We loved to dip our fingers and hands into the large jar of mercury and feel the full impact of Archimedes principle.

A favorite trick was to partially fill a pipette with nitric or hydrochloric acid and then surreptitiously sneak the tip into a mate's pocket and let a few cc's of the acid dribble out. There was usually a short delay until the victim felt the sting and burn, and with experience he generally could be out of his short pants and heading for the sink in less than 5 seconds. Happy was understandably opposed to this practice, not only for the disruptions caused to the class but also because occasionally an irate parent would have the audacity to complain about ruined clothing and Happy would politely inform them that as his pupils were destined for university he was not responsible for their conduct any longer.

One thing Happy undoubtedly did regret was the day he taught the class how to make gun-cotton. This is a mildly explosive compound used originally in crude weapons. After perfecting the process we selected one of Happy's most valuable sturdy glass tubes about 3 feet long and proceeded to charge it with a generous load of guncotton, backed up by a nicely-fitting piece of solid glass rod. We did have the good sense to take it outside and point it away from the building, but nevertheless its trajectory crossed the exit door to the lab. Just as I ignited the wick Happy emerged from the lab to see what we were up to. My heart sunk as the weapon discharged its projectile with impressive force. Happy was no slouch and sized up his predicament immediately, leaping at least four feet into the air as the glass rod passed harmlessly beneath him and shattered to smithereens on the steps ahead. He took the event in good humor however and in classic understatement admonished us to be more careful in the practical applications of our knowledge.

Sport was a big deal in Rhodesia and I always privately cursed my poor co-ordination and awkward movement. The words geek and nerd had not yet been invented, but certainly they would have applied to me and a few other academics who did not make the cuts for the various sporting teams. Whereas academic accomplishment was encouraged, sport was the main topic of conversation and set a school's prestige. Prefects were normally chosen first from the best sportsmen, as they commanded the most respect regardless of intellect. In those days all pupils took an IQ test when they entered high-school and the results were not concealed. Whereas there were some all-rounders who were gifted academically and physically, there were those who made the team purely on brute strength and endurance, two qualities very useful when playing rugby. Most of the boys had insightful nicknames alluding to their physiques or personal talents.

During rugby season every second weekend the teams would travel by train to other towns in the country to play those schools, but on weekends that the games were on our home fields the townsfolk turned out in force to cheer their sons to victory. The school was well endowed with numerous playing fields but the first team always played on the main field with a nice terraced pavilion. Tea was served at half-time by the school kitchen staff. The highest level I attained was the Warthogs, a selection of the least-gifted players but amusing to watch and fun to play. We occasionally got to play early in the afternoon as a curtain-raiser to the main match, but most of the time our games were on weekdays against ourselves.

Having a pool at home, at school and downtown, swimming was big in our family. This did not require any eye-limb co-ordination and so I was able to perform reasonably well. The school had competitive swimming galas and there were public galas in the municipal pool. Umtali had some first-class swimmers and divers who went on to compete at national level. In our last year at school a buddy and I decided it would be useful to get our lifesaving medals. Whereas all pupils were taught the basics of lifesaving, our enthusiasm was materially enhanced by the fact that the instructor for the medal course was a girl about our age. At that time the saving technique involved pacifying the victim and then turning him/her belly up. The saver then came underneath on his back and secured the victim under the arms, using only the legs for propulsion. The instructor had to play the role of victim, and as savers we did not lose the opportunity to secure her by placing our hands on her breasts. She took this reasonably well as long as we stayed on the outside of her swimsuit, but if our grasp became too invasive we got slapped. We naturally undertook to learn at a slow pace but eventually got the medals.

The school had a band which played at various functions and school dances. Mum had long-since abandoned her dreams of having a violin-playing son and after long negotiations had settled for an accordion. After several years of lessons on the violin both the teacher and I agreed that my talents were insufficient for the instrument to ever afford even minor enjoyment to myself or others. The accordion was in a different league and not even considered to be a bona-fide musical instrument by Mum, but considering the torture the whole family had been subjected to during my hours of violin practice, she relented. After consulting with the local accordion expert in town, Dad bought me a very nice Scandalli and set me up with lessons. Whereas my skills were limited, at least clean notes could be struck and I did achieve some measure of proficiency. The band consisted of the usual three electric guitars, drums, piano, trumpet and accordion. A couple of the members fancied themselves as Elvis and various other contemporary rock singers and we had good fun. At the school dances, held in our nice Gledhill Hall, the caliber of the music was irrelevant, the main requirement being a beat so that aspiring suitors could wrap their arms around the girls and make appropriate movements. They were good examples of the British playwright's observation that "dancing is a vertical expression of a horizontal desire".

Of course the school dances were subjects of great discussion before and after by both sexes. As contact with the opposite sex was limited by the separate schools, selecting and inviting a guest was a delicate affair for those who did not have established relationships. The physique, attire, make-up and behavior of every girl were analyzed in detail at group discussions. The potential for various favors was vigorously disputed and from time to time bets were placed. The problem was always proof other than reliable witnesses, so certain conditions were agreed upon for collection of the debt. One year a group of resourceful seniors decided to gather more solid evidence of the various girls' real preferences and so a microphone was concealed in the girls' toilets which fed an amplifier and speaker in the boys' toilet. This proved to be an invaluable source of information, which brought great joy to some boys and made laughing-stocks of others.

Officially alcohol was not permitted on school property but this was regarded as a pedantic infraction of every senior's human rights by boys and staff alike during dances. The only condition set by the staff was that its procurement, storage and consumption should be more or less covert so as not to blatantly offend the few over-zealous parents who might delude themselves that little Johnny did not enjoy a beer now and then. Whereas most of us went along with this, there were those who seriously misjudged their tolerance for alcohol and ended up making asses of themselves during the dance. However, a few beers certainly livened up the crowd and removed some of the inherent inhibitions we may have had regarding our dancing skills and capacity for appropriate conversation with our partners. The band's performance was definitely enhanced by the consumption of beer and our music got exponentially better as the evening progressed.

1962 saw more political changes. Unhappy with the opposition Dominion party which had been defeated at the 1961 referendum, the conservatives formed a new party, the Rhodesian Front. Its mandate was to secure independence from Britain so that we would have complete control of our own affairs. At the next election this party won a majority and elected Winston Field as Prime

Minister. Dad was guardedly optimistic and joined the Manicaland branch as Party Secretary.

As part of the negotiations over the impending break-up of the Central African Federation, the Southern Rhodesian government requested complete independence from Britain as had been promised to Northern Rhodesia and Nyasaland. At a bizarre meeting in a railway carriage parked in the middle of the bridge over the Zambezi at Victoria Falls at the end of June, 1963, Rab Butler, the British minister representing Harold MacMillan, gave a verbal assurance that this would be forthcoming without preconditions. However, he refused to put it in writing, fearing repercussions from the newly independent black states. He asked Field to take it on trust, which he did. It soon became obvious that independence would not be granted until Southern Rhodesia guaranteed a one-man-one-vote franchise. At this point Ian Smith took over the leadership of the ruling Rhodesian Front party in an effort to talk sense into the British. The Central African federation was dissolved on 31st of December 1963, giving full independence to Northern Rhodesia and Nyasaland and leaving Southern Rhodesia without its promise of independence and with a huge debt.

Ian Smith was a decent man, born and raised in Rhodesia and a true patriot. He flew Royal Air Force fighters in the Second World War for his mother-country Britain, was shot down, survived and flew again. He ran a large farm well and gave employment, housing and medical care to a large workforce. The contemporary media depicted Smith and his ministers as small-minded, naïve country bumpkins vainly and obstinately defending a failed regime. In fact the opposite was true, the rest of the world was naïve as events have undisputedly proven. Had Smith's government been allowed to rule Rhodesia without interference, today it would be the shining star of Africa and a grand example to the rest of the continent and the world. Blacks would have fair and equitable representation and the country would be exporting food and other commodities. Not a cent of foreign aid would have been necessary.

1963 was my last year of high school and we all had to think what lay beyond that. From a young age I had a passion for all things mechanical and enjoyed working with my hands as well as my head. It seemed natural that I would seek a career in some type of engineering, most likely mechanical. Dad and Mum supported this as they knew me very well after having supplied me with various Meccano sets, tools and materials. The three courses I had selected for my last years fitted well with the university requirements for engineering. Dad had scrimped and saved enough to pay for my education but I knew it meant he went without things he needed and I hoped I could do well enough to get at least one of the several scholarships offered in Rhodesia. Scholarships depended firstly on final year exam results so I did my best to pay attention in class.

Umtali Boys' High Prefects 1963

In September 1963 I again joined Coney's camping trip, this time to Northern Rhodesia (now Zambia), Nyasaland (now Malawi) and Mozambique. We had a slightly different group of boys, but many of the same teachers. We headed north-west through Salisbury and Sinoia to cross the Zambezi at Chirundu. Again, Coni had many old buddies on the route, and we spent the first night on a nice farm in southern Zambia. The next day we drove to the magnificent Luangua game reserve and set up camp just outside the reserve on the banks of the Luangua river. Another of Coni's friends, Norman Carr, had been warden at Luangua for many years and he had kindly ordered several grass huts to be built at the campsite so we would have some measure of protection. The park was not fenced, so although technically our camp was outside the boundary, the game was unaware of this and were all around us.

The heart of the park was the Luangua River and right below our camp it was teeming with hippo and crocodiles. Our only means of bathing was the river, so we went in groups and kept to shallow water, making lots of noise. The strategy seemed effective, as no-one was attacked. One of the boys, Frank, who happened to be a bugler in the cadets, was assigned the duty of playing Reveille every morning at 6.00am to awaken the camp. However, he soon perceived that the hippo did not enjoy his bugle-playing during the day as they raised their heads from the water and made loud roars of objection. He teased them by blowing louder and moving closer until one matriarch took exception and left the water at surprising speed to pursue Frank. Fortunately Frank was a good rugby player and quick on his feet, so he was able to scramble up the steep bank to safety, but from then on bugle playing was restricted to Reveille.

After breakfast each day we walked in groups into the reserve in the company of a black ranger. These rangers knew the bush well, but in case of emergency they carried Greener 12-bore shotguns loaded with buckshot. Of course their primary objective was to avoid confrontation so they made it clear that their instructions must be strictly obeyed. The virgin lowveld bush has a beauty all of its own and to really appreciate it one must walk, not drive. We moved slowly on game-paths and reveled in the sights, sounds and aromas. Many of the larger species have poor eyesight and rely mainly on smell to sense danger, so by keeping the wind in our faces we were able to get very close to rhino and elephant. There were also a myriad of small treasures from scorpions to dung-beatles to observe and learn about.

I did not personally observe this incident because I was in a different group, but one morning Coni and his group watched a pride a thirteen lions attack and bring down a large, lone bull buffalo. Coni captured the entire event on his 8mm cine camera so when we got home, all of us could see it. A bull buffalo is a formidable beast, but the lions had a well co-ordinated attack and one lioness was able to jump on the buffalo's back, snag his snout with one paw and twist his neck to bring him down. After that it was all over and the lions started eating as the unfortunate beast was drawing his last breaths. I arrived on the scene after the lions had eaten their fill and the hyenas and vultures had moved in. The lions did not like this and periodically one would get up and rush at the carcass, driving the scavengers away. It was a losing battle however as nature intended, and within a few short hours the carcass had been picked clean.

We spent a wonderful week in Luangua and heard some of the stories about Norman Carr. Coni related a humorous occasion which had occurred on one of his previous visits. Norman had rescued two lion cubs which he named Big Boy and Little Boy. When these became full-grown they returned to the wild, but continued to greet Norman when he passed nearby on his rounds. They liked to ride on top of the Land Rover, and when he whistled they would come and climb up there. Coni had Norman in one of the school Land Rovers on that trip, with the two black cooks and some schoolboys riding in the back. They came upon the two lions, and Norman whistled. The black cooks were unaware of the special relationship and were understandably horrified when the two lions trotted up and calmly stepped amongst the occupants of the bed of the Land Rover on their way to their perch over the cab. It was claimed that they turned white for a few seconds!

From Luangua we drove to the small Nyasaland town of Lilongwe where Coney had yet another buddy who ran a tobacco processing facility. We spent a pleasant night on his farm and proceeded to the shores of Lake Nyasa where we camped on the beach. The lake had nice sand beaches and clear water and a friend kindly furnished his boat and ski-board so that all of us had an opportunity to demonstrate our skills. As none of us had any experience with skiing due to the bilharzia in Rhodesia, this was a wonderful and spectacular challenge for each to show his stuff before a crowd of unsympathetic and vocal spectators. The boat owner was very patient, and by the end of the stay everyone could do the requisite figure-of-eight without falling.

At that time Nyasaland was still part of the Central African Federation and had a relatively small population of permanent white inhabitants. The country had no minerals to speak of and was basically an agrarian and fishing economy. The whites grew tobacco, coffee and tea as cash crops and the blacks had their cattle and cultivated small plots of maize and millet. It was obvious that the Federation was a failure and was about to be dissolved, which indeed occurred on December 31st that year. Power had effectively passed from British hands to a new local government headed by Hastings Banda in May 1963 and in July 1964 Nyasaland became the independent country of Malawi.

As Nyasaland had never been a colony and had few natural resources it made the transition from British to local rule relatively smoothly. Many of the whites were British civil-servants and regarded their home as England. Hastings Banda had been born in the country but had spent most of his life away in South Africa, the USA and Britain. Of all the newly independent nations in Africa, Malawi probably suffered the least. This was primarily due to Banda, who had had sufficient education and exposure to European culture to understand his position. He was effectively a dictator but knew that he needed to maintain good relations with Rhodesia and South Africa because his country was very dependent on them for trade, investment and transportation. However, like most dictators, he was not opposed to treating himself and his friends extremely well and securing lucrative partnerships in all the large industries. His first order of business was to construct a large palace for himself . The next was to make it clear to the large corporations that their businesses would encounter far fewer government restrictions if they donated half the stock to him or one of his selected ministers.

From the lake we headed south to Blantyre, the largest town. This was a typical colonial-African town with tree-lined avenues and the normal country club where sports were played enthusiastically and celebrated with even greater vigor after the games in the bar. Here we visited our former maths teacher Silky who had accepted the position of headmaster of the local high school.

From Blantyre we headed south to cross the Zambezi at the Portuguese town of Tete. Rhodesians did not have much respect for the Portuguese, considering them befitting of the Afrikaans description "see-kaffers". Our opinions were validated by the fact that it took us four hours to clear Mozambique customs and immigration formalities, during which we remained in no-man's-land on the bridge. Tete was hot and humid so we continued south and made camp in the bush. This was the one occasion where nobody had any friends to call on. The next day we crossed back into Rhodesia at Villa Manica and went to our homes for the first hot shower in three weeks.

On Saturday, November 23rd 1963 I was working on my Skoda when Dad rushed out of the house to tell me that John Kennedy had been assassinated the day before. With the 8-hour time difference with Texas we only heard about it on the morning news the next day. Dad had not liked Kennedy as a president because he considered him inexperienced, liberal and naïve but of course we all felt sorry for his young family. Dad was very skeptical that this was merely the act of a single malcontent, as many Americans were and still are. Dad thought even less of Johnson and hoped that Barry Goldwater would defeat him in 1964.

In December I had to write the final exams of my school life, the English Higher Schools' Certificate (HSC). I wrote this in four subjects, English (mandatory),

mathematics, physics and chemistry. I also applied for
a scholarship from the Anglo American Corporation,
one of the world's largest mining conglomerates. Anglo
evolved from the holdings of Cecil John Rhodes and continued to maintain its headquarters in Johannesburg. It
had vast interests all over the world in almost every mineral and precious stone. After making it through the first
selection process I and my close friend Bugs were invited
to the Salisbury office to participate in a series of tests
and interviews designed to check our IQ.

Anglo's offices in Salisbury were in Charter House,
a high-rise on the corner of Jameson and Kingsway. For
the coming year only 12 scholarships would be awarded
to boys in Southern and Northern Rhodesia. These
were coveted awards as Anglo paid the full four years
of college tuition, board, lodging, books and a monthly
stipend of cash. Anglo wanted good engineers for its
many mines and this was a means of attracting the best.
The deal was that after graduation Anglo would get
four years of service, but as these jobs were coveted
as well, this was an added attraction. Other industries
also gave scholarships on this basis and it made a lot of
sense.

We assembled in the foyer of Charter house with
some trepidation, keenly assessing the competition. The
testing process involved speed and precision and we
spent the day doing all kinds of tasks to measure these.
I thought I did reasonably, but by design, no-one was
expected to get a perfect score. Dad had saved diligently
to accumulate enough cash to pay for college for his

children, but it would be a great help to him if I got this scholarship, so there was a strong incentive for many reasons.

The results were going to take some time, so the family embarked on a scheduled holiday to South Africa. This would turn out to be the last time we all took a holiday together. In 1963 Dad had proudly purchased a large 1960 Chevrolet Brookwood station-wagon imported from the USA by an American subsidiary operating one of the tea estates in the Honde valley in the mountains of Inyanga. This was a spacious vehicle, white on top and turquoise below. Dad mounted the full-length roof-rack on top and we loaded the car up with all our personal items, tools, spare-parts, camping gear and fishing tackle. This turned out to be a formidable weight, so Dad purchased and installed rubber boosters which fitted inside the rear springs to lift the rear back to normal height.

We had a great trip down to Coffee Bay in the Bantustan of Transkei, camping en route. Transkei was one of the theoretically independent black states created by Apartheid and was the ancestral territory of the Xosa tribe (of which Nelson Mandela is one), lying north of the Kei river and south of Zululand. It is a beautiful area of rolling hills and long, unspoiled coastline punctuated by sheltered bays between rocky peninsulas. The blacks living there had been stirred up by various agitators and we were met with sullen stares from some that we passed along the road but most were their normal happy selves. The Xosa women dress in colorful blankets and roll their hair into red clay dreadlocks so they were quite a sight.

We left the main national road at Umtata and proceeded on dirt roads to our hotel at Coffee Bay.

Europeans operated in Transkei at the pleasure of the black government, but in practice tourism was a valuable source of income and white-owned hotels which had operated for many years were left undisturbed. Dad & Mum had had many holidays on this coast, the first (which I don't remember) at Mazeppa Bay, and another, when I was four, at Kei Mouth. All these resorts were simple but unspoiled and many Rhodesians holidayed there. To the south was the port of East London, a fairly large city where everything was available, so from time to time we would take trips to buy essentials and see the sights.

Our hotel was on the side of one of the hills overlooking the bay, with about 200 yards down a sandy path to the beach. The beach was pristine, about a half mile long with rocky outcrops at each end. The water was clear and the large rollers came in uniformly in clean unbroken lines, perfect for board and body surfing. The hotel fare was all-inclusive with three excellent meals a day, so our routine was beach after breakfast until lunch, then other activities such as fishing, hiking, games until sundown. Sundown was a favorite time for because that was when Dad broke out the dumpy Lion beer and he and I would enjoy a couple of these while Mum had her sherry and the rest of the family had soft drinks.

Dinner was a formal affair with four to five courses served by waiters in crisp white uniforms. After dinner we would have various activities on the beach or in the hotel. There was another hotel at the opposite end of the bay and we would often go over there to visit the other crowd. Most families stayed at least two weeks, so both parents and kids made firm friends. Once a week one or the other hotel would hold a dance which was a grand opportunity to expand the circle of attractive girlfriends.

The rugged Transkei coastline had a large selection of beaches and fishing spots so from time to time groups would take several cars and picnic at these. One particularly memorable spot was Hole in the Wall, so named because of a huge rock in the ocean with a large hole worn by the constant wave action. Dad, Butch and I loved the fishing and hiked over the rocks to get as far out in the ocean as possible. At that time red bait was still available from the rocks at low tide and we enjoyed timing the swells to rush down between them and cut open the shells to get the red flesh inside. Transkei also had crayfish which the local tribesmen caught and delivered to the hotels. When boiled in seawater these are one of the finest crustacean delicacies, more flavorful and succulent than lobster.

From Coffee Bay we drove down the coast to Plett, stopping on the way to stay a night with Mum's cousins on their farm close to East London. Although these visits were rare, when they occurred it was always a wonderful reunion and adults and kids celebrated accordingly. We stopped again in Port Elizabeth to visit another cousin, and from there proceeded to Plett. The drive from Port Elizabeth to Plett was one of our favorites, with the road winding down and up through the Groot Rivier and Bloukranz passes. Both passes had steep, narrow roads and we were always sure to encounter several troupes of baboons. At the bottom of the Bloukranz was a secluded small settlement with a long beach known as Nature's Valley. This was a special spot for Dad, as he and his family had camped here on a vacation in 1928. The tree under which they had camped was still standing, situated next to the small river which fed the lagoon.

From the high ground after the Bloukranz the road dropped down to the Keurbooms river which fed the lagoon at Plett. The first sight of the Bay from the top of this descent was spectacular and we stopped the car to admire the view and inhale the fresh, salt air. Plett was considered equivalent to heaven by all of us, and we continued down into the village in great spirits. Dad had dreams of retiring here and had purchased about 15 acres of land a little west of town overlooking the long promontory of Robberg. He had had a shed constructed in absentia, but at that time it was impractical for the family to stay there. We therefore took rooms with our old friends the Jerlings, who had a farm a little further west and rented to tourists.

The Jerlings, like most Afrikaners, were the most hospitable folks one could hope to meet. We had met them on a previous holiday and stayed a few days, but on this occasion they truly became family. Their youngest son Kobus was my age and their grand-daughter Elise was Ev's age so we had a grand time together. Mrs. Jerling was a fine cook and served up sumptuous breakfasts and dinners every day. Sometimes at night we would assemble around a fire outdoors and sing traditional Afrikaans and English songs accompanied by Mum on her ukulele.

In early January we received a letter from Anglo American advising me that I was on the short-list for a scholarship and would need to travel to Kitwe, Northern Rhodesia for a final interview. As we were at the end of our holiday, Dad decided that the whole family would head home via Salisbury and from there I would fly to N'dola and on by car to Kitwe. In Salisbury we visited the clothing store to purchase appropriate attire for the interview. Those were the days of the pure nylon shirt and we were impressed with the crisp, wrinkle-free appearance and bought one. There was a very good reason that these shirts never became popular, as a few minutes after putting mine on I realized that it created a little sauna environment of its own around my chest. After a couple of hours I was surrounded with the aroma of a hyena and no-one dared get close.

However, this minor issue was far overshadowed by the prospect of my first flight. Salisbury had built a new airport out beyond our old Hillside house and there I boarded the Air Rhodesia Viscount twin-engined turbo-prop. This was a special treat because until recently the fleet had consisted of a few Vikings, the British equivalent of the DC3.

The Central African Federation had just been dissolved, much to Dad's delight and the old Central African Airways had been split into three separate companies, one for each country. There were two more scholarship aspirants on the same flight, my competitors perhaps but also perhaps my future colleagues. We got window seats and held our breaths in trepidation and awe as the engines screamed, the plane gathered speed and then rose up into the clear Highveld air. For the first time we got spectacular aerial views of Salisbury and picked out the obvious landmarks. The Viscount cruised at about 300 mph and 20,000 feet so we had good visibility all the way, across the Zambezi and up to N'Dola. The landing was equally exciting and we exited the plane and were met by the Rhokana Mines driver who took us to Kitwe.

Salisbury 1963. Charter House in the center.

Kitwe had a reputation for fast-living and free spending. It was effectively the center of the Copperbelt, which stretched from northern Northern Rhodesia to southern former Belgian Congo. Rhokana was based in Kitwe but there were other mines and other companies in the surrounding area. In 1964 it was known that Northern

Rhodesia would be granted independence later in the year, and the word was out to get as much copper out of the ground as possible before that date. Miners were paid generous salaries and housed in mine houses, but beyond that there were hefty bonuses based on footage mined and powder saved per day. Young miners ended up with lots of money in their pockets and minimal expenses, so like most young people in this situation, they spent on pleasure. Mining is a dangerous business and rigid discipline is required underground. Perhaps for this reason the miners were known for their exuberance during free time. All forms of sport and entertainment were available and the mine club was popular, with plenty of drinking and gambling in the bar. This was facilitated by the wise British custom of prohibiting women from bars.

We were interviewed individually by the Chief Engineer and Mine Manager and happily all of us in that group were accepted. That evening the Chief Engineer invited us to his home for a braaivleis and put us at ease. We all flew home to prepare for the move to Kitwe. Of course Dad & Mum were ecstatic that I had made the cut, not only because I was one of only eight in the country to be selected, but also because this relieved Dad of a large expense. We celebrated in proper form and the next day drove home to Umtali. There I was delighted to learn that my schoolmate and friend from standard-2 days, Bugs, had also been awarded the same scholarship.

Chapter 15:
KITWE

There was not much to pack because I did not own much. The main thing on my plate was to prepare my aged Skoda for the trip. This required machining the rear of the gearbox casing to accept a modern oil-seal and other general maintenance, but this was soon accomplished. Bugs and I loaded up our two small suitcases and set off. I imagine Mum & Dad felt some strong emotions as their eldest son drove off into the unknown and dangerous world of deep-level mining, but like good English custom demanded, they did not let it show. I gave Mum, Jen and Ev hugs, shook Dad's and Butch's hands and drove away.

The Skoda was incapable of any high speed, so we drove along at the leisurely pace of about 50 mph. The weather was clear so we did not have the top on and enjoyed the clear air and sun on our shoulders. We drove to

Salisbury and then took the road north through Sinoia, the Hunyani hills and on to Karoi, where we spent the night at the local hotel. Traffic was light and we motored along happily, contemplating our new lives with great enthusiasm. The next day we drove down the Zambezi valley escarpment and crossed the river at Chirundu, over the impressive suspension bridge. After clearing the border formalities, we drove on through Lusaka, the capital of Northern Rhodesia, and up to my uncle Jim's farm just south of Broken Hill. This part of Northern Rhodesia is Highveld like Mashonaland, pretty much flat with Msasa trees and grasslands.

After spending a couple of enjoyable days with uncle Jim we drove on to Kitwe. The mine owned a large block of flats at the top of Central Street, and the nine student engineers from out of town moved into three of these. I shared with Bugs and a fellow from Bulawayo. We met the other fellows, four from Salisbury, one from Gwelo and one from N'dola. Two more and one girl in the group were from Kitwe and lived at home. The first order of business was to evaluate the club bar, and after an appropriate number of beers each, we all became good friends.

The policy of large companies financing the education for future employees made good sense and ensured a steady supply of hand-picked professionals. The traditional policy for Northern Rhodesian students was to attend universities in Britain. Because the British term began in August or September, the mine decided that the interim period from February until this time should be beneficially filled by working through all the departments on the mine and also attending classes equivalent to the first year in engineering school. After a short orientation period teaching us about the mining business in general, Rhokana in particular and required safety practices, we were each assigned a department and sent to work. Our lodging was free, but we had to supply all our other needs. The mine paid us a salary of thirty four pounds a month to cover these.

My first job was in the huge mine workshops, which suited me very well. As Kitwe was somewhat isolated and big mines cannot afford to wait on repairs and equipment, these shops could pretty much build anything. They were divided into mechanical, foundry and electrical. I started off in the mechanical shop as apprentice to a journeyman fitter. We overhauled the immense motors which powered the winding-engines hauling men and ore up and down the mine shafts. My journeyman was a real professional from the mines in South Africa and he took great pains to impress upon me the importance of doing the job right.

After the shops I was sent to Mindola shaft, about five miles from the city center. At six am each morning I joined the other miners and collected my battery and helmet light from the charging station. We then went to the shaft head and loaded into the cages, two decks with sixty men per deck. The cage dropped like a stone and in just over a minute we reached the intermediary 2,000 foot level. Because of the increasing weight of the cable as the cage descends, this is about the limit for a single shaft. The 2,000 level had a huge open cavern, brightly lit and painted blue. Here the intermediary winding engine was mounted at the next shaft, going down to 4,000 feet. I had been assigned to the main pump station, the lowest point in the mine. The Mindola shaft spewed about nine million gallons of water per day, and this had to be continuously removed to prevent flooding. Nine huge multistage pumps sent this water to the surface and into the lake constructed for this purpose. At any given time, six pumps were running, two were on standby and one was undergoing maintenance.

The fitter responsible for the day shift at the pump station was a Scotsman named Bill. Bill worked 12-hour shifts seven days for fifty weeks a year and in the remaining two weeks he went hunting. Bill was delighted to have an aspiring engineer with him as he and his hunting buddy George were involved in an ongoing dispute regarding the stopping power of rifle bullets. George, another Scotsman, was a high-velocity man, whereas Bill was a slower, heavy-bullet man. As we had plenty of free time once maintenance had been completed, we decided to investigate the difference scientifically. The chamber in which the pumps were located was long and spacious. At one end we suspended a large metal plate rigged with a small finger at the bottom to measure deflection. We marked a clear white cross in the center and set up the rifle at the far end, clamped to a heavy workbench. It took a few rounds to get the aim perfect, after which the testing began. We picked a plate thickness that George's high velocity .3030 would penetrate but Bill's slower .458 would not. Behind the plate was a barrel of sand to absorb George's bullets. No-one questioned us taking rifles into the mine.

To Bill's delight, testing revealed a far greater deflection of the plate with the heavy bullet than the high-velocity lighter bullet which passed through the plate, which was a simple demonstration of Newton's laws of physics. Despite these irrefutable data, George remained unconvinced.

I was fortunate in that during my time with Bill he invited me to accompany him on the next hunting trip, coming up in a few weeks. This happened to coincide with the international rowing regatta on the Kafue river the weekend before Bill's trip. More about the rowing later, but after the regatta I set off alone in my old Skoda to drive from Lusaka to the Kafue game reserve where Bill and George had a hunting concession. He had given me rough directions and I turned off the main highway on to a dirt road leading to the reserve. The road was rough and dusty and the car was in a continuous slide as it bounced over the corrugations, but with long experience under these conditions I held it more or less on track. After a few miles a black fellow in a nice business suit flagged me down for a ride, so I stopped and advised him that he was welcome, but in the open car he would get some dust on his suit. This did not deter him and he climbed in and held on for dear life as the car skidded from side to side. Once in a car, these hitch-hikers are often content to go as far as you are going, and so it was.

He never revealed his intended destination. After a few hours of choking dust and bone shaking we arrived at the small village of Mumbwa, close to the border of the park. My passenger's dark suit was now a uniform red/brown, but he did not seem in the least bit concerned and thanked me profusely. I filled up with gas and headed into the park.

Bill's directions were pretty good and I followed the tire-marks of his Land Rover and George's 7-ton truck until I arrived at a pleasant camp at the edge of a large dambo, an area of grassland with water at some times of year. The only problem was that the camp had obviously been abandoned. There were a multitude of tracks radiating in all directions, and as it was getting late in the afternoon I did not want to waste gas and time checking them all out. I decided to drive back to the gate and see if anyone had information on the new campsite. Fortunately the gatemen, once reminded, remembered that Bill had left a message with them. They assigned me a small boy of about six years old to guide me. He rode happily on the front mudguard of the car and pointed out the route. There were no actual roads to follow, just tire-tracks between the trees. The old Skoda had good ground clearance so we bounced along, avoiding the larger obstacles. Just as the light was fading we reached the camp.

Bill and George saw no need to rough it when hunting, and had hauled along a very nice caravan to sleep in, several tents for kitchen, lounge and bar, chairs, tables, a paraffin refrigerator and a generous supply of food and liquor. To assist with the hunting and cooking, Bill and

George had brought along their household staff, who were more than happy to escape the drudgery of working under the "madams". It was understood that my guide would be happy to stay with us until such time as we saw fit to return him and he joined our assigned park ranger whom he obviously knew.

The hunting concessions were sold by territory and animal, with strict limits. Bill and George had purchased their limits of each animal they wished to kill, some for meat, others for trophies. The ranger accompanied every hunt and checked off each animal on the permit as it was shot. If the animal was wounded, the ranger demanded every effort be made to pursue and kill it. If it escaped however, for permit purposes it was checked off anyway. Our ranger was a little skittish, as during the hunt before Bill's, a bull elephant had been wounded and charged the group. The ranger had managed one quick shot before the enraged beast seized one of the party and trampled him to death subsequently collapsing itself. The ranger had done his best, but nevertheless he held himself responsible. He refused to go after elephant in this concession because he correctly judged the herd to be unusually hostile after losing its bull so recently.

Bill and George had already shot their warthogs and various species of antelope, so the camp was rich with the aroma of drying skins and smoking meat. The servants had constructed a framework of green tree-limbs about three feet above the ground, and laid strips of salted meat on it to dry for biltong. To discourage flies, hyenas, jackals and any other scavengers, they kept smoky fires smoldering under the meat around the clock. Biltong is generally air-dried without fire, but under the circumstances there was no choice and the end product tasted delicious anyway. With George's 7-ton truck we were well equipped to haul all the meat and trophies back to Kitwe.

The black people were generally a happy bunch. They enjoyed good humor as much as anyone, particularly when it involved the misfortune of another. While driving through the bush the next day in the Land Rover, the fellows in the back spotted a beehive high up in a tree. Honey is a rare treat, and lots were drawn to see who would undertake the formidable task of climbing the tree to dislodge the hive. The loser accepted the role with good grace, scaled the tree and dropped the hive. Of course when he got to the ground, the angry African bees were all over him. Swatting them with his hands, he ran for the Land Rover. His colleagues, not wanting to risk a single sting, insisted that we drive away before he reached us. As they beheld their unfortunate friend sprinting in desperation, they were consumed with mirth. When we finally stopped well out of range, the badly stung victim staggered up with a huge smile on his face, enjoying the joke as much as anyone.

We dined on grilled warthog that evening, washed down with cold Castle beer and followed up with Bailey's Irish Cream liqueur. After the long and dusty trip it was delicious! There was not room in the caravan for me, so I unrolled my sleeping-bag on the soft grass near the truck and went to sleep. There were several fires going near me so I was not disturbed by hyenas. In the morning the cook produced a fine breakfast of eggs and bacon, after which we set off to hunt buffalo. The terrain in the area the ranger took us to was more broken, so I rode on top of the Land Rover to spot obstacles and alert Bill. Finally we came down a gentle decline leading to a small stream and spotted a herd of buffalo on the far side. There was little wind, but the ranger determined that from here the hunt must proceed on foot, with only he, two skinners, Bill and George. I stayed with the Land Rover and had a perfect view of the hunt. The grass and shrubs were severely trampled and afforded little cover, so the five moved downwind and slowly worked their way closer. The African buffalo is considered one of the most dangerous animals to hunt because not only is it large and hardy, but if wounded it takes strong offense and will circle behind the hunter and attack him if possible.

Bill's buffalo, Kafue 1964

Bill and George had previously tossed a coin and George won the first shot, to be followed immediately by Bill before the herd had a chance to flee. He would now have his opportunity to prove the stopping power of his high-velocity bullet. His .3030 held five shots in the magazine and I watched him and Bill stop and line up the shots. I saw the rifles kick and a few moments later heard the shots and the strikes. One buffalo went down after a few steps, but another put its head down and started trotting towards the hunters. I heard five more sharp cracks from the .3030 and the beast kept coming. I then heard one louder shot from the .458 and this stopped it dead. The rest of the herd had fled, so I drove the Land Rover over the river and up to the bodies, which were about 100 yards apart. Bill's had one shot to the shoulder with no exit wound, whereas George's had seven entry wounds and six exit.

The skinners made short work of removing the entrails, saving some tasty morsels for themselves. The vultures were already circling above the stinking masses, so we dragged the carcasses under a large tree limb, using the Land-Rover and a heavy chain. Bill had thoughtfully brought along his block and tackle, which he suspended from the limb. Even minus its guts, a grown buffalo probably weighs1200-1500lb and we struggled to winch the two beasts into the truck, severely overloading it. The descent to the river was steep, and the opposite bank even steeper, so we had to unload the beasts, drag them across and load again on the other side. We finally got back to camp just before sundown and the skinners lost no time in stripping the carcasses and spreading the meat to dry. We dined on fresh buffalo steaks that night. George was officially stripped of his title "One-shot" which he had held until that day.

The next day it was agreed that I should make a run to Mumbwa to return our young guide to his parents and collect ice. The two of us set off in the Skoda after lunch, but halfway to the gate I had to stop for a herd of elephants in my path. We had no way of knowing if this was the same herd responsible for the killing the week before, but I was not keen to test them. Unfortunately they continued walking slowly towards us, so I tried to back up. The Skoda was not at the forefront of technology when it was built, but its designers had attempted to give this appearance by installing a column shift. This had never worked well, but reverse had always been particularly problematic. I tried in vain to get the gear without the customary banging and slapping, but to no avail. We had no choice but to keep still and quiet as the herd casually ambled right across our nose, less than ten feet away. Animals generally pay no attention to vehicles, but I was concerned that the open convertible would be an exception. Fortunately it was not, and we continued the trip without further incident.

The rest of the hunt was enjoyable but we were unsuccessful in getting any lion. We used a zebra carcass as bait for them, but for reasons unknown the only takers were hyena, jackal and vulture. We actually did not ever even see lion, only their spoor. The last night the truck had been loaded with all the dried meat so the fires were not kept up. About three am I was awakened by a loud crunching noise and turned on my flashlight to see several hyenas at the foot of my sleeping-bag chewing on discarded bones. My only weapons were full beer-cans in a box near the bed, so I hurled a few of these at the scavengers. They moved off a little, but then commenced on the beer, piercing the steel cans easily with their strong jaws and teeth. They developed an immediate taste for beer and lapped it up with great relish. I had no option but to rekindle the fire and keep it stoked until daylight.

Back in Kitwe we were enjoying our new-found freedom and first paychecks. Zorb and I decided to pool our money and buy an old Matchless 500 motorbike which a friend had dismantled but never reassembled. We paid him five pounds and proceeded to assemble the engine in Zorb's flat. We soon discovered that the crankshaft was badly worn, and after evaluating options to build it up in the mine shop, we decided to abandon that engine and bought a Norton 500 engine from one of the miners who had raced bikes in his youth. He offered to assist us in modifying the Matchless frame to take the Norton engine. We cut and welded and eventually mounted the engine and connected it to the gearbox by chain. Impatient to try our new creation, one night in Zorb's flat we connected the final wires and gas-line and decided to see if it would start. We had not yet figured out the necessary modifications to the exhausts, so the ports on the head were wide open. To our delight, after a few kicks it started with a tremendous roar, spewing blue flames out of the ports. In a few minutes there were irate neighbors beating on our door, so we decided to take it outside and go for a spin.

We only had a pint or so of gas in the tank, so we drove down to the local Caltex station to buy more. The attendant was not at all deterred by the long blue flames, and in fact complimented us on the magnificence of the stripped-down contraption as he nonchalantly pumped gas into the tank while the engine ran.

During the construction process Zorb had been assigned to work with one of the rigging crews. These crews were responsible for lifting large equipment into tight spaces using cranes, cables and blocks and tackle. This was a very dangerous field and required a great deal of skill and experience. The riggers regularly changed the cages for the ore-hoppers on the main shafts and periodically had to drop and lift the locomotives and ore trains to and from the underground haulages. The boss of Zorb's crew was Joe, known to us as Joe the Rigger. Joe was a tough South African who wore glasses with thick, violet-colored lenses. He was an expert welder and helped us with the rework of the engine mounts for the bike. We enjoyed visiting Joe, as not only did each job end with a celebration at Joe's house with unlimited alcohol of various types, but Joe's wife was a fine looking woman who dressed very much in accordance with our fashion preferences.

Bugs, Zorb, me & Square-eyes

We completed the bike in due course and two of our mates bought bikes for themselves, so we enjoyed touring together and riding to and from work. One afternoon we were riding in a residential neighborhood when a large dog rushed out and started biting the front tire. He was out of range for a kick, no doubt having learned from experience, so we had to stop and encourage him to return home by means of shouting and hurling a few stones. The next week we had another such encounter with a different dog, so we concluded that it was high time the Kitwe dogs go through an education program regarding motorbikes. We made up two long whips of rope and set out with the three bikes, all with pillion riders. We started at the known houses, and revved the engines until the dog appeared and went for the lead bike. The other two bikes came from behind on both sides and the pillion-riders proceeded to give the dog a good whipping before he retired howling.

We were making good progress in this re-orientation effort until in an act of excess enthusiasm one of the riders whipped a sausage dog on a leash, being walked by its owner. The owner was irate and did not buy the argument that his dog was a potential future hazard. We were duly summoned by the chief of police who kindly informed us that any future dog-whipping would result in confiscation of our bikes and a stiff fine.

With our parents 700 miles away and no family or friends in town to feed back information, we considered it the ideal time to start beer drinking in earnest. We encountered various young girls in town and would visit their homes as a group, usually four to six of us. Being aspiring young engineers bound for a company-sponsored college degree, both the girls and their parents were quite receptive to these visits. The more astute fathers soon realized that the more beer they offered us, the more frequent our visits and so even the least attractive girls with smart parents could count on competitive courtship. Some of the parents went even further, offering us fine meals in their homes. One particularly enthusiastic mother let it be subtly understood that not only her quite attractive daughter, but indeed she herself also could be available for more intimate involvement with any or all of us. One of our group did take advantage of both offers and received quite an education in the process, which he kindly shared with the rest of us.

Our appetites for courting were further whetted by our frequent visits to the local nightclub. Kitwe was a popular venue for an impressive variety of nightclub performers from all over the world for the simple reason that the miners had plenty of money to spend and little to spend it on. Coming straight from high school we were very happy to watch the voluptuous strippers and dancers perform their acts. Most of the performers appreciated our undisguised admiration as opposed to the blasé attitude of the veteran clubbers, and during intervals we were very well treated by the girls. One in particular impressed us, Pamela the Tassle-Tosser. This young, blonde English girl obviously had precise control of her pectoral muscles, and during her act attached a long tassle to each nipple. In perfect time to the music she could rotate these tassles in the same or opposite directions while at the same time gyrating the rest of her body provocatively. During her intervals she was kind enough to give us close-up explanation of her technique.

At first we had only one car, the Skoda, between six of us. This had been constructed as a two-seater convertible but frequently had to transport five or six when going to the movies and visiting girls. The local black police constables made a habit of stopping me and complaining about overloading so I lodged a formal complaint with the chief of police claiming police harassment. He listened attentively and promised to look into the matter, but regrettably that very night he himself pulled me over for having eleven people in and on the car, riding on the hood, the trunk and both mudguards. He explained that under the circumstances, including extreme inebriation of most of the passengers, that he considered my harassment claim without merit. We therefore decided that another vehicle must be procured, and settled on an old Vanguard estate-wagon which we jointly purchased for fifteen pounds. We repainted it a bright blue and it did yeoman service.

We also decided that due to our early rising requirements and absence of parental supervision, we would all grow beards. After a couple of weeks without shaving it was apparent that not all beards were the same and there were those amongst us that the Good Lord did not intend to have beards. Whereas most of this underprivileged group accepted their misfortune and started shaving again, Bugs our flat-mate refused to accept this conclusion and believed that he only needed a little extra time. As the weeks passed by, by even the most lenient standards, his attempt at a beard was pitiful. The straggly patchy tufts of hair grew at random without form or quality. We renamed him Arseface in order to more accurately describe his countenance, a nickname he retained under protest for many years. Political correctness was an unknown concept and our one Jewish student was soon nicknamed Nose. His flat-mate broke his leg during a hockey game and thereafter became known as Pegleg.

After my stint in the pump-station at Mindola I was assigned to one of the shift-bosses to learn the intricacies of mining. Each afternoon after all the miners got to surface, the explosive charges were fired remotely. The mines were blasted in "stopes", large caverns which followed the

seams of copper-bearing rock. Pillars were left at appropriate intervals to support the roof of the cavern. These
stopes got larger and larger until a limit had been reached.
Depending on the richness of the ore, stopes may be
back-filled with rubble from the mills and then the pillars
removed too. It was the responsibility of the shift-boss to
enter the mine after each blast and verify that it was safe.
A regular miner accompanied him with a long pry-bar,
and any dangerous hanging rock was pried loose and fell
to the floor.

Once the shift-boss certified the mine safe, the hauling crews would descend. The loose ore would be pushed
to a series of steeply inclined small tunnels which ultimately led to a haulage containing tracks and a small train.
Grids across the tunnel mouths prevented oversized rocks
from entering and blocking the tunnels. These large pieces would have to be broken up with hammers or blasting.
The personnel cages on the hoists would be swapped for
large ore-hoppers and the trains would haul the ore to
the shaft and dump it into the hoppers. The headgear on
the surface hoist was designed to tip the hopper when it
reached the top, dumping the ore into another train which
hauled it to the crushing plant. Removal of ore went on
all night.

In the morning the cages were attached again, the
haulage crews brought to surface and the drilling crews
sent down. They would drill new sets according to the
shift-boss's instructions and then set the charges and the
cycle would start again. I was not allowed to drill or set
charges but I accompanied the shift boss. He sometimes

would send me down the ore-tunnels to check for obstructions. I did not like slithering alone down narrow
tunnels of solid rock 4,000 feet underground with my
helmet light the only source of illumination. The problem was that if I could not clear an obstruction, I had to
work my way up again going backwards on hands and
knees. He also sent me down the ladders on each shaft to
check for air and water leaks. There were no safety rings
behind the ladders, only the rock wall, so a missed grip
could lead to a long and deadly fall. However, safety in
the mine was very strict and accidents were rare. There
was no horse-play or bending the rules underground. The
rock on this mine was very stable and timber support was
rarely required. If Mum and Dad had any concerns about
this work they never mentioned them to me. Mining was
a time-honored profession in southern Africa and the
South Africans were considered the best miners in the
world, with some mines 13,000 feet deep.

Although Kitwe was a relatively small town, there
were plenty of cultural and sporting options. The town
boasted a first-class theater and drama group who put on
fine performances at regular intervals. We played our part
by assisting with the construction of the props and the
consumption of the beer. Some of our group were skilled
cricketers and rugby players, but three of us, Eyes, Zorb
and I, opted for rowing. Due to drought, the Mindola lake
had shrunk to no more than half a mile long, but this was
enough for us to practice on. The rowing club had a nice
boathouse and a selection of craft, from a single-skull
to eights.   Most of the competitive rowing was done in

fours with a coxswain and one of the laboratory fellows made up our fourth. We had an enthusiastic club president who had us out every weekend competing at different lakes around the Copperbelt. The Mindola lake had a well appointed clubhouse, and after practices on Sunday mornings the barman would have our personal pewter mugs full of Castle beer as we entered the bar, with the second bottle open on the side. Nothing tasted better.

As our skills improved with time we had reasonable success in the inter-club regattas. The culmination of the season was the big regatta between Northern and Southern Rhodesias, held that year on the Kafue river south of Lusaka. The three of us planned to drive down in the old Skoda, Eyes sitting in the back on a cushion. The night before our departure we were returning from a party when I took a wrong turn and ended up going a short distance down the railway track. We noticed severe bumping over the sleepers, but thought little of it. As we progressed south the next day I noticed when we stopped for gas that one rear tire had worn completely bald. This was alarming, as it was almost new, so I realized that the railway ride had bent something badly. As we were close to Broken Hill, we stopped at uncle Jim's farm to evaluate the damage. The Skoda had independent rear suspension and checking with strings we found one side badly bent. Uncle Jim had a very impressive sledge-hammer, so we held a stout log against the half-axle and Jim wielded the hammer. After a few blows everything was nicely lined up again, so we fitted the spare and continued on our way.

The regatta site was nothing more than a clearing in the bush with access to the river. The first boat to venture upstream to the starting point got a nasty surprise when an irate hippo suddenly emerged in front of them and crushed the bows of the boat in his huge jaws. The rowers reacted well and backed up at high speed, probably setting a record for a four in reverse. There was no budging the school of hippos, so the race had to be shortened to allow them their wallowing hole.

The first day, Saturday, was designated for practice. We rowed up and down, judging the currents and getting our strategy perfected. The coach was very pleased and we turned in some excellent times. That night all the crews attended a braaivleis on the banks of the river, washed down with unlimited quantities of beer. Pretty soon the other type of boat-race commenced, with each crew lining up beers on a table and drinking them in rapid succession against another crew. As the night progressed the singing commenced, each song filthier than the last. We had a good repertoire of awful songs from our cadet days, and these were sung with varying degrees of musical talent. Well after midnight we collapsed in our clothes on the grass, to be rudely awakened by a kick from the coach the next morning.

We were not in prime condition for a very strenuous race, but our assessment was that neither were any other crews. This regatta must probably rank as one of the most pitiful performances in the history of rowing, as rowers fell over getting the boats on the water and were jerked overboard when they lost timing. We came in dead last and the coach was irate, but everyone recovered well and lived to row another day. We made close friends as only drunks can, and redeemed ourselves at the re-match in Salisbury later that year.

In July seven of our group left to attend university in England. The remaining five of us preferred to attend the University of Cape Town, which had a southern-hemisphere curriculum starting in late February. Cape Town had an excellent engineering faculty and is one of the most beautiful cities on earth, with the Atlantic Ocean on one side of the peninsula and the warmer Indian Ocean on the other. We therefore had an extend-ed program at the mine, ending just before Christmas. This also afforded us a longer study period. We followed a correspondence-course based in Johannesburg and various specialists at the mine gave us classes and re-viewed our work. We were required to complete assign-ments by specific dates and send them to Johannesburg to be graded.

We had all completed the Cambridge Higher Schools' Certificate exams at high school, so theoretically we were one year ahead of the South African students who com-pleted Matric, the requirement for university entrance. This meant that the correspondence course was ploughed ground and we worked through it with little effort. Anglo expected this to qualify us to write first-year university supplemental exams in February and assuming these would be passed, go directly into second year. This would mean we would graduate in three years instead of the cus-tomary four. This was a reasonable theory, but in actual fact impractical for engineering students because neither high school nor the correspondence course included first-year mechanical drawing, a vital course.

In late October we finished our correspondence course and were sent to Salisbury by bus to take the required exams. This was a twenty-four hour bus ride on a nice Mercedes bus. When my father heard about the proposed trip he requested that I bring him an African Grey parrot, a bird he had always coveted but was unable to find at a reasonable price in Southern Rhodesia. These were plentiful in the Congo, and blacks would catch them and sell them by the roadside in Northern Rhodesia. I was lucky to find a nice young bird whose eyes were still brown and paid the princely sum of ten pounds for him. We took him back to our flat and made him a nice stand with a perch in the mine workshop. By common assent he was named Joseph. Although still technically a chicken, Joe did not take kindly to his new perch. He bit viciously whenever we attempted to touch him, so the mine had to come to the rescue by unknowingly donating us a pair of heavy leather welding gloves. Joe hated the gloves too and would scream when we donned them to catch him, biting hard wherever he could.

It was illegal to transport these parrots across borders because they could carry dangerous avian diseases, so we had to come up with a plan to conceal him from other passengers and smuggle him through customs. We did not spend a lot of time on this plan, and when it was time to catch the bus I placed Joe in a carry-on cardboard suitcase, which he did not like at all. Once closed and therefore dark however, he accepted his predicament and became quiet. We spent the daylight hours on the ride drinking beer and playing poker. Every hour or so some-one would enquire "How's Joe?" I would lift down the suitcase from the overhead rack, carefully lift a corner to peek inside and then replace it, proclaiming Joe's good health. After a few of these checkups, the other passengers became very curious, all craning their necks to try to get a glimpse of "Joe" each time we checked.

Parrots are smart birds, and before too long Joe figured out that he had been in the dark for more than twelve hours and something was wrong. He therefore set about investigating the cause of this anomaly and proceeded to use his strong beak to chew away at the corner of the suitcase during the night. We passed through customs at Chirundu about midnight without incident, and shortly after this the passengers were rudely awakened by an irate scream from Joe as he poked his head out of the hole he had chewed and surveyed his surroundings. The passengers received him well and he made the remainder of the trip perched on the back of my seat, behaving himself with unusual decorum. Dad was delighted with him and he became a beloved companion for the next thirty years, speaking English, Shona and Afrikaans quite fluently.

Our two dogs did not like Joe at all. Like most animals, they were jealous of his exalted position and the fact that Dad seemed to favor him by letting him sit on his shoulder and nibble his ears. They also suspected that Joe was getting better food, and pushed their snouts against the wire of his cage to get a better look and smell. This was a risky business because a nip from Joe on the soft part of the nose could be very painful. In fact dogs do not normally like unshelled peanuts but when offered them they ate them with obvious distaste, pulling up their lips. The dogs could not distinguish between Dad's and Joe's voices and Joe took great pleasure in ordering them about, principally telling them to "get outside". They obeyed without hesitation but seeing no sign of Dad, were suspicious that they had been duped.

In Salisbury we were housed at the Ranch House complex on Rotten Row. This was owned by Anglo American and set up to host various liberal functions, mainly for black aspirants. Our hostess was a fine lady who seemed delighted to take care of five young men and she lost no time in making us welcome. Not surprisingly the welcome included a prolonged cocktail hour and dinner, and about midnight we crawled to our rooms and lapsed into the blissful sleep of the truly inebriated.

The next morning we dragged our abused carcasses to the Queen Elizabeth girls' school where the exams were to take place and tried to get our addled brains to function. This routine lasted for three days but we all made it through intact. After a couple of days visiting our respective parents, we returned to Kitwe on the same bus. Notwithstanding the fact that the bus was a fine Mercedes, the owners had obviously not followed the instruction regarding routine maintenance and after an unscheduled stop on the isolated highway between Lusaka and Broken Hill to pick up a friend of the driver, the bus refused to start again. Fortunately that stretch of road was level, so all the passengers disembarked and pushed the bus until it eventually fired up and ran.

Back in Kitwe there was much excitement because of the transition to "independence"which had occurred in our absence. After tortuous negotiations between the Federal government, the respective local governments and the British government, it had been decided that the Federation should be dissolved. This was no surprise to Dad, who had correctly judged it an ill-conceived arrangement from the start. Northern Rhodesia was to become the new state of Zambia under the dubious new "democratically elected" government of President Kenneth Kaunda. As this situation was beyond our control we took little interest in it other than to marvel at the concept of a country of virtual peasants with absolutely no understanding of the democratic process electing a group of men with no experience in governing anything to run the country.

It happened that after Zambia became independent on October 24th, 1964 that Kitwe held its annual show where agriculture and all manner of commodities and products were on display. One of our student engineers nicknamed Zorb because of his resemblance to Zorba the Greek had volunteered to man an educational display of optics which was housed inside a dark tent. He noticed President Kaunda and his group approaching and offered to give him a demonstration. Kuanda beamed as only he could and stepped inside the dark tent unnoticed by his bodyguards. Zorb took his time explaining the physics to an uncomprehending Kaunda and then proceeded to dazzle him with the magic of optics. When the presentation was over, they exited the tent to find the whole fairground in pandemonium as the bodyguards frantically searched for their lost president! Kaunda laughed heartily and thought it a marvelous joke, reprimanding his bodyguards as they hung their heads in shame.

As Northern Rhodesia had never been a colony of Britain, under its Protectorate status there was no doubt that at some point the government of the country would be turned over to the indigenous population. It can be argued that to do this in 1964 when the population was far from prepared for democracy was realistically a great disservice to all inhabitants. However, Zambia had never had a large expatriate population and although many of the immigrants had put down deep roots, the transition to independence was accepted with sad resignation. There were even those who believed it was wonderful, but this notion was soon dispelled as the country effectively regressed into anarchy over the next ten years.

The Copperbelt consisted of various big mines spread over a large area, following the reefs of copper ore. These reefs extended up north into the Katanga Province of what had been the Belgian Congo. After Belgium abruptly abandoned its colony in 1960, all hell broke loose. The many different tribes went at each other with spears, pangas and what guns they got their hands on. They slaughtered themselves and many unprotected whites, particularly the good nuns who had given their lives to helping them. They destroyed their own schools and other valuable infrastructure. In a misguided effort to subdue them the United Nations sent in force of "peacekeepers" and these simply contributed to the mayhem. In Katanga, because of the valuable minerals, the big Belgian mining conglomerate Union Miniere supported a local politician, Moise Tshombe, to declare Katanga a separate country. He hired an intrepid band of mercenaries to bring back order. These were tough South African, American, French and various other nationalities and without the restraints of the Geneva Convention they were very effective. The world would not accept Mr. Tshombe and a separate Katanga however and after three years Tshombe was sent into exile and Katanga rejoined the republic.

With the reputed collaboration of the Belgian government and the CIA, the elected president, Patrice Lumumba was overthrown and assassinated. Lumumba had enlisted military support from the Soviet Union which sealed his fate. With the support of the west, the head of the Congolese army, General Joseph Mobutu, became the dictator of the Congo and presided over continuing strife while enriching himself from the diamond and copper mines to the tune of billions of dollars which he wisely deposited in Swiss banks.

Those Belgians who had not fled before independence now found themselves in untenable circumstances. A steady stream drove south through Kitwe fleeing the disaster, telling horrific tales. Many flew out from the various airports in the Congo, leaving their cars at the airports. Enterprising young miners from the

Copperbelt drove up and collected these cars, keeping
them or selling them. Our group decided to drive up
and scout the territory but I was not allowed through
the border because I had neglected to bring my vaccina-
tion certificate. This was clearly a solicitation for a bribe
which I was not prepared to pay, so I hitch-hiked back
to Kitwe and the rest went up to Elizabethville. They
had a grand time and were well received by the few
Belgians remaining. In 1974 the famous Rumble in the
Jungle took place in Kinshasa. The winner, Muhammad
Ali, when asked by Howard Cosell how he liked returning to the continent of his ancestors, reputedly gave the
very candid reply "I'm just glad my grandpappy got on
that boat".

Our partying on weekends covered the entire
Copperbelt and the capital of Northern Rhodesia, Ndola.
We had rowing regattas in most of these towns and got to
know the local girls. One Saturday we attended a party in
Ndola and for some reason I drove home to Kitwe alone
in my Skoda. I must have fallen asleep, because suddenly
I was aware of severe irregularities in the ride and opened
my eyes to see long grass being mowed down in front
of the car and a loud scraping sound emanating from
the front wheel. I stopped and climbed up on top of the
trunk to look around. All I saw was grass and darkness. I
got out and inspected the car as best I could in the pitch
black night, finding the front mudguard pushed against
the wheel. I was able to pull it away and then there was no
alternative but to turn the car around and follow the path
of flattened grass back to the road. Surprisingly this was

quite a long distance but the terrain was reasonably flat except for the initial descent from the road.

In Southern Rhodesia the politics were getting really hot as the Rhodesian Front strove to talk some sense into the British government. It was clear that the promise of independence given by Butler during the strange meeting held in a railcar at the center of the bridge over the Victoria Falls in June 1963 was worthless. The party replaced Field with Smith as Prime Minister in April 1964 and Rhodesians were hopeful that their country could be saved from the disasters of all the newly-independent nations in Africa.

Of course Dad was skeptical of British promises which were never developed into written documents. Smith and his ministers fought valiantly for the cause of responsible government, but Britain was not interested in logic, reason or the welfare of its 250,000 white and six million black subjects living in Rhodesia. As South African minister Pik Botha wryly proclaimed, the negotiations between Rhodesia and Britain resembled a prolonged game of rugby which continued until the winners lost.

In December 1964 our sojourn in Kitwe was complete and we all returned to our respective homes. I spent Christmas with the family and submitted my application to join the mechanical engineering class at the University of Cape Town. At that time there was no issue regarding acceptance at the South African universities. If you had passed the Matric or HSC you were assured of a place in the class. Annual tuition was about $360, which was paid by Anglo American. All five Kitwe boys applied for the same residence on campus, the venerated Smuts Hall. As agreed with Anglo, we were to write the first-year supplemental exams in late February. These were for the purpose of providing those who had failed certain classes to re-write the exam so that they could progress to the next year's classes. In our case we were to write all the first-year exams except mechanical drawing.

Chapter 16:
CAPE TOWN

One residence opened early to accommodate those writing "supps" and inasmuch as February is prime time for the Cape Town beaches, Bugs and I decided to leave Umtali in early February in order to spend as much time as possible on the beach. Dad was concerned about my taking the old Skoda to university, believing that having convenient transportation to the beach would be too great a temptation. He therefore prevailed upon me to sell it, promising me his Borgward if I passed the first year successfully. The old Skoda was duly sold for the princely sum of twenty-five pounds, but Dad's plans were thwarted to some extent because Bugs bought a car.

Bugs and I packed our few belongings into his Fiat and set off south. The shortest route from Umtali took us through tribal trust lands (TTL's) to Fort Victoria on the traditional nine-foot wide tarmac road in wide use throughout the country. We passed the large irrigated black farmlands of Nyanyadzi where Dad worked with the black farmers to create co-operatives which pooled resources and negotiated for the best sales of the crops. Dad worked in several TTL's within a hundred-mile radius of Umtali on the same basis as part of the Rhodesian government's effort to assist black farmers. He enjoyed this work and due to his financial background was adept at ensuring the farm produce fetched fair prices. The blacks liked and trusted Dad. They perceived that he would never deceive or exploit them.

Beyond Nyanyadzi was the resort of Hot Springs. This was a popular spot in winter, because the altitude was much lower than Umtali and the average temperature higher and also because the hot sulphur springs fed a large swimming-pool. There was nothing better than leaving Umtali on a cold Sunday morning and spending the day picnicking around the warm pool with other Umtali families.

The road crossed the large Sabi river via the impressive Birchenough suspension bridge, a huge steel arch visible from miles away. This was financed by the Beit Trust, whose chairman was Sir Henry Birchenough. The Beit brothers Alfred and Otto were business partners of Rhodes in the British South Africa Company which administered Rhodesia until 1923. The bridge is an impressive engineering feat considering that it was completed in 1926 in a remote location with almost no basic resources.

We drove through the small town of Fort Victoria, where a handful of British soldiers and farmers had held off the Matabele warriors in 1893. The small fort still stands in the center of town as a reminder of those few brave men's courageous defense of the Shona tribesmen in the area

We crossed the Limpopo on another Beit bridge, this one with conventional columns, and continued to the small Transvaal town of Potgeitersrus where we spent the night. Most of these small towns had one prominent hotel which also served as the social nucleus. The locals were always delighted to see guests from out of town who brought them news and good company. The Afrikaans are very hospitable folk by nature, and Bugs and I were warmly welcomed to the bar and plied with drinks, which we did little to resist.

We spent two more nights on the road and finally arrived in the magnificent city of Cape Town. We both had roots there, Bugs having been born in Rondebosch and raised there until his family moved to Rhodesia and my mother having lived there for some years, attending Rustenburg high-school and studying music at the university. The university, founded in 1829 as the South African College in the Gardens area of Cape Town, moved to its present site on the Groote Schuur, estate of Cecil John Rhodes, in 1928. The campus is one of the most spectacular in the world, perched on the side of Table Mountain overlooking the Cape Flats with the Hottentots Holland mountains in the distance.

We were assigned to rooms in the new Driekoppen residence. The old Driekoppen was a collection of former barracks, affectionately known as Belsen because of its Spartan accommodations. The new building was modern and comfortable, conveniently located close to campus on Woolsack road. Bugs and I moved into our allocated rooms and then immediately set out to evaluate the various beaches both in terms of geographic and human attractions. We soon concluded that the best combination was Clifton, with its four sheltered coves at the bottom of a steep cliff. Here the young ladies of Cape Town tanned and paraded their bodies in brief bikinis and competed for the attentions of the men ogling them hungrily. As Clifton is on the Atlantic side of the peninsula, the water is cold year round but the sheltered location makes it a tanner's paradise.

In a few days the other three members of the Anglo team arrived and we were pleased to see that they all had acquired cars, so we had no transportation problems. We soon discovered that the huge university hospital of Groote Schuur was conveniently located on De Waal Drive, a few minutes from Driekoppen. This was propitious because the large university hospital had a large number of young nurses in training who were all well acquainted with the male anatomy and desirous of male company.

Despite our theoretical objective of writing the supp exams, this task did not weigh heavily on our minds and we set about making the most of our few weeks of "vacation".

Our days began at Clifton, where we descended the many steps down the cliff to First Beach below the

Clifton Hotel. The sand was fine and white and the ocean clear and cold. After a suitable period of warming ourselves and reviewing the day's selection of girls, we took to the waves. Clifton waves are usually average in height and break fairly close in due to the slightly shelving beach, but they break clean and are easy to ride. We had no boards, but enjoyed good body-surfing for as long as we could stand the cold, emerging blue and shivering to soak up some more sun.

We left the beach at about eleven and climbed the steps to the hotel, where we established ourselves at a table on the balcony overlooking Table Bay. The waiters were happy to see us as they were assured of good tips after serving many beers. After several hours on the beach, the cold Castle or Lion beer went down very smoothly. We drank happily and usually ate a hamburger or sandwich before returning to the beach for a nap.

The afternoons were particularly pleasant because Clifton faced west and the sun would set over the ocean, warming the wall behind us. We left after sunset and returned to the residence for a shower and dinner.

After dinner it was time to visit the nurses' home. It was important to actually know one or two nurses so that they could procure others for us and we were fortunate that Bugs and I knew one from Umtali and Banger knew one from Salisbury. We had to confront the matron in the hallway of the residence each night and ask for the girls we knew. They would come down and negotiate and after a brief waiting period they and their friends would appear ready for the evening's festivities. Girls are not stupid and our friends took great care never to invite any girl they considered more attractive than themselves. This was not an issue with our Umtali friend for she was very good-looking, but Banger's friend was not as blessed and generally delivered inferior friends.

The student nurses were under no misconceptions as to the nature of the outing. It was tacitly understood that we paid expenses and they delivered enjoyment in one form or another. Being engineers whose minds worked by logic and reason, we believed that the first thing to establish in a potential relationship is physical compatibility. This is rapid and easily assessed, so there is no point in continuing if this is unsatisfactory. Intellectual compatibility is more complex, and indeed sometimes can never be accurately assessed.

For girls we had not met before we saw no reason to invest heavily. Our standard evening's entertainment consisted of driving out to a remote beach with a couple of dozen beers, a gallon of red wine, several loaves of bread and a few yards of boerewors.

We built a fire of driftwood, drank the beer and wine and cooked the wors on sticks over the fire, then consuming it between chunks of bread. During the drinking and cooking phase we made exploratory moves on the girls. We met with different degrees of success and soon figured out which girls to place on the "invite again" list. On one occasion, at the isolated beach of LLandudno, after "dinner" the men decided a swim in the cold Atlantic would be just the thing to prepare for the continued consumption of cheap red wine. We trotted down to the waters' edge and stripped off our clothes, after which we went for a short jog down the beach to warm up. Unexpectedly an elderly couple was strolling peacefully a little way ahead, and as ten naked men padded silently past them they forgot their age and fled in terror. When we returned cold and wet to where we had left our clothes they were gone, the thieves soon identified as our dates, dancing around the fire. If they expected some degree of coyness they were sorely disappointed as we walked slowly and nakedly up to the fire to retrieve our stuff. A few girls remained to admire us and the rest fled giggling and shrieking.

After two weeks of beach and partying I began to feel weak and noticed that my urine had turned brown and my eyes yellow. Bugs' brother was in his third year of medical school at Groote Schuur, so we consulted him. He was horrified and immediately arranged for me to be admitted to the infectious diseases ward with a serious case of hepatitis. The rest of the group was very sympathetic and visited me each evening, bringing with them several six-packs of beer which we rapidly consumed together. After a week the doctors were perplexed that I was not showing any signs of improvement. Providentially our pretty Umtali nurse visited me the next afternoon when the buddies were there and observed the beer-drinking in utter disbelief. No-one had informed us that any alcohol was poison to a hepatitis patient and the doctor was duly summoned to give us a stern lecture on the subject.

The hospital stay happened to coincide with the supp. exams, so I missed them all. My colleagues may as well have missed them too because not one of them passed. I emerged from Groote Schuur several pounds lighter and with strict instructions from the doctor not to touch a drop of alcohol for six months. This was a verdict almost equivalent to a death sentence for a Newman, but without recourse. I was duly assigned the duty of designated driver.

After hospital we all moved into our permanent residence, the venerated Smuts Hall. Smuts was the original residence built on campus at the same time as the university, and dedicated by the Prince of Wales in 1928. It was a stately stone structure consisting of a large rectangle divided in the center by the dining hall, creating two courtyards. The lodgings were divided into flats, each having ten rooms on three floors, two at the bottom and four on the other two. Each floor had a basin and toilet and the showers were on the ground floor. The exceptions were the corner flats which had four floors and the area above the common-rooms which had a row of rooms above the upper common room. At the far end of the rectangle was the warden's house.

In those days there was a definite system of initiation for new students at all the South African universities. This was a time-honored strategy to promote bonding and a sense of community as it effectively forced interaction between all members of the residence. New members, imaginatively referred to as Newmen, were immediately reminded that they were the most pitiful and useless human beings on earth. In the evening of move-in day all Newmen were assembled in the upper common room and given a stern lecture by the chairman of the House Committee. This began by stressing that we did not belong there at all and we had effectively taken the places of personal friends of the seniors totally against their recommendations to the admissions clerk. This was followed by an inspection of our persons by all the seniors, who did not flinch from pointing out in loud voices every real and imaginary defect of our bodies and attire. We were then instructed to make large circular name tags out of hardboard with our personal information in large lettering and these were to be hung around our necks at all times. Furthermore, to mitigate the miserable appearance we presented to the public, we were to dress in suits at all times and wear bright green ties to clearly identify our lowly status as Newmen.

All this was not unexpected and taken in good humor, the various quips and insults generating some spirited repartee. The next morning we appeared punctually at seven am in our suits for Formal Breakfast in the dining hall. The hall was set up by flat, with ten to a table, nicely laid with white linen and an impressive array of cutlery. Uniformed waiters delivered each of the three courses with aplomb, different each day in the true English/South African style. The London Savoy could have done no better. No-one could begin until the warden arrived and seated himself at the head table.

The campus at that time consisted of two rugby fields above de Rhodes' Drive with Rugby Road separating them from the two residences Smuts and Fuller. From this level a huge flight of steps led up to the main campus with the centerpiece being the Jamieson Hall. The original academic buildings spread out both sides of "Jammie", everything in nice stone construction. At our time two modern buildings had been added for the science and civil engineering faculties. This must be one of the best campuses in the world, with a fifty-mile view in front and the spectacular Devil's Peak mountain behind. A short distance up the mountain is the Rhodes' Memorial with an even better view. The tennis courts were across Rhodes' Drive, accessible via a tunnel, and the swimming pool and squash courts were along Woolsack Road.

All this campus originally was part of Rhodes' estate Groote Schuur, meaning Great Barn in Dutch. This was Rhodes' official residence as prime-minister of the Cape Colony and after his death it reverted to the state and served as southern residence for the prime-minister of the Union and later the Republic of South Africa. The Northern residence was in Pretoria. Below the estate was the village of Rondebosch which served as the primary shopping and drinking venue for most of the university faculty and students. Not surprisingly there were many hotels with bars in the vicinity, but the closest and favorite was the Pig and Whistle.

Cape Town loved its university and the students who brought life and vigor to the city and the permanent residents were amazingly tolerant of students and their pranks. The proprietor of "The Pig" was no less indulgent, deriving most of his income from the meager allowances of his young cliental. The pub opened out on to a nice courtyard and in good weather this was the preferred area. The Pig formed the off-campus social club where men and women could meet, eat and drink freely. The residences were strictly segregated and except on the formal dance occasions, members of the opposite sex could not cross the thresholds. Transgressions were punished by expulsion. At the Pig drunkenness, noise and bawdy behavior were all considered normal and any guest of the hotel portion could not contemplate sleep before the closing hour of eleven pm.

One of the first items on the university agenda was the annual Rag. This was ostensibly a parade of floats through the center of the city to raise money for the main University charity, SHAWCO, the Students' Health and Welfare Organization. Founded in 1943 by a medical student, this had grown into a major contributor to the impoverished townships surrounding Cape Town. The Rag gave the students a great opportunity to party for a week while applying their skills and ingenuity to float-building and the results were generally impressive.

Preparation involved deciding upon a theme, procuring materials and then building the float. The thought-process was enhanced by consuming copious quantities of various alcoholic beverages. As most students were strapped for cash, the criterion was simply the most effective result for the lowest cost. Rhodesians were predominantly beer drinkers, there being no wineries in our country. The Capetonians had access to a wonderful variety of local wines, ranging from world-class to awful. Our first year we were persuaded that the wine was definitely the drink of choice and one of the cheapest was Liebestein. This was a sickly, sweet white wine which delivered the alcohol to our systems with limited enjoyment and disastrous after-effects. However, the first night of float-building we were unaware of this, and each purchased a gallon demijohn of Liebestein. As the evening progressed we deteriorated rapidly and the next morning suffered terribly. That was the end of the wine-drinking for a while and we returned to our trusted Castle beer.

Rag took place on Saturday morning with the parade down Adderly Street, the main street running from the Gardens down to the Foreshore. The entire student body of about six thousand turned out in various imaginative attires, some wearing less than others and some wearing very little at all. The girls correctly deduced that the less they wore, the greater the donations they received from the men in the city. Some were on top of the floats, sing-ing, dancing and drinking and others roamed the street and pavements soliciting donations. One predominantly Rhodesian float had the message "We want a white Christmas" emblazoned along the length, a sign of the failing negotiations between Ian Smith and Harold Wilson regarding Rhodesian independence.

The town fountain was on Adderly Street at the Heerengracht and as the parade reached this point it rapid-ly was transformed into a giant wading-pool with drunken students stumbling and fighting one another as part of the entertainment. Normally entering the fountain was an offense punishable by law, but on this happy day the police turned a blind eye. The parade ended on the Foreshore in front of the harbor and the students dispersed to rest before the evening festivities at the Rag Ball.

The Rag Ball involved the appointment of a Rag Queen and Drum Majorettes and this year one of the majorettes was a beautiful and vivacious girl from Bergvliet, a suburb of Cape Town. Bugs was entranced by the obvious attractiveness, wit and character of this girl and he resolved to acquaint her with his impressive physique and many talents. This was no easy task because about a thousand other young men had similar intentions. Perseverance paid off however and Bugs was duly acclaimed as the preferred suitor.

The average day at UCT consisted of formal breakfast and classes from 8.00am to 1.00pm. Classes were typically 40 minutes, this period being considered the maximum for maintaining concentration. Lunch was informal and we took the next available place at an incomplete table. After lunch we generally relaxed in one of the courtyards, but this relaxation was often rudely interrupted by someone dropping a large water-bomb from a top-floor window. When this occurred there was a frantic scramble to catch the perpetrator and this became an accepted form of midday sport. Being enterprising fellows, we developed more sophisticated bombs and means of delivery as the term progressed. The end-point was reached when a fifty-pound bomb was launched from a fourth-floor window on to a colleague's convertible as he and his date innocently drove along rugby road. The bomb fortunately missed the occupants but did severe damage to the hood of the car and the expense incurred deterred further development.

After lunch most of us had tutorials which lasted a couple of hours, after which we did various sporting activities. Dinner was at 7.00pm and required suits and academic gowns. The doors closed at this hour and any-one arriving later went hungry. The warden presided and the five course meals would generally rival those served at Buckingham Palace. If service was not immediate, all the diners would beat their spoons on the tables until the situation was rectified. For this reason Smuts spoons were of reduced capacity, being severely flattened over the years. From time to time if the warden appeared to be in a less than commodious mood, every time he looked down at his plate the entire group would lift their tables as one and edge them closer to the head-table. This continued until all the tables were pressing up on the high-table and we were eyeball-to-eyeball with the warden.

After dinner we did our assignments, but as Newmen, at 9.00pm we were required to serve tea to each senior flat and recite jokes to the seniors. At first this was a daunting experience, for regardless of our tal-ents at preparing tea, the seniors chastised us unmerciful-ly for the poor quality and service. The joke-telling was even worse. As we delivered the punch-line the assem-bled group would glare at us in stony silence and then launch into a carefully orchestrated tirade as to the poor taste and complete absence of humor in our jokes. This was a definite testing process whereby the responses of the Newman in his defense were expected to be vigorous and witty. Some Newmen took this in good spirits and recognized the challenge and others were petrified and dreaded the encounters.

After a couple of weeks of serious hazing the seniors informed us that in order to conduct an effective evaluation of the new intake we would all have to fight one another in an evening of boxing in the gym. A roster was posted on the notice board showing the pairing. Not surprisingly, the smallest and weakest were paired with the biggest and strongest and this led to great trepidation on the parts of the faint of heart. After dinner on the appointed night we were all lined up in the outer quad and inspected for attire and attitude. Bugs had procured a red silk dressing-gown and attached the word "Bugs" to the back and arrived at the line-up skipping and feinting like Muhammad Ali. This infuriated the seniors and a spirited shouting match ensued. We were then marched to the gym and the fights began. Of course the real pairing was fair, and I found myself pitted against a hairy Greek about my weight but shorter and stockier. There was no question of mutual restraint, the seniors crowded around us and bellowed encouragement and criticism. The three-minute round seemed like an eternity and by the finish neither of us could lift our arms, let alone deliver a blow. We were both excoriated for our pitiful performances but the evening was considered a great success by most and we certainly got to know one another better.

The next ordeal was the Newmen's Sports Day. This pitted the four men's residences against one another on the sports field across from Belsen. Sports are very important in all aspects of South African life and this event was taken seriously, with mandatory training for a month. The seniors accompanied the progress closely, shouting abuse regardless of performance and drawing attention to any real or perceived defect in the individual's anatomy or technique. On the appointed Saturday we were all lined up for inspection in the outer quad and threatened with terrible consequences if we stained the honor of Smuts in any way. The competition itself was quite an orderly affair with some excellent performances and the Smuts team won the day. We marched back to the residence in good spirits, only to be met at the door by furious seniors equipped with fire-hoses. We were given a stern lecture to the effect that our great performances had actually caused grievous insult to the seniors because last year the team had not won and we had tried to show that we Newmen were better than the seniors. We were instructed to get on our hands and knees and crawl into the residence in shame while the seniors took great delight in cooling us down with the fire-hoses.

To the casual reader the "initiation" process might appear to be abusive. Perhaps for some individuals it was. However, the majority understood the primary objectives of putting life in perspective and bonding with everyone. Under the circumstances of hardship and "abuse" people talk to one another and the strengths and weaknesses of each are defined. The system also tests the mind, as quick and witty responses on both sides make life more interesting and enjoyable. The residence becomes a big family and lifelong friendships are forged.

The Kitwe Five had certain advantages over most of the Smuts Newmen. Firstly, we were one year older than other residents. Secondly, we were not fresh out of high school and the ties of mummy's apron-strings, the mining experience having given us a good perspective on real life. Thirdly, because of our earnings on the mine and our all-expenses scholarships we had more money than most. Not surprisingly we were therefore less tolerant of the prolonged initiation process, and after the sports day humiliations we initiated a Newmen's revolt and encouraged all Newmen to abandon the suit and tie at all-times rule. The seniors did not take this well at all and they proclaimed that not only were we to retain the dress code for the entire academic year, but furthermore on Saturday nights we were grounded and had to report to an appointed senior every hour. This only lasted for one Saturday however, because we arranged rides for everyone to the local pubs, drank rapidly and returned to report every hour. As the night progressed the degree of inebriation outpaced the hours on an exponential scale and by closing time the Newmen were crawling and staggering to report and had lost all semblance of respect for the unfortunate senior. As there was a real risk of accident if this routine continued, the seniors wisely rescinded it. We did wear the suits for the whole year.

The other undergrad residences were Driekoppen and College. College House was situated off campus on Main

Road in Mowbray, the town adjoining Rondebosch. College had a reputation for an initiation program a little more demanding than Smuts, and several of our friends were subjected to this. It so happened that there was a large movie theater about two hundred yards west of College House on the other side of Main Road. Next to this theater was the Mowbray police station. As a time honored rite of passage, College Newmen were required to run the Flaming A course. This involved stripping naked, whereupon an obliging senior would stick a rolled newspaper between the Newman's legs and light it from behind. The Newman was then required to run down Main Road, make a U-turn at the movie theater and return to the gates of the residence without dropping the flaming newspaper. This program was timed precisely to coincide with the Saturday night movie hour when lines were longest.

There were a number of challenges involved for the Newman. The first was to secure the newspaper between the legs while running. The next was running fast enough that the time and tailwind kept the flames from reaching the sensitive areas of the anatomy. The most challenging however was avoiding arrest by the Mowbray police who patrolled at this hour with increased diligence. They were true sportsmen however and never used their dogs to run down a Flaming A contender. The police did catch men from time to time and when this happened, the entire College House, in a show of unity, would surround the police station and sing bawdy songs at high volume until their man was released. It was a respected game which everyone approved of.

The student body was effectively divided into two groups; the Engineers and everybody else. The Engineers held regular "smokers" to ostensibly provide a cultured setting for intellectual discussion. These were normally on campus on a suitable lawn, but also took place in various pubs close by. Beer was served in unlimited quantities and smoking of every type was encouraged. There was an impressive array of pipes, cigars, cheroots and cheap cigarettes and a heavy blue haze enveloped the group. The discussions seldom reached the expected level of intellect regarding technical matters, but generally focused on sports and women. As at that time there were only two female engineering students and they had the choice of joining in or boycotting the smokers, both had the good sense to participate, notwithstanding the fact that their anatomies, personalities and perceived sexual preferences were widely and openly debated.

The Engineers had full curricula and therefore had no interest in or time for frivolous political demonstrations. At this time there was a strong liberal movement in all the South African universities, led by the small but energetic body NUSAS, National Union of South African Students. Whereas most students paid no attention to their liberal agenda, this proved to be a mistake because they were able to push through various acts of defiance to the government with little resistance. There were marches and demonstrations organized by the local chapter which we engineers wanted no part of, but dreamy liberal students rose to the cause in rapturous bliss. The first change was to ban all social functions on campus as long as the University continued in its policy of not admitting "non-whites". This meant that there were no more dances in Jammy, a great shame for everyone. If there were any liberals in Smuts they were far outnumbered by men with common sense and most found little sympathy with liberal ideals. Smuts did not fall under the jurisdiction of the SRC, Student Representative Council and we held our annual Smuts Formal Ball as always.

Across the parking-lot from Smuts was the twin female residence of Fuller Hall. This was strictly off-limits to any male, but of course this challenge was met in various imaginative ways. In years before a tunnel had been started so that a group of arduous lovers could gain access to their mates, but this had been discovered and nipped in the bud. Others furnished their girlfriends with ropes that were lowered from upper-floor windows at night so the suitors could climb up and pursue their instincts. One of our flatmates, Jakes, had not been lucky in love and continued to complain about his misfortune. One Saturday morning, after a prolonged session of beer-drinking at the Pig, Jake's complaints called for remedial action by his buddies. We stuffed his ample body into one of the Smuts laundry baskets and secured the lid. We then loaded this onto a large trolley and rushed the entrance of Fuller, leaving the trolley in the middle of the outer quad before escaping. The girls were not sure what to make of this Trojan Horse, a laundry basket rocking and emitting muffled roars. The matron, a large and powerful Afrikaans lady, was duly summoned. She released the lid and the naked form of Jakes sprang out like a grotesque jack-in-the-box, hurling drunken abuse at all around him. It took four campus police to subdue him and return him to Smuts, but the exposure was clearly worthwhile as his attributes had impressed certain young ladies who subsequently became more responsive to his advances.

The annual Smuts Formal Ball was an auspicious occasion enthusiastically anticipated by all. This was the one time each year that members of the opposite sex were permitted to enter the stately portals. The system was well designed to encourage the maximum opportunity to imbibe and enjoy the favors of one's partner in a truly Roman orgy environment. Newmen were not permitted to invite girls as they were required to serve as barmen for the seniors. The bottom two rooms of each flat were lavishly decorated and set up as a lounge and a bar, with an impressive variety of themes ranging from posh to jungle. Vast quantities of every type of alcohol were procured. The favorites were beer, cheap wine and cane-spirits. The last was favored because at about 180-proof it rendered very rapid and spectacular results.

F-flat Formal 1967

The dress started off as very formal, with the
men in full dress attire and the women in long gowns.
Recreational drinking began early in the morning and got
serious at seven pm when the ladies arrived. From then
on the evening rapidly deteriorated in comportment and
attire. Jackets and bow-ties were cast aside and trampled,
make-up was smeared and elaborate hair-dos were demolished. Even the most reserved (of which there were very
few) became ardent and vociferous and every man considered himself irresistible to the ladies. The dining-hall
was set up as a huge ballroom and decorated appropriately. A local band provided the music. The revelers staggered to and from the ballroom and made every attempt
to keep time to the music, falling over periodically and

dragging their partners down with them. They normally contrived to fall on top of the girls and did not rush to get up again.

This first year I was assigned to barman duty in a seniors' flat like every other Newman. I possessed a beautiful cream tuxedo, purchased a few months before in Salisbury in a moment of extravagance. I donned this with great pride and honestly attempted to fulfill my barman duties diligently. It was accepted that barmen drink as much or more than everyone else, not having the distraction of partners. It was also accepted that the maids were welcome to attend the formal and participate in the drinking.

For those unfamiliar with the Cape Colored, a little digression is necessary. In the early days of the Cape Colony there were few Bantu in the area. The indigenous population consisted of small tribes of Bushmen and Hottentots. Both of these were small of stature and difficult to domesticate. As the Cape was essentially a re-supply station en route to the Far East, on the return voyages Malay's were brought to the Cape to serve as virtual slaves and perform the unskilled tasks. The Dutch and English sailors and residents, in the absence of sufficient women of their own, found the Malay women quite attractive and proceeded accordingly. These liaisons produced offspring which, over time, formed a group of their own, known as Cape Coloreds. They were, and remain, a special people, neither white nor black with a character all of their own. Both men and women have a great proclivity for wry humor and hard liquor.

Our maids were Katie and Rosie, who considered themselves surrogate mothers to all the "boys" and constantly castigated us for our errant ways. Formal night was a grand opportunity to celebrate and both of them proceeded to get stumbling drunk, cursing in Afrikaans and English and falling over every second step. They mingled freely with the guests and were not reticent in giving their opinions on the perceived potentials of the invited girls. This was all taken in good spirit and most of the comments were hilarious.

I conducted my barman duties as diligently as possible and tried to keep up with the drinking. I must have been quite successful, as my last memories were groveling in the mud in combat with a fellow barman. I awoke next morning in a full bathtub, my ruined tuxedo now a shade of dirty red from the mud fight. Despite the cleaner's best efforts, it was never cream again. The next three formals were with partners and the new crop of Newmen as barmen. I would like to say that we matured with age, but this would be incorrect. We had wonderful times with many pranks and quick humor.

As many Rhodesians elected not to go home during the short break in April because of the time and expense involved in the 1600-mile trip, we sought other diversions to amuse ourselves. One of these was the Hobo Hop, an informal party held in the garage under Smuts Hall. This garage had obviously been constructed without regard to the true dimensions of future automobiles because the entrance on Rugby Road was barely wide enough to admit a Mini Minor. For this reason no cars were parked there.

Unmindful of the obvious fire hazard, the Hobo Hop involved construction of a number of cubicles using bales a straw, one cubicle for each group. A space up front was left clear for dancing with a trestle-table for a bar against the wall.

The evening involved a prolonged period of beer-drinking followed by some unimpressive dancing and terminating with each couple doing what they enjoyed most amongst the straw inside each cubicle. There were many smokers but the odd small fire was extinguished quickly. In order to preserve some semblance of order, one senior was delegated to attend the function, which he did most willingly. In our case it was Porch Pike, so named because he had a proclivity for waiting in Smuts entrance, known as the porch, to dispense unwelcome advice to Newmen returning from long evenings. Porch was an impressive figure, short but tremendously powerful, who played lock-forward on the rugby team. He sat on the bar like a blond Buddha, consuming a can of beer about every five minutes. From time to time he felt disposed to intervene in various small fights that broke out on the dance floor, effortlessly lifting each combatant by the shirt and hurling him against the straw bale walls.

Sport was considered more important than academic achievement and pretty much everyone participated in one sport or another with varying degrees of aptitude. I had learned from my school days that any sport involving a ball was not for me, and therefore decided to pursue the rowing that I had begun in Kitwe. Zorb and Eyes joined me and with one more we formed our own foursome.

The University had a very nice rowing and sailing club located on a peninsula on Seekoe Vlei, a few miles to the east near Muizenberg. The club had a good fleet of single and double sculls, fours and eights. We practiced on the water three times a week and ran up the mountain behind the campus another three, resting on Saturdays. Competitive rowing is an arduous sport involving all the large muscles and fitness is essential. I rowed number three, just ahead of the stroke who set the timing. At full speed a rower is stroking 55-60 times a minute and timing must be perfect or one gets thrown out of the boat by the oar.

Seekoe vlei is quite a large body of water and at times the wind would whip up small waves which made practice difficult. The shells have very little freeboard and the clearance of the blades to the water is tight. On these days we practiced in the "Tub" a clinker-built boat, heavy and cumbersome but with much greater clearances. Once a year all the universities' teams assembled for the intervarsity championships. These were great fun and boatraces occurred on water and land. My first intervarsity was in 1966 and Wits (University of the Witwatersrand) was the host. We had to spend a week in Vereeniging prior to the race in order to adjust to the high altitude and we took full advantage of the opportunity to meet our competitors and party. Our coach became a little concerned that we were not dedicating ourselves sufficiently and called a meeting in our room to lecture us on the perils of over-indulgence in beer. Just as he reached the punchline there was a knock on the door and a waiter entered bearing a tray loaded with beers which we had ordered previously, at which point the coach conceded defeat. We also rowed for Western Province at various venues. These were very serious affairs as to lose to another province was a major disgrace, so we trained hard and drank less.

Chapter 17:
UDI

On November 11th 1965 at eleven am, Rhodesian
Prime Minister Ian Smith declared unilateral independence from Britain. This was considered an act of
last-resort after every effort had been made by Smith
and his cabinet to talk some sense into the British.
Everyone in Rhodesia realized that there was risk and
sacrifice involved but this was considered preferable to
the alternative of political suicide. Dad was elated but
had his doubts that the western world would allow the
independent Rhodesia to survive. He was convinced,
probably correctly, that the USA was intent on dismantling all the European empires in order to open these
up to US trade and for president Lyndon Johnson to
show support for the escalating Civil Rights movement. This indeed has happened, with the enthusiastic
assistance of the USSR. Little did Russia realize that

eventually its own empire would implode after seventy years of misery.

As the Rhodesian Front had a mandate, the decision to declare independence was not put to a referendum. The whites were divided into three basic groups. There were those who believed that this might buy enough time for the English and American politicians to come around to some common sense and accept it. Others, while not liking the prospect of black rule, believed it was inevitable simply due to numbers and the sooner the whites handed over power to the blacks the less resentment and chaos there would be. The third group believed that black rule would be wonderful and everybody would live happily together forevermore. They were all disappointed.

The Rhodesian Front saw no need to compose its own declaration of independence because a perfectly good version was available from the USA, well drafted by Thomas Jefferson in 1776. They tweaked it a little but in essence regarded the situation as very similar. The day and hour were selected to coincide with Armistice day to remind Britain that tiny Rhodesia had sent a greater proportion of its men to defend Britain than any other country. Rhodesians could not understand why their mother country, their own people, their own families would betray them after all the loyalty given over the past 75 years. They could not understand why Britain would destroy a loyal ally in favor of a government promoted and assisted by Russia and China. Of course many in Britain were totally opposed to the Government's policies, but politics trumped common sense. Smith was astonished that during the initial negotiations it was the Conservative Party under Harold MacMillan that had refused to grant Rhodesia independence. Once Labor took control he knew the chances were very low and UDI was the only option left.

Rob Smith, Ian Smith's stepson, was a resident at Smuts and in my same Mechanical Engineering class. All of us were delighted by Ian Smith's action and most South Africans were very supportive. "Smithy" was congratulated effusively and the Rhodesian contingent at Smuts was very proud. There was never any question of military action by the UN or any western democracy. Most European and American troops would refuse to fight against decent people who had done no wrong and had been their most reliable allies. The expected action was sanctions to cripple the country financially. For Rhodesia to survive in the face of these expected world sanctions it was essential that South Africa and Mozambique refuse to collaborate with the UN. Smith had secured promises from Hendrik Verwoerd and Portugal's Salazaar that this would be the case. The Shah of Iran had agreed to supply oil. There was a lot of excitement in the air and South Africans flashed their lights in approval when they saw the Rhodesian registered cars on the streets and highways.

Sure enough, in a short time, the UN Security Council convened and announced a program of crippling sanctions against tiny Rhodesia under the ridiculous charge that the Smith government posed a "threat to world peace". These included a British blockade of the

Mozambique port of Beira to stop crude oil supplies to the pipeline across Mozambique supplying the Feruka refinery near Umtali. To put the situation in perspective, a world body responsible for preserving world peace was advocating the destruction of one of the most decent, peaceful and well-administered countries in the world in the name of democracy! There was no question that sanctions would hit the black population hardest and the final objective of removing responsible government would guarantee many decades of anarchy, slaughter and starvation for them. Rhodesia posed no military threat to the world. We had no weapons of mass destruction. There was no maniacal group of rulers conducting purges. Rhodesia was very well run, had low unemployment, low debt, low crime and excellent education for all. The result of black rule in Central Africa was well known. Kenya, Tanganika, Uganda, Rwanda, Burundi and the Belgian Congo were all in turmoil after being granted "independence" and huge slaughter had occurred and still occurs today.

The Rhodesians set about sanction-busting and soon had a cunning system in place to export their tobacco and minerals via South Africa and Mozambique and receive needed supplies of fuel and other necessities the same way. In addition to this, many small businesses were set up to supply things that were previously imported. Pretty soon there was Rhodesian wine, all manner of manufactured goods and substitutes for non-essential imports. Britain had lost a good customer and the huge exports of chrome which were needed by the USA now reached its steel plants via Russia. The atmosphere was almost euphoric as the population circled the wagons for a long siege. Dad was cautiously hopeful but in his heart he knew that 250,000 decent people could not survive for long in the face of world opposition. Smithy joined our flat at Smuts and during vacations we visited him at the Prime Minister's residence in Salisbury where Mr. & Mrs. Smith received us all very graciously.

During these vacations all the Rhodesian Cape Town students got together frequently in Salisbury. The days would usually begin about 11 am on the sun-deck of the Monomatapa hotel on Kingsway as the bar did not open before then. The waiters would happily deliver trays laden with Castle or Lion beer as they knew we were there for a while and would tip them well. In the evenings we would generally congregate at one of the homes of local residents and have a few beers there before going out for dinner. Those whose girlfriends lived in town would invite them to join the group and the rest of us had to fend for ourselves. The Park Lane hotel on Jameson Avenue was a favorite first stop and there we would be served by a dwarf waiter bearing the name of his illustrious ancestor Lobengula. Lobengula was a great character and enjoyed the regular banter he received from his customers. His head was barely at table level but in his mind he was six feet tall.

After dinner we had the choice of two main night-clubs. The oldest, Le Coq d'Or, was generally known as The Golden Penis and offered good dancing and strip shows. La Boheme was a little less sophisticated as the name implied, but offered very good entertainment too. Those without girlfriends could often encounter some company here and after the many beers some of the less attractive girls became quite desirable. Salisbury in those days was a fun town and we thoroughly enjoyed our times there.

Chapter 18:
THE KRAUT

In my second year in Cape Town my sister Eveleigh enrolled in a secretarial college down town and took up residence at the city YWCA on St. George Street. She became friends with a local girl enrolled in the same course and introduced me to her. Ingeborg was pure German whose parents came from Hamburg. Her father had worked for a German film company and had been transferred to Cape Town when Inga was small. Inga's father had died before I met her and she, her mother and elder brother lived in a house overlooking Camp's bay. Inga was fun to be with and loved the beach which was just a short walk from her house and after a few weekends of getting together we started dating. To us, all Germans were Krauts and Inga immediately became known as The Kraut to all our Smuts group, including their girlfriends. I was a little more romantic and called her Borgie. She seemed pretty happy with this nickname, perhaps being relieved after noting that my sister Eveleigh was nick-named Bograt, a legacy from home.

By this time most of our group had made their choices of girls and we had a grand time on weekends at the beaches and at the local hotel functions. My routine soon involved arriving at Inga's house after lunch on Saturdays, where in summer I would be greeted affectionately at the front door by Inga in her bikini, which was always a welcome sight. Inga loved the sun and her house had a beautiful front verandah overlooking the bay where she spread herself out to tan. Germans are proud people and convinced that if one wants the best quality product, it has to be made in Germany. Pretty much everything in Inga's house conformed to this philosophy, from the Grundig sound system and VW car to even the can-opener in the kitchen. Naturally the meals were also German, with lots of potato, mutton and sauerkraut washed down with good German beer or wine. The family still spoke German at home and because of my knowledge of Afrikaans I could follow some parts of conversations.

After a suitable period of continued tanning and listening to music we would go to the beach at Camp's bay or Clifton where we would normally find friends from Smuts. Clifton was great in the evening and we consumed our beers with our backs to the warm sea-wall and admired the sun setting over the ocean. We would usually eat dinner at Inga's house and then join our friends for the evening's entertainment. Most of the larger hotels had dancing every Saturday night with good bands and lively music and we would invariably agree to meet at one of these. We had a large choice all over the peninsula, all with different attributes and music. The hotels were happy to see us because notwithstanding our limited budgets, beer was always a high priority and we were good customers. Our enthusiasm for dancing increased as the evening progressed regardless of the quality of the music.

The Clifton Hotel was one of our favorite dance spots because in addition to the spectacular situation over First Beach, at that time they had very good music, supplied by the Ronnie Singer band. Not surprisingly, Ronnie was a singer but he also was a very talented performer on the electric organ and composed many of his own songs. Our group got in the party mood by rapidly consuming drinks made from cane-spirit and bitter-lemon, a pleasant-tasting cocktail with formidable alcohol content. Once warmed up, our group rudely took over the small dance floor and performed our own drunken routines which were generally not admired by other patrons. The Clifton also offered a sumptuous seafood buffet on Sunday nights, but as this was out of reach on our normal budget we reserved it for special occasions.

I was fortunate that this second year Dad's fears of irresponsible exuberance on my part had diminished to the point that he made good on his promise to give me his Borgward station-wagon which had run up a high mileage as his work-vehicle visiting all the farmers' co-ops in the Tribal Trustlands. This good German car met the full approval of Inga's family and her brother confided to me that had Mercedes directors not bribed Hitler to get the lion's share of the war contracts, Borgward would now be the leading manufacturer. Notwithstanding this high praise, the company went out of business the next year. This station-wagon, although not considered the ultimate in curb-appeal, was a fine workhorse which could comfortably haul four couples and several cases of beer while getting excellent gas mileage.

The evenings did not end when we left the dance-halls and indeed from my perspective the best was yet to come. After dropping off any other couples, Inga and I parked at a nice secluded spot half-way down from Kloof Neck to her house and indulged in unrestrained demonstrations of our affection for each other. Finally I left her happy and disheveled at her front door and returned over the Neck to Smuts. Despite the drinking I never had any kind of accident and neither did any of our friends.

Sunday mornings were normally taken up with rowing practice and we all met at the boathouse on Seekoe Vlei. The sailing club shared this boathouse and we were always amazed that whereas the rowers were on the water five minutes after arriving, the sailors spent most of their time on land rigging and un-rigging their boats. We rowed vigorously for a couple of hours and then returned to Smuts for lunch. Sunday afternoons were spent with Inga at her house or one of the many beaches around the Cape. From Camp's Bay there are delightful drives along the rugged coast with a great selection of secluded small coves and long stretches of pristine beach. On weekends when everyone was free we would get several carloads of couples and venture into the mountains or further along the coast and have a great time hiking, swimming, drinking and loving.

We were fortunate in that several of our colleagues in Smuts had access to beach-houses owned by their families. These were of course favorite destinations and well used by our group. Our family had "the shack" at Plettenberg Bay which was pretty rustic and a six-hour drive away, but Jakes, Smithy and Don had houses nearby. Smithy's family had a house at Kommetjie, a small village at the mouth of the Kom river down the coast of the peninsula on the Atlantic. There we had access to a number of surf kayaks, designed to sit on and ride the waves. They had a raised rear as a backrest and to give greater area for the wave to push on. It was convenient to paddle out on the Kom river where the deeper water prevented the waves from breaking and then circle around behind the backline of waves and surf back in to the beach. Kommetjie was at the southern end of Long Beach, a long, barren expanse of sand where we sometimes body-surfed.

Jakes' and Don's parents had houses at Hermanus, a beach and fishing resort about an hour east of Cape Town on the Indian Ocean. These were nice houses and had the added attraction of ski-boats which we could use on the lagoon. We had many good weekends at these houses, sometimes when the parents were there. Jakes' parents were real characters who enjoyed seeing the university crowd. Jakes' mother was an excellent cook and looked after us very well. One night we arrived back at her house very late after a night of partying. Like all mothers, she was attuned to the return of her son and called out from her bedroom "Son, are you all drunk?" When Jakes managed a slurred "yes Mum" she simply said "there are meat pies in the oven, just heat them up for yourselves and go to bed quietly without waking your Dad".

Jakes' dad was a big, strong South African who had farmed in Kenya until its independence in 1960 and then set up a marina on Lake Kariba, the vast body of water created by damming the Zambezi River below the Victoria Falls. He enjoyed water-skiing and allowed himself the luxury of a wetsuit which he made clear was for his exclusive use. One weekend we were down at Hermanus by ourselves on a cold but calm day and the lagoon was mirror smooth and ideal for skiing. Jakes could not resist the temptation and squeezed his ample frame into his dad's wetsuit, stretching it to the limit. Jakes liked to slalom and cut hard which invariably resulted in some spectacular falls. The wetsuit was pushed beyond its limits and Jakes emerged from the water with it hanging on his body in tatters. This posed a real problem because we could not afford a new one, and even if we could, Jakes' dad would notice. After some deliberation we decided to repair the original suit with the special adhesive available for that purpose. We thought we had done an admirable job, with the tears barely visible.

A few months' later the old folks arrived at their beach house for a few weeks' vacation. The first thing they noticed was that the single beds in the master-suite had been tied together using dad's dressing-gown cord. I had done this on a previous visit and forgotten to undo it. The next thing was various female undergarments under the bed in Jakes' room. On our next visit they mentioned these infractions in good humor and it was decided that we would all go skiing. As it was still quite cool, Jakes' dad, in a magnanimous gesture, offered his wet suit to one of us. With great pride he produced it from its storage area but his congenial beam of pleasure immediately turned into a snarl of rage as he perceived the vast array of repaired rents in his prized suit. We all had to chip in for a new suit to calm him down.

In June 1966 Robert Kennedy visited South Africa and was invited by NUSAS to give a speech at the University of Cape Town. NUSAS was a very liberal student organization strongly opposed to the government and most of us detested it. However, it is always smart to know your enemies and so we attended Kennedy's speech in front of Jammie. Dad had no use for the Kennedys, regarding them as rich boys living on their trusts who had never held a job and had little understanding of the real world. Robert Kennedy's speech left no doubt that he totally disagreed with the Apartheid system although he had absolutely no experience in Africa and knew nothing of the problems confronting us. After listening to Kennedy I was inclined to agree with Dad.

In September 1966 I was driving into Cape Town to pick up Borgie from the secretarial college. My route took me close to the houses of parliament where I noticed a large commotion. I turned on my radio and discovered that South African Prime Minister Hendrik Verwoerd had been stabbed by a deranged Greek parliament messenger. He was rushed to Groote Schuur hospital but was dead on arrival. Verwoerd was the main architect of the Apartheid policy and revered by the Afrikaners for having finally secured complete independence from Britain in 1960. His death marked a turning point in South African politics and there are those who believe it was not simply the act of a troubled messenger.

Chapter 19:
ACADEMICS

The University of Cape Town was recognized as one of the best seats of learning on the African continent and we were privileged to have excellent professors on each faculty. Whereas the University of the Witwatersrand in Johannesburg was the leader in Mining Engineering, Cape Town was tops in Mechanical and Civil. These courses were four years of hard work with classes every day from 8 until 1 and tutorials and lab or workshop in the afternoons.

Our 1965 Mech-Eng class started off with fifty-five students, some of whom were first-year repeats. Of these, only four of the original green intake graduated after four years. Most of the others finished in longer periods, but some dropped out altogether or switched to easier degrees. For those of us with Rhodesia's Higher School Certificate, first year was a breeze because we had covered all the ground except for the mechanical drawing. Second-year came as a big shock and we had to severely curtail our time at the beach. In the mid-year exams one of our group was disappointed to find that the sum of his marks in all subjects came to ten. Not surprisingly he failed the entire year and took five years to graduate.

Our professors were all very dedicated and came from various countries. The Dean was South African, but others were from Germany, Switzerland, England and Texas. We also had grad-students instructing us in the lab work from time to time. First year was the same for all engineering students, after which the classes were dedicated to each discipline. There were certain classes such as mathematics which were common throughout the course and here we got to know the students from the other branches.

Our Mech-Eng classes got smaller and smaller each year until at final year there were only seventeen of us. This made for excellent instruction and we had very good access to each professor. As electronic calculators were just coming on to the market and were very expensive, all our calculations were done using the simple slide-rule. Computers in general were still in their infancy and we did basic courses using the old punch-cards. All drawing was done with pen or pencil and paper using a large board which we carried to and from classes.

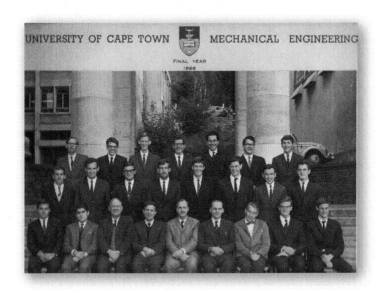

The curriculum was tough for everyone and after a day of classes and some sporting activity we worked most nights until midnight preparing our assignments. Exams set a high standard in both speed and complexity and it was rare that anyone scored over 75%. Having come from high school where I was consistently top student it was a rude awakening to find myself far outclassed by other members of our Mech Eng class. On many occasions I would not be smart enough to grasp the full meaning of a topic during class and would have to rely on further explanation from my classmates. They were always very generous with their time and went to extraordinary lengths to get me comfortable. We had a very close group and thoroughly enjoyed our courses and social interaction.

During the summer vacations I usually spent some time in Cape Town and some with the family at our shack in Plett. While in Cape Town, to earn some money, I worked as a limo driver for a local car-hire company on Buitekant street. This was a rich experience as I got to drive an amazing variety of passengers from celebrities to drunks and prostitutes. I got to know the city and surrounding areas very well, the good, the bad and the ugly. Some of my fares were generous in inviting me to accompany them at whatever party or festivity they were going to, paying for my time as well.

The times at Plett during this period were great fun too because it was a prime destination for students and it seemed that half the university was there during Christmas. All our family was there until Jen married, after which it was just the five of us. Several Smuts friends had houses in Plett and so we had good times fishing, surfing and partying. The Plett area is spectacular with a wide variety of beaches, lagoons and fishing options. Our buddy Curly was an avid fisherman and his father had a house on Robberg beach and a large property west of Robberg with cliffs overlooking the ocean. Robberg itself offered some excellent fishing and we would leave very early in the morning to hike to our favorite spots. One of these was the Island off Robberg. This was on the windward side and generally had large swells so one had to be alert not to get swept off the rocks. We fished for Galjoen which were medium-sized and took red-bait. The rocky bottom was tricky and our tackle got snagged frequently, usually meaning loss of hook and sinker. The other options on Robberg were Sterkstroom, a deep gully, the Point, a long shelf of rock and the Meidebank, a sheltered cliff on the leeward side. Curly always brought along his gilly Johnnie, a colored fellow who had been born and raised in Plett. Johnnie was an experienced fisherman who hired himself out to give advice and assistance to less experienced enthusiasts. These fellows knew where the fish were biting, the best time and the correct bait. Like all coloreds, they had sharp wits and kept up an amusing banter.

The Point at Robberg is a gently sloping shelf of rock descending into the water. It is a favorite fishing spot because Robberg extends about a mile into the ocean and the fish have to go around the point to access the bay. There is a fishermen's shack which can be rented for those who wish to overnight there. It is a majestic spot and so far unspoiled, but a long walk home over rough terrain if many fish have been caught.

In the other direction there are also magnificent rock formations to explore. We accompanied Curly and Johnnie to some of these. An hour's drive east through Nature's Valley and the Bloukranz and Grootrivier passes is the Tsitsikama forest. We had to leave the car at the end of a track and then hike down the cliff to Kraaibek (crow's beak), a pair of rock formations jutting out into the surf. One had to time the passage carefully between swells as there were low points which got covered with water. Because of the difficult access few people fished here and there was still abundant red-bait to be had on the rocks. We fished from sunrise until about nine am, after which the fish generally stop biting.

In the evenings we all usually assembled at the long bar in the Beacon Island hotel. This structure has since been replaced with a more modern building but the new bar cannot compete with the old in ambience. The hotel had a spectacular situation on a small island separated from the mainland by the Piesang river. Originally a whaling station, the whale-boats launched from here to hunt the abundant Southern Right whales which still come into the bay. The bar building was single-storey brick with a green corrugated-iron roof and women were not permitted inside but could be served outdoors at one of the various tables on the lawn. The internal drinking normally degenerated quite rapidly due to various games that encouraged rapid consumption. A typical warm-up involved 8-12 beers in about an hour, after which we would join our girlfriends for dinner and wine.

In my second year the class was joined by those who had failed this year previously which included our Smuts buddy Bert. Bert's dad was a successful entrepreneur and had seen fit to share his good fortune by purchasing a new Alfa Romeo for his son as he entered second year for the first time. Bert and his contemporaries were full of energy and formed a wild group whose passions were scuba-diving and recreational bomb-making. The new car gave extended range to the diving and seriously detracted from the studying to the extent that the year was an academic failure. Shortly after this became evident, Bert's dad came to town and invited his son and buddies to dine with him at the Mount Nelson hotel. The evening was a great success but at the farewell proceedings Bert's dad asked for the keys to the Alfa. He threw them far out into the spacious gardens and advised his son and guests that they could ponder their future dedication to studies on the five-mile walk home to Smuts. He sold the car the next day.

Without his car and mindful of his dad's wrath, Bert applied himself and passed second year whereupon his dad presented him with a new Toyota sports car which had just been launched. At Easter in third year a large group from Smuts set off for Plett and I elected to ride with Bert and two more buddies. We set off after classes at high speed and stopped about every thirty minutes at suitable bars to fortify ourselves with brandy and coke. Bert had only two accelerator pedal positions, on and off. In the on position the car reached speeds of about 115 mph which was not too bad on the straights but downright scary through the mountains. The breaking point came just after the town of George where there is a long descent to the Kaaimans river bridge. This is a rare curved bridge and it was clear that the tires had reached the limit of their lateral traction under the severe g-forces. Pappy, normally intrepid, could not stand the pressure and emitted a high-pitched scream of terror as the carload of drunks entered the bridge sideways. Bert's face broke out into a magnificent smile of satisfaction as he expertly drifted the car over the bridge and admonished Pappy for his disappointing lack of confidence. Not wanting to tempt fate too far, I found a more sedate ride back to Cape Town.

Fishing was not confined to Plett. Once a year the engineering class hired one of the colored fishing boats out of Cork Bay to go snoek fishing off Cape Point. The snoek is a delicious fish and a vicious fighter, with huge teeth that would take one's finger off. Most of them ranged from 10-15 lbs. The trip was usually preceded by some serious preparatory fortification in the form of brandy at one of the Rondebosch pubs, after which we drove down the peninsula to Cork Bay harbor. The boats left about midnight so as to arrive over the fishing grounds at dawn. There was no fancy equipment involved, the colored crew simply supplied each of us with a roll of 100 lb nylon and several large hooks attached to the line with steel traces. Around the boat were wooden posts to loop the line over so that one had some friction if the fish fought hard. As we motored out, the crew prepared bait from mackerel they had caught previously.

The Cape is notorious for its large ocean swells and some of our classmates did not take the combination of alcohol, diesel-fumes, fish aroma and wild rocking too well. After a surprisingly short time we had several casualties but the colored captain paid no attention at all other than to direct them to the leeward side of the boat. Some got so weak they simply collapsed on the deck with their faces in the slime and fish entrails and succumbed to blissful unconsciousness. I was always fortunate and felt no ill-effect, perhaps because my brandy-soaked stomach was already in motion of its own.

When we reached the fishing grounds the captain slowed the engines and the crew instructed us how deep to set our hooks, measured out in arm-lengths of line.

We looped the line around the posts and felt the tension on the tight side to be ready for a strike. When the snoek hit we had to react quickly to set the hook, otherwise he would spit it out. Once hooked well, we started to bring the fish in as rapidly as possible because the sea around us was full of seals eager for a free meal. There was no question of sportsmanship or "playing" the fish, we merely used brute strength on the heavy line. I was a little slow the first time and was incensed to see a seal bite off 90% of my first catch just as I was about to bring it in. I ended up with only the head on my hook. When we got a whole fish in the boat, there were two techniques for removing the hook. The crew favored bringing the fish in between their legs and clamping it tightly with their thighs while they freed the hook from the vicious jaws. To most of us this involved unnecessary risk, so we favored the under-arm method where we clamped between upper-arm and ribcage. This meant using the left hand for hook removal, but we managed most of the time. Once free, the fish was killed with a sharp blow to the head to avoid it biting our feet. These trips usually netted about 30-40 nice fish and those who lived in residences took them back to the main kitchen for all to enjoy.

For all South Africans and Rhodesians, rugby is the sport that is most loved and respected. This is a sport for men, with no sissy pads to protect the body, no breaks for commercials and no substitutions just because a player gets tired. You go out on the field in your jersey and shorts and you play as hard as you can for each 45-minute half. The game is fast-moving and requires some quick-thinking, not just brute strength. Varsity rugby is some of the best because these players are academics and not enrolled for their sporting abilities. Many of them go on to play for the Springboks.

Obviously in this environment the annual game between Cape Town and Stellenbosch universities was for us the most important game in the world. UCT students were known as Ikeys because we had the largest proportion of Jewish students, although that percentage was low. Stellenbosch students were the Maties, maat being the Afrikaans word for friend. The Maties on the rugby field were far from friendly and being predominantly big, strong Afrikaners they comprised a formidable foe. The Ikeys normally lost this game but now and then we had a win due to superior strategy. The game alternated location between the two towns, our home field being the Newlands stadium and the Maties home field their university stadium. Each group of spectators had its own designated area in the stadium because experience long ago had shown that intermingling rapidly degenerated into ugly fighting in the stands. Although the main game usually began at four in the afternoon, the stands were full by 10 am as lesser matches were played and beer was consumed. Each side had an impressive repertoire of filthy songs designed to humiliate the opponents and these were sung simultaneously at great volume throughout the day. By four o'clock the spectators were in a frenzy and the teams trotted on to the field to great cries of exhortation. Once the game begun, advice from the stands was constant and often very amusing. In all honesty, there are certain sports that simply must be described in Afrikaans because English does not have the phonetics to adequately convey the spirit of the occasion. Rugby, fishing and hunting are prime examples as the language has a rich vocabulary to apply to every conceivable situation with guttural enhancements and word combinations which add immensely to the enjoyment. Because of our time in Umtali with Afrikaans students, Bugs and I spoke the language reasonably and thus were able to participate fully.

To the Maties the Ikeys were a bunch of pampered sissies and they made their opinion clear at every opportunity. After the intervarsity game it had been customary for opposing residences to conduct raids on each other, but the year before our arrival there had been a very nasty car accident as Maties sped towards Smuts and all occupants were killed. The authorities at both universities then wisely banned these raids. The Maties considered this yet another sissy rule and so they decided to walk the 35 miles from Stellenbosch to Smuts. This they did, but were so exhausted upon arrival that their fighting spirit had given way to a tremendous thirst, whereupon they gladly became our best buddies in return for unlimited beer. Not to be outdone, the next year Smuts decided to walk to Stellenbosch as a gesture of friendly reciprocation.

It was decided that it would be less arduous to walk at night owing to lower temperatures and less traffic. After dinner we all went down to the Pig & Whistle to fortify ourselves for the ordeal and the walk commenced at midnight, straight down the N2 highway. The first few hours were pleasant enough, but by daybreak the pace had slowed and blisters were beginning. As we turned off the N2 to Stellenbosch we were positively dragging and it was a very sorry group that limped and crawled into the courtyard at Eendrag residence. A bus returned us to Smuts and after licking our wounds we prepared for the evening's festivities. I drove painfully to Inga's house and crawled up the many stairs to her front door. When she opened it in full evening attire and saw the pitiful wreck on hands and knees her strong Germanic disdain for weakness gave way to sympathy and we spent the evening at home. It took a long time for my Achilles tendons to return to normal.

We also had games between the UCT residences. It was well known that my athletic abilities involving ball games were extremely limited and for this reason our team thought they were playing it safe by assigning me the position of goalie in a soccer game against Belsen residence. The teams were pretty evenly matched and the game was nearing its end with no score when the Belsen goalie made a good save and then punted the ball high over the players. Our defense was caught off guard and the ball hit the ground, bounced a few times and started rolling towards my goal. A sigh of defeat went through our team as they watched helplessly as the ball approached me. I lined up on it nicely and with my legs spread wide, reached down with my hands to catch it. My reflexes were not quite right and the ball escaped my hands, rolled between my legs and just made it over the goal line. There was an enraged roar from the team and I had no option but to sprint for my car and flee. I waited several hours until I was sure they were at least on their third beers down at the Cecil, and then joined them.

In our final year a series of international rugby matches was held in the various big cities. In Cape Town the venue was the stadium at Newlands. A much sought after job from the students' point of view was that of barman in the players' lounge of the stadium. Zorb, Jakes, Eyes, Smithy and I were fortunate to be selected. It was understood that the barmen were entitled and indeed expected to drink along with the players in the spirit of celebration of the game, regardless of which team prevailed. It was also understood that at the end of the party, empty bottles of hard liquor would be counted with the full ones to ensure none had been removed from the premises. We accordingly accumulated a number of empties of the preferred whiskey, brandy and vodka and smuggled these into the bar before the game. At the end of the festivities we took an equivalent number of full bottles out. Zorb, being possessed of a greater thirst than the rest of us, saw fit to arrive in his sheepskin jacket which had capacious pockets. After cleaning up, he filled these with bottles but discovered there were a few extra. He therefore stuck these inside his trousers and secured them with his hands. All went well until we arrived at the exit, where the president of the rugby union saw fit to shake our hands in appreciation of the fine service we had given. Zorb had no choice but to offer his hand, whereupon a bottle of scotch was liberated and slid down his leg to crash open on the floor. The effusive farewell changed into a strip search and we all had to surrender our ill-gotten gains. Being fine sportsmen at heart however, the officials took no offense and insisted on a couple more drinks to show their magnanimous spirits.

All too soon final exams were upon us. Our normal exam technique, honed to perfection over the years, was to cram mercilessly the few weeks before exams started to compensate for lack of attention during the classes. In this way we got the entire year's study in perspective and it was amazing how everything suddenly made sense. The schedule usually involved two exams per day, so each night before we would cram these subjects exclusively. We discovered that neat brandy consumed continuously throughout these evenings materially enhanced our ability to focus and stay awake. We each had study partners who had exams on different days and in my case I had Jakes, a Civil Engineer in the room next to mine. It was each partner's job to ensure that the other studied diligently, did not slip off to the Pig and did not fall asleep prematurely.

Jakes, being a man of robust stature, was liable to consume more than the required dosage of brandy and had to be watched carefully. One evening when I went to check on him he was not in his room, but the window was open and I could hear muttered obscenities outside. Sure enough, Jakes was perched on the 12" ledge fifty feet above Rugby Road. I leant out to coax him inside but he was in a belligerent mood and tried to pull me outside too. It took me thirty minutes of gentle conversation to get him back inside. When exams were over we counted seventeen empty bottles of brandy, a small price to pay for our engineering degrees.

In order to keep our bodies in reasonable shape during exams, about five each afternoon we would don our tennis gear and take the short walk under Rhodes' Drive to the tennis courts. There we would play continuously until just before dinner time. My preferred opponent was our flat-mate Quadro, an intrepid Englishman with royal bearing. Our tennis was of an inferior standard but we were equally matched and had enjoyable games.

Apart from his intellect and quick wit, Quadro was also valued highly as a friend because he never drank alcohol. We had no problem with this because he enjoyed himself just as much as everyone else and at the end of evenings when we knew we were in bad shape, Quadro could be counted upon to get us home safely.

Graduation was held in Jammie, with engineers on the right and everyone else on the left. It was customary to sing the traditional varsity songs during the assembly period which were explicit adaptations of Gilbert and Sullivan musical pieces referring to the manly qualities of the UCT students and their prowess in sports and love. Most graduates' parents came to town for the event and after receiving our sheepskins and taking the obligatory series of photos, we assembled at various restaurants to celebrate. Our group met at Arthur's Seat Hotel in Seapoint and a fine time was had by all.

Several marriages were scheduled right after graduation, among them those of our close friends Bert
and Erica and Bugs and Lorna. These were fine affairs, Bert's being held on Erica's father's estate near
Somerset West and Bugs' at the Vineyard Hotel in
Newlands. Large groups of graduates attended these
and it must have been a great way to start married life.
In my case I was not quite ready to tie the knot with
Borgie and the following year she got impatient and
married someone else.

The four years in Cape Town were some of the
most enjoyable of my life and passed all too quickly.
After graduation I went back into the mining business to
start earning some money. By 1968 it was obvious that
Rhodesia could not ever be the same again and South
Africa's days were numbered as a first-world country. I resolved to save my money for three years and then tour the
world in search of a new country. Jakes and I left Cape
Town in February 1972 on the Windsor Castle bound
for Southampton and spent six months travelling all over
Europe in an old bright orange VW combi we named
'Mbusi, Swahili for goat. I left for the U.S.A in August
and Jakes returned to South Africa. After travelling the
entire country and parts of Canada for three months on
the Greyhound bus, in November I was offered a good
engineering position in Richmond, Virginia and remained
with this fine company until my retirement. This job involved considerable travel and during a long project in
Brazil I met and married my beloved wife Nemezia, another good German girl whose family had emigrated to

Brazil in the late 1800's. Together we raised two wonderful children and continue to enjoy our lives in the U.S.A and Brazil.

My misgivings regarding Rhodesia were unfortunately fully realized. Russia and China started supplying arms and training terrorists to overthrow Smith's government. The world seemed to approve of this, calling these groups "freedom fighters". The terrorists infiltrated the country from training camps in Zambia and Tanzania, intimidating the local villagers and attacking isolated farms. They were no match for the Rhodesian armed forces but inflicted a high cost on the country in terms of arms and manpower. The final blows came in 1975 when Portugal abruptly pulled out of Mozambique and in 1976 when the new black government of Mozambique closed its borders with Rhodesia and hosted the terrorists. In September 1976 South African Prime Minister John Vorster was persuaded by Henry Kissinger to also close the borders with Rhodesia. At this meeting in Pretoria, Ian Smith was left without recourse and obliged to agree to the principle of black majority rule within two years. It is claimed that Kissinger had tears in his eyes when he told Smith it was with deep regret that he had to force him to commit political suicide. These two events effectively cut off Rhodesia from all trade and there was no way out. It was also a sad day for Mozambique, which erupted into 16-year civil war which decimated the country. At this point, with great sadness, Dad sold the house and moved to his plot in South Africa. The terrorist war continued but it was clearly a lost cause. Smith tried his best to negotiate a reasonable transition, consulting the chiefs and offering to include bishop Abel Musurewa in an interim government. The world would not accept this and in 1980 insisted on a general election which resulted in a victory for Robert Mugabe.

Everyone born and raised in Africa feels the strong affinity for the land and it is something that cannot be dwelt upon but also cannot be eradicated. It is as though I have had two lives, the one in Africa and the one since. We wonder what the long-term future for Africa is. White Rhodesians have spread all over the world in modern-day Diaspora. Only about 20,000 remain in Zimbabwe. Of those, some elected to stay for love of the country and some had no choice for lack of funds to emigrate. In general, those who left have done well, using their good education and adventurous dispositions to make their ways in agriculture, commerce and industry in many different countries. Dad disagreed with the Rhodesian Front administration in one important respect. He believed that the party knew early on that the country was not going to survive. If this was so, he felt that white Rhodesians should have been free to leave with all their moveable assets. Instead, the government placed severe restrictions on movement of currency and large assets, virtually forcing many to stay and watch everything they had fall prey to devaluation, vandalism and expropriation. Sister Jennifer was one of these, having worked all her life as a schoolteacher and entitled to a comfortable pension. Because of the rampant inflation caused by Mugabe's corrupt government ministers and mismanagement her pension is not enough to buy one loaf of bread and she must continue to work the rest of her life.

There were those who believed that majority rule would be wonderful and everyone would live happily together. It can only be said that these optimistic views were due to a failure to learn the lessons of history and a lack of understanding of Africa. Unfortunately everyone has had to pay the price and the damage is largely irreversible.

EPILOGUE

There are wonderful people of every race but regrettably there are also those who, given the chance, inflict terrible harm upon their fellow humans. Most humans love power but few have the self-discipline to use it wisely. Decent people would like to live according to Abraham Lincoln's second inauguration address near the end of the Civil War, "With malice toward none, with charity for all...." Unfortunately human nature does not work this way. Dad used to often remark that the world could be a paradise for everyone if only humans could behave reasonably. Practical politics must therefore accept that the human is a complicated animal and large groups must be managed bearing this in mind. The concept of equality is a naïve dream. Nobody knows quite what equality means in the broad sense. The only sense in which it can be applied is equal treatment under the law. Every country will have its dissidents and malcontents regardless of the well being of the majority.

No two human beings are identical in every respect. For this obvious reason there will always be rich and poor and those somewhere in between whom we refer to as the middle-class. The only thing a government can do is to provide an infrastructure and enact laws which give everyone an opportunity to make the best of his life. The government cannot guarantee success or happiness. These depend on multiple factors which it has no control over. A major factor is core beliefs which are commonly referred to as "culture". A society which promotes honesty, decency, compassion, hard work and individual responsibility will be far more successful than one which has no moral foundation and expects others to support it. Historically the major religions sought to teach their adherents basic moral behavior. Communism and its derivatives are bound to fail eventually because these core values are abandoned.

Various rulers and governments have sought to improve the lot of "the poor". Poor is not necessarily an unhappy state unless it involves starvation. It is also very subjective. In the USA poor is defined as a family of four whose annual income is less than $23,000. A Bushman living in Namibia considers himself rich if he owns a knife. In the 90 years of colonial rule in Rhodesia the average tribesman was lifted from virtual savage status to a decent life with adequate employment, food, shelter, medicine, education and justice. He was ruled by a responsible government which wished him well.

The human is an animal that operates partly by common instinct and partly by individual thought process. Success in life requires definition, but if this means the ability to survive in reasonable comfort for a reasonable period of time, success depends on good planning. Any project goes better if it is planned well, and life is no different. There are many theories as to why certain groups of humans plan better than others, but the most logical is climate. In harsh climates with very cold winters, preparation must be made each summer in order to survive the winter. Over the centuries inhabitants of these regions have adapted and learned to look ahead and understand the consequences of their actions. In hot climates no planning is required and the high temperatures tend to make every creature more lethargic. If this is accompanied by high humidity the effect is greater. This is readily observed in counties which span high degrees of latitude.

The other important factor is culture. Regardless of physical differences or similarities, ethnic groups may have very different ways of looking at life. These involve inherited values and priorities, religious teachings, politics and local conditions. They affect the way people relate to others, their ethics, their sense of humor, their food preferences etc. There are those who believe that formal education can homogenize all these differences. This is clearly not so. If left to themselves, members of each group tend to associate with others of the same group and retain their historical cultures regardless of their level of formal education.

Anthropologists lead us to believe that homo sapiens originated in Africa. From there various tribes moved gradually all over the world and over time adapted to their various environments. Central and Southern Africa have reasonably temperate climates and little forward planning is required for basic survival. Thus life there continued in basic form for centuries until the colonists from the north arrived.

Politicians and heads of state must also plan intelligently. Unfortunately most humans are not concerned with events beyond their elected terms or life-spans. They instinctively prefer immediate certain rewards to future potentially better ones. This has had dire consequences in the forms of war, environmental damage, demographic shifts and runaway cases of transplanted flora and fauna. It is the culture of the people which makes a country successful. If large numbers of immigrants from different cultures dilute the national culture sufficiently, the country will change. This can be good or bad depending on the respective cultures.

Starting with the colonization of the Cape by the Dutch in 1656, southern Africa gradually became stable and was thriving by the mid 20th century. Its rapid deterioration over the last fifty years is due to the foolish actions of European and American politicians who should have known better. The infamous "winds of change" speech by Harold McMillan in 1960 was an astounding admission of complete failure to comprehend the basic principles of human progress which the once mighty British had held so dear for centuries. The consequences of the post

World-War two policy in Africa were completely predictable to anyone with basic knowledge of the area. Did the western politicians who wrought this catastrophe on Africa realize what they were doing? It's difficult to believe they were that naïve. One must therefore conclude that this was a deliberate policy to promote a different agenda, which was sold to the public as a "human rights" initiative. In Zimbabwe the only people who have retained their "rights" are Mugabe and his ministers.

Rhodesia has gone from the iron-age to first-world and back in a short 100 years. My father was born in 1912 shortly after the colonization and died in 1999 having seen the country rise from virgin bushveld to first-world status and then reduced to chaos. I started writing with the intention of simply documenting my life growing up in Rhodesia. Whereas there was nothing special or outstanding in this, I wanted my children and their descendants to be aware of another time, which, as in the novel *Gone with the Wind*, is gone forever. This was a good time during which decent people worked hard together to build their lives and a country which all could enjoy and take pride in.

As I embarked on this project, it became increasingly apparent that not only have times changed considerably since then, but also the entire accepted philosophy of the civilized world. Mankind has gone through many flawed contemporary behavioral patterns in the belief that they had merit and that somehow their generation had discovered something that their predecessors had missed. Occasionally they were correct, but more often than not these turned out to be passing fads which made little sense. Perhaps due to the horrors of the Holocaust, post WW2 politics focused on encouraging different ethnic groups to intermingle and treat one another fairly in the naïve hope that this would create a harmonious group all living happily together. This is known as "diversity". The predictable result is that everyone involved equalizes at the lowest common denominator. As Winston Churchill predicted for communism, "equal misery for all".

The western world is now shackled by the illusion of "political correctness" which is a term coined by the media to discourage people from airing their true beliefs in public. It is a softer form of the propaganda machines of Nazi Germany and Soviet Russia where anyone who spoke up against the Party was liable to be turned in by his comrades. The key word in this strategy is "racist". The word racist is now considered an unconscionable insult and is used by anyone who is not completely white to protest any perceived or real mistreatment or disadvantage. If racist means acknowledging that different ethnic groups in general have differences other than physical appearance then every observant human is a racist. However, if it is construed to mean a person who mistreats or disadvantages another without having any other provocation or knowledge than appearance, the correct terminology is xenophobia. This certainly exists, as do all other human failings, and no laws will eradicate it. A decent, moral society will condemn it naturally.

For all of the known history of mankind, the strong, diligent, smart and unscrupulous have exploited the weak, lazy, apathetic and stupid. This has varied only in terms of degree. No laws can change human nature, only human behavior to some extent. There are those who believe that all humans are intrinsically good and will treat one another well if only given the chance. Nothing in history or individual experience supports this theory, but it is a noble dream. The dreamers are often academics who spend most of their lives in the company of other academics and artists who have a proclivity for dreaming. Another group which espouses the liberal cause is those who have inherited great wealth and while living privileged lives far removed from the man in the street, seek to embellish their own reputations by promoting his cause via various forms of philanthropy. The "have-nots" will always want to share the assets of the "haves" and will vote for a government which redistributes the wealth. Looking at recent history, the greatest atrocities ever visited upon mankind have begun with liberal agendas which rapidly degenerated into vicious dictatorships. Zimbabwe is just one more example.

The reality is that all living creatures are programmed for survival and they will fight for this using any means at their disposal. In a civilized society the laws punish those who cause harm or disadvantage to others. For most this works reasonably well, but for those who live for the moment and do not think or plan ahead it does not. They follow their instincts without considering the consequences and everyone pays the price. The difference between successful nations and those who live in constant turmoil is related to the degree to which its citizens and leaders think ahead and obey reasonable laws.

All groups of humans need good leadership and management in order to be successful. Left to themselves without laws or codes of behavior they tend to lapse into anarchy and obey their basic instincts. This can be clearly seen every time there is a major power-cut or other disaster in large cities throughout the world. As soon as certain segments of the population perceive that law-enforcement is compromised they commence looting and destroying. Installing good leadership is not simple and many a leader has started off well, only to abuse his power once he realized that he could.

The civilized nations promote their systems as liberty and freedom for all. Of course this is an illusion, they are the most regulated societies in the world. Freedom for every individual to pursue every desire without restriction would be a complete disaster. Reality is that civilized nations have laws which try to ensure that individuals can only do things that do not adversely affect others. This is a difficult balancing act because a great deal is subjective. However, in certain countries they have reached a point where it works reasonably well. In Africa this balance has been destroyed.

Freedom is a word used by politicians to delude their constituents into believing that they are privileged. In fact freedom is relative, not absolute. Even a person living alone in the wilderness is not free to do as he pleases. He must work and struggle to survive. The U.S.A., which proudly proclaims itself "the land of the free" has so many laws protecting the freedom of its citizens that almost every activity is unlawful. The myth that Africa was "free" before colonization is believed by many. In fact Africa was one of the harshest continents on earth where population remained small for centuries owing to war, natural disaster and disease. When the Pioneers arrived in Mashonaland in 1890 the total population of what is now Zimbabwe was estimated to be less than 500,000. These tribes had no clothes, no shoes, no written language, no wheel, no permanent structures, no medicine and only crude spears for protection. After only 90 years of colonization, at the time of "independence" in 1980, the black population was over 7m and the infrastructure was first-world. British colonization was the best thing that had happened to them.

In the late 1960's Chris Kristofferson composed the country ballad of Bobby McGhee which was performed by Roger Miller, Gordon Lightfoot, Janis Joplin and others, reaching the top of the charts several times. The chorus goes "Freedom's just another word for nothing left to lose, nothing ain't worth nothing but it's free…." The people of Zimbabwe have now realized complete freedom by this definition. Most of them have nothing left to lose. Law and order is totally gone. They are back where they were one hundred and twenty years ago when the Matabele tribe was free to plunder, rape and kill the Shona and other tribes with complete impunity. The beautiful land my grandfather and father helped build to first-world status has regressed to total anarchy.

The question that arises often is: which group of people has the right to control a country? Almost none of the world's surface is currently occupied by the same ethnic group that first set foot upon it. Populations have moved continuously and to claim ownership based on historical habitation has never automatically conferred control or possession. The stark reality through the ages has been that land is controlled or "owned" by those who are strong enough to do so. The earliest known human inhabitants of Rhodesia were the Bushmen or San. Other tribes migrating from the north displaced them. The Matabele would probably have displaced the Shona had the white man not intervened. So simply being born on a piece of land does not guarantee perpetual ownership. If it did, the next question would be: how much land around the birthplace is owned? Just as the lion marks his territory, it is only his for as long as he can stave off the competition. The same goes for humans. So do the Shona have a "right" to control the piece of land designated as Zimbabwe simply because they outnumber other groups? No more than anyone else. It is only theirs as long as they can hold it. They did not control it when the whites arrived and one man controls it now, having been put in place not by his own courage or wisdom, but by naïve western politicians.

A large part of the African continent is in turmoil. Few true democracies exist. Few good leaders have emerged. Corruption, destruction and slaughter are the norm. At the time independence was granted to each, the countries were productive and had decent infrastructures.

Most are now beggars and instead of building, have destroyed. Despite billions of dollars of aid from taxpayers of western nations, starvation, displacement and disease are commonplace. The most likely eventual outcome is that the Chinese will gradually assert themselves and take over those countries which can furnish them with needed minerals and other commodities. They are already in countries with attractive natural resources and are rapidly increasing their influence. The naïve European nations handed over their hard-won possessions on a plate.

Whereas the colonization of many parts of the world was conducted by Jesuit priests in a quest to bring religion to the primitive inhabitants, we should not delude ourselves into believing that the era of empire-building in the African continent during the nineteenth century was for any purpose other than financial and strategic. Africa is rich in resources and controls vital sea routes. The civilization of the local inhabitants was simply a by-product, and it can be argued that the entire experience was not in their best interests. However, it is a fact that colonization virtually eliminated inter-tribal warring, eradicated most human and animal diseases, sharply decreased child mortality and raised the standard of living. It also began the process of preparing indigenous Africans to take their places in a civilized and technical world.

It is true that the colonists placed their own interests before those of the indigenous tribes, as conquerors are prone to do. It is also true that the tribes were treated unjustly in some respects. Many of their prized cattle were expropriated without compensation and cattle driven over the Zambezi to Bulawayo by colonists in 1896 brought the lethal rinderpest virus to Rhodesia which devastated the herds. The subjugation of the tribes was in part facilitated by the confiscation and decimation of the cattle which were the mainstay of the local society. Whereas most British colonists treated the blacks well, there were those who abused them. However, these deprivations were nothing compared with their historical treatment by other conquering blacks.

The colonization of various parts of the world over the centuries had nothing to do with skin color. It involved vast differences in culture. Robert Mugabe was born in 1924 which means his father was probably born when Mashonaland was still in the iron age. It took Europe millennia to go from the iron age to the industrial revolution. Is it reasonable to expect in Africa this could be accomplished in one generation?

Current public opinion put forth by the media leads us now to regard the colonists as evil exploiters of a defenseless continent. The tragic current disaster of the entire region is blamed squarely on the colonial era. The colonists are depicted as a group of indolent white masters living lives of luxury while the black masses toiled in abject poverty to support them. The western world is now living in a strange period of self-delusion, which few people really believe in but are reluctant to vent their true feeling for fear being branded racists and bigots.

The facts of the matter are that all the development on the African, American and Australian continents was conceived, financed and executed by European colonists.

In Africa, the local inhabitants provided manual labor, and in doing so, learned valuable skills and earned money to improve their lifestyles. Except for the northern portion, the continent had absolutely no infrastructure when the first Europeans arrived in the 15th century. In those countries which were granted independence in the 60's, much of the infrastructure has already been destroyed. Nice paved roads are now potholed dirt tracks. Water and power supplies are unreliable. Many structures are damaged and looted. Productive farmland has given way to semi-desert or reverted to virgin bush.

The American Declaration of Independence contains the statement that "all men are created equal". Thomas Jefferson, the primary author of this document, certainly did not contemplate extending to his slaves the rights to life, liberty and the pursuit of happiness. It is equally obvious that all humans are unique and have different characters, talents and shortcomings. The only sensible philosophy is that all men should be treated equally when applying the laws of the land and the laws should not discriminate. Laws must be fair and just, but life itself is not always fair or just and humans must understand and accept this.

The historical application of democracy had wisely limited the electorate to persons who were likely to vote responsibly. Early in the 20th century, probably linked to the industrial revolution, pressure from unions and women's groups opened up the franchise to all citizens in Europe and North America with mixed results. As has been demonstrated in Africa, universal suffrage is not for everyone and those countries which were at peace and prosperous in 1955 are all now all ruled by virtual or actual dictators, with varying degrees of incompetence and self-indulgent exploitation of their people and assets. The principle of one-man-one-vote was applied to peoples totally unsuited to it against the wishes and advice of those who governed the countries well and understood the people the best. Starting in the late 1940's, under pressure from the United Nations, European powers granted "independence" to one colony and protectorate after another with disastrous results. In Africa, huge amounts of arms and landmines poured into the continent and ugly tribal wars ensued. Millions of humans perished and many millions of animals were indiscriminately shot or killed by landmines. Much of the valuable infrastructure that had been established by the colonists was wantonly destroyed or simply left to deteriorate through lack of attention. The mess continues with no end in sight.

Southern Rhodesia had been a self-governing colony since 1923 and was governed very well. At the break-up of the Central African Federation in 1963, Britain refused to grant full independence to Rhodesia until "majority rule" was guaranteed. In 1965 the Rhodesian government declared its independence unilaterally (UDI) in order to preserve the country for all its inhabitants. However, after fifteen years of crippling international sanctions and a terrorist war sponsored by both east and west, in 1980 a "democratic" election was held which gave power to the China-sponsored party of Robert Mugabe. Mugabe, an avowed Marxist, became prime-minister and shortly thereafter declared himself president. Whereas, unlike some other new African presidents, he did not publicly state that this was an office for life, in practical terms that was what has occurred so far. The west hailed this as a grand accomplishment and Mugabe was knighted by the Queen of England in 1994 (revoked in 2008). At this time of writing, he is regarded as one of the worst rulers on earth.

Shortly after his party came to power in 1980, Mugabe made a deal with North Korea to train an exclusive brigade of Shona troops to be under his personal command. This 5th Brigade was then sent to Matabeleland with orders to slaughter and starve the region into submission. The world press which had been so critical of the Smith government had nothing to say about this massacre and there is no accurate record of deaths. Estimates range from 20,000 to 40,000. This action effectively silenced Mugabe's main opponent, Joshua Nkomo and his Matabele-based party, whose terrorists had been financed by Russia. The Russians, Chinese and North Koreans lost no time in setting up their embassies in the re-named capital of Harare. The story goes that a young Shona boy asked his father "Dad, why does everyone call one another Comrade now?" "I'm not sure son, but I think it's Russian for Kaffir!"

From the onset of Mugabe's rule, redistribution of land was a major issue. Whereas before independence a large portion of the country had been declared Tribal Trust Lands for the exclusive use of indigenous blacks, a clamor began to transfer white farms to blacks, on a willing buyer, willing seller basis. Some farms were purchased on this system, most going to black ministers, but in 2004 Mugabe's popularity was waning as the country deteriorated and he instituted a major land-grab, literally sanctioning the expulsion of white farmers from their own productive farms by force, using ragtag bans of undisciplined "veterans". The great myth being propagated was that the blacks all yearned to be farmers and would use the stolen land wisely and productively. The reality is that farming is hard work which requires good planning and involves risk and few of the blacks aspire to it. Most want to be in the cities and after expelling the white farmers, looting their houses and equipment, the "veterans" abandoned the formerly productive farms which have now reverted to bushveld and produce little.

After UDI, many white Rhodesians, including myself, who are ethnically totally British, were stripped of their British citizenship. I was fortunate to be granted South African citizenship through my mother, but many were left stateless unless they elected to remain in Zimbabwe and become Zimbabwe citizens. The spineless British politicians who caved in to pressure from the USA and newly-independent nations in the United Nations will doubtless be poorly judged by history for selling their own citizens down the river.

As I write this in 2010, Zimbabwe, as Rhodesia is now called, is a corrupt, starving dictatorship under the maniacal and fanatical rule of an aging Robert Mugabe. He is kept in power by a ruthless military and a small group of unscrupulous international tycoons who exploit the assets of the land without restraint and share the spoils with Mugabe and his henchmen. Massive starvation has only been averted by huge infusions of foreign aid at the expense of the taxpayers of other countries. Many of the wild animals in the beautiful game-parks have been eaten or poached for ivory. The forests have been decimated for firewood. Erosion is prolific and diseases which had previously been eradicated have resurfaced. Power and water supplies are sporadic due to broken pumps and power-stations. The roads are falling apart and the trains don't run. The damage to the country is largely irreversible and it is in danger of becoming an arid wasteland. The currency has been abandoned and American dollars have taken its place. Except for a small number of politicians, every human, animal, plant, field and stream in the country has lost. Law and order are subject to the whims of politicians. Many Zimbabweans have simply fled to South Africa to avoid starvation. To those of us who were born and raised in colonial Rhodesia the current disaster was entirely predictable the moment "majority rule" was forced upon us.

How and why did this happen? Was it not obvious that Africa was not ready for universal suffrage? Of course it was. Democracy, as Winston Churchill correctly pointed out, is the worst form of government, except for all the others. In the original Greek concept, only male citizens of good standing were qualified to vote, a system the Greeks called aristocracy, meaning rule by the best. As Socrates wrote, universal suffrage was unthinkable and would result in mob rule to the detriment of all inhabitants as the Russians discovered during 70 years of "communism" and the slaughter of millions of their own people by their own elected "leaders". Democracy becomes self-destructive at the point when the majority of voters receive more in government benefits than they contribute in taxes. This majority will elect a government which will continue these handouts and the productive taxpayers will be taxed to death until the whole system implodes and the country is bankrupt. In effect it kills the goose that lays the golden egg.

True democracy assumes a decent, honest, well-informed and involved electorate whose primary objective is the common good. This is an unrealistic assumption, but the degree of success of the system depends on to what extent it is unrealistic. The American and European democracies are to a large extent illusory most of the time, but the electorate does have the means to force change peacefully when things get too far out of hand. Most "democracies" are driven by small groups of powerful men who control the media and large corporations and who can contribute large quantities of cash to promote their candidates. The general public is faced with a choice of self-serving candidates and is largely apathetic or led along by the nose. The system bungles along until the population becomes extremely dissatisfied. In Africa, forcing universal suffrage on primitive peoples prematurely has resulted in a farce of vicious dictatorships, causing more death, starvation and suffering than ever seen before.

The demise of the European empires had its genesis within the famous Fourteen Points presented by US President Woodrow Wilson in 1918 as conditions for the armistice of the First World War. Wilson was the first US president to deviate from the non-interventionist policy adopted by the US government since the early 1800's. Point 5 effectively required full representation for all peoples of the colonies, as it was Wilson's aim to spread democracy throughout the world. These points were considered in the Treaty of Versailles between the Allies and Germany. Ironically his own congress refused to ratify this treaty and the USA never joined the League of Nations that Wilson hoped would guarantee world peace indefinitely. It became a toothless entity which sat by and watched Germany openly flaunt the terms of the treaty and re-arm to fight the Second World War.

The treaty of Versailles was forced upon Germany and encountered some opposition but nevertheless was signed by the European allies and Germany, rearranging Europe according to the various language groups and taking no account of historical possession. Germany was stripped of its colonies and was subjected to huge cash reparations which it had no possibility of paying. This foolish and unnecessary war had accomplished nothing positive, had cost millions of lives, destroyed an incredible amount of property and left the taxpayers of all participants to foot the immense bill. The world had been irreversibly changed and tiny Rhodesia was to feel the consequences.

The other school of thought is that one group of people cannot control a larger group of people indefinitely and "the majority" must ultimately prevail. In fact all countries are controlled by small groups, the only distinction being the composition of the two groups. In most countries the general population does not like the government. In the USA today the approval rating for Congress is 9% which means that 91% of the population disagrees with the way the country is being managed. How can this be when the electorate has the power to select members of Congress? It is because of a largely misguided, misinformed and apathetic electorate and the fact that over the years, in an attempt preserve the seats of one party or the other, voting precincts have been manipulated so that many seats are virtually guaranteed regardless of performance. The process goes by the unlikely term gerrymandering, which apparently is more acceptable than the true terminology, which is vote manipulation. In addition to this, elected members of congress are funded heavily by special-interest groups in a process known as lobbying, which is the political term used for bribery. The Founding Fathers' worst dreams have materialized, whereby Congress does not represent the people, have allocated themselves lifelong privileges unavailable to the electorate and any five of the nine unelected Supreme Court justices can interpret the Constitution to reflect their own philosophies with complete disregard for the clear language of the document. In Zimbabwe, as demonstrated in the 2008 election, Mugabe has retained power using more traditional methods, intimidating, killing and beating his opponents and rejecting vote counts that did not favor himself and his party.

The question must be asked, what should have been done? As I hope the narrative will have demonstrated, white Rhodesians were, for the most part, perfectly normal people who loved their country and intended no harm or deprivation to any of its inhabitants. Our culture was English and I like to believe that we had a good system of government based on a qualified franchise which set reasonable standards.

In the mid 1950's it was plain to all who lived in Rhodesia that there were two possible courses of action for the long-term success of all inhabitants. Already at that time, within the Land Apportionment Act, a large portion of the country was reserved for blacks only, based on historical tribal territory. These areas could have been declared separate nations with virtual independence, on the same principal as South Africa's Apartheid system. Apartheid has been translated to mean all kinds of different things, but in fact it is simply the Afrikaans word for apartness or separate development. Most of the world has operated on the apartheid system since the first group of cavemen elected to break away and form their own tribe. There is nothing intrinsically wrong or evil with the principle. Had the apartheid system been implemented, blacks would have had autonomy in their own lands and whites in theirs.

Apartheid got a bad name because of the segregation laws which had been practiced throughout Africa and the United States for centuries. These laws were necessary to maintain standards which the whites had set for themselves but the blacks were unaccustomed to. Certainly they were discriminatory, but the realist will understand that everything in life is discriminatory, it is only the basis that varies. Apartheid could have worked. It failed in South Africa because the South Africans wanted it both ways and the European and American governments forced it to fail. South Africans wanted the blacks to work for them, but they did not want them to have any rights where they worked. The rest of the world also wanted it to fail and imposed harsh sanctions on South Africa to collapse the economy. Had Rhodesians divided the country equitably and done their own work or had a guest-worker program, separate nations could have existed if the rest of the world had not interfered. However, although valid in theory, apartheid would inevitably have led to comparisons between black and white ruled countries and blacks would continue to feel disadvantaged. There is no solution to hurt feelings, but the proximity of viable and stable white states would have certainly been beneficial to the independent black states.

The other option was a defined path to the enfranchisement of more blacks within the same state. From its inception Rhodesia had never excluded citizens from voting based on race. The franchise requirements were based on education, income or property-ownership and applied equally to all inhabitants. This was a good system which set reasonable standards. If it had been allowed to work over time, eventually many blacks would have earned the vote and been able to participate in shaping the future of the country.

Smith and his ministers worked tirelessly to save Rhodesia but the world was not interested in logic or reason. The declaration of unilateral independence in 1965 was a last resort but the world would not accept this and imposed crippling sanctions. It also financed and encouraged a terrorist war, the main victims being isolated farmers and rural blacks. Rhodesia fought bravely but it was a lost cause and in 1980 responsible government ended with the election of Robert Mugabe. Amazingly, the incompetence and massive corruption of Mugabe's regime is blamed on the "colonists". Robert Mugabe is a well educated man and he alone is responsible for his behavior. In contrast Abraham Lincoln had only two years of formal schooling. In retrospect, even if Britain had granted full independence in 1964, the United Nations would inevitably have objected to the responsible government and imposed sanctions just as they did on South Africa, so the result would have been the same.

There are those who believe that had Rhodesia not agreed to majority rule, massive insurrection would have occurred amongst the blacks and the whites would have been slaughtered. This was a risk since the Pioneers set up camp in 1990, but was never really likely. There are always malcontents and agitators in every society and Rhodesia had its share of riots, demonstrations and random attacks on isolated farms but these were not widespread. The infusion of foreign capital and arms to terrorist groups after 1964 made the situation a lot more serious but had it not been for the international sanctions, the Rhodesian armed forces would have prevailed. The majority of the population was reasonably happy with adequate food and shelter. They were arguably the best-off in Africa. The agitators were a relatively small number of radicals trying to stir things up, whose leaders were well known.

World politics is planned, not accidental. What Smith and most Rhodesians did not realize at the time was that the U.S.A and U.K had a very different agenda than what was publicly disclosed. No informed and reasonably intelligent person cold have possibly believed that granting "independence" to a government made up of inexperienced, self-serving and blatantly corrupt instant politicians could result in anything but disaster for all. The real agenda had nothing to do with "human rights" or the welfare of the general population. It was simply to remove good and responsible governments in order to render these countries ripe for exploitation. It has been successful in accomplishing these objectives. The Chinese have moved in. It is astounding that Europe and the USA deliberately transformed countries ruled by loyal and competent allies into chaotic dictatorships for sale to the highest bidders. Ironically, the public justification for Europe abandoning its colonies in Africa was supposedly because it felt that if it did not support the "self determination" of the local tribes then they would turn to the communists for help and Russia, North Korea and China would get a foothold in Africa and turn it into another Cuba. They are well on the way. To compound the problem, many of these African countries are now open to Islamic radicals who are losing no time in setting up terrorist cells to attack the developed world. The whole world must now go through incredible inconvenience and expense to protect themselves from this tiny group.

7262976R00192

Printed in Great Britain
by Amazon.co.uk, Ltd.,
Marston Gate.